A Guide to Industrial Archaeology Sites in Britain

A Guide to Industrial Archaeology Sites in Britain

Selected by
Walter Minchinton

GRANADA
London Toronto Sydney New York

Granada Publishing Limited
8 Grafton Street
London W1X 3LA

Published by Granada Publishing 1984

British Library Cataloguing in Publication Data

Minchinton, Walter
  A guide to industrial archaeology—Great Britain—
  Directories
  I. Title
  609'.41   T26.G7

ISBN 0-246-11781-8 (hard covers)
ISBN 0-586-08387-1 (paper covers)

Printed in Great Britain by
R. J. Acford, Chichester, Sussex

Contents

Introduction

Industrial Archaeology in Britain

Everywhere the impact of man on the face of Britain can be seen. Over the centuries he has exploited the resources available: he has cultivated the soil, cut down trees and planted them, harnessed the natural sources of power, mined and quarried for minerals and stone and clay, developed a transport system, created settlements and established industrial and commercial activities both for work and for recreation. Over time the face of Britain has changed and never more rapidly than in the past half century when earthmoving machinery has enabled man to transform the appearance of the countryside more rapidly and radically than ever before.

In one way or another man has always been interested in his past and spasmodically has done what he could to preserve evidence of former ways of life. The lives of our ancestors in the remote past have attracted interest and prehistoric sites have been explored and preserved. Among the most familiar of tourist sites is Stonehenge, and other prehistoric sites of various types from one end of Britain to the other have become places of pilgrimage. We have long recognized too that castles and cathedrals, country houses and civic buildings form part of our heritage that we should preserve, though our perception even within this range has been influenced by changes in taste and fashion. Victoriana, which but a generation ago was looked on with scorn, is now viewed with critical appreciation. And since 1945 we have come to appreciate a wider range of sites which reflect the ways in which the ordinary people of this island worked, lived, played and carried on their lives. Though many would include industrial sites going back to prehistory within the scope of such interest, by and large attention has tended to be concentrated on the physical manifestation of what we have come to call the Industrial Revolution, that process which by a speeding up of the rate of economic change made Britain the first industrial nation. And from Britain these forces spread their way around the world so that key industrial sites have become of interest not only to the inhabitants of Great Britain but also to visitors from overseas. In 1979, when it celebrated its bicentenary, Ironbridge, the Shropshire town where the first iron bridge in the world was erected, was visited by people from all over the world.

To describe this area of interest, the term 'industrial archaeology' was invented in about 1950. Clumsy and unsatisfactory as it is, it is now too late to think of a different term for this particular enthusiasm. Not only has it been widely adopted in the English-speaking world – though the Americans spell 'archeology' thus – but it has been accepted by other countries as well. Thus the French speak of l'archéologie industrielle, the Germans of industrie-archaologie, the Italians of l'archeologia industriale and the Belgians of industriele archeologie. The term 'industrial archaeology' is thus one of the successful British exports of the postwar world.

The growth of this interest in Britain has been evidenced in three ways: by the formation of local industrial archaeology societies, and of a national Association for Industrial Archaeology; by the publication of journals both locally and nationally and of series of books by a number of publishers, as well as individual volumes; and by a greatly expanded effort to preserve key items of interest of our industrial past. In this the central government (through the agency of the Department of the Environment), local authorities, the National Trust, private charitable trusts and commercial enterprises, have played their part. And despite much destruction the range of preserved artefacts is widening.

But what is the scope of industrial archaeology? Chronologically, it stretches from prehistoric times to the present day for it is concerned with the preservation of examples of the way in which man operated in the past. So the prehistoric mine is of as much interest to the industrial archaeologist as the first-generation nuclear reactor or oil refinery. If the furthest time boundary is vague so is the most recent. When does a process become obsolete? While the dirt archaeologist gains his information by excavation, in the best of all possible worlds the industrial archaeologist would be able to forestall the demolition or destruction of examples of past technology and the physical context in which such activities were carried on.

The subject matter of industrial archaeology has been classified in a number of ways but quite a workable method is to deal with its scope under the following categories:

1 *Sources of power*: these include the natural sources of power which our ancestors employed such as the human treadwheel, the animal gin, the windmill, the watermill and the tidemill as well as more modern forms of power supply, such as the steam engine, the internal combustion engine, electricity and nuclear power.

2 *Extractive industries* such as quarrying for building stone, lime-

stone, slate, and so on, and mining of coal, iron and the various non-ferrous metals, such as copper and lead, and the processes associated with their extraction.

3 *Manufacturing industries* include rural and urban crafts, agriculture, textiles (cotton, linen, silk and wool), metal manufacturing, engineering, building, leather, soap, glass, paper, pottery, food and drink, clothing and footwear as well as the more recent industrial developments such as chemicals, electronics and so on.

4 *Transport* ranges from the improvement of roads including tollhouses and roadside furniture, the construction of canals and the improvement of river navigation, the building of the railways and later tramways and the development of ports to the fixed installations of the air age, airfields and airship hangars and the like.

5 *Public services* such as gas, electricity and water supply, drainage, sewage and waste disposal, post and telecommunications.

6 *Commercial buildings* including shops, corn exchanges and others such as theatres and cinemas.

7 *Social buildings*: the homes erected for workers, industrial settlements, workhouses, gaols, mansions built by industrialists and commercial magnates, and buildings for worship, leisure and entertainment.

Some accounts of industrial archaeology consider one or more of the categories listed above, others deal with the whole range that can be seen in a particular area. Examples of both kinds of book are listed in the bibliography at the end of this volume.

Reflecting a growing interest, the boundaries of preservation have been gradually widening. Some things are comparatively easy to preserve because they are relatively small, are in isolated positions and have acquired a romantic aura. Some of these activities have acquired preservation societies of their own. Within this category must be included windmills and watermills – the Society for the Protection of Ancient Buildings (SPAB) has a wind and watermill section – and there are numerous societies concerned with individual mills; beam engines also have their *aficionados* and there are railway preservation societies, motor vehicle societies, canal trusts, tramway societies and so on. Some small items such as limekilns or tollhouses are more vulnerable

and the preservation of roadside monuments is not easy. The sites of early industrial processes – china clay, coal, slate-quarrying, iron, paper, pottery and textiles – are also preserved. What is more difficult is to preserve more recent technology, for the frontier of appreciation has not yet brought them within the ambit of consideration. There is an urgent need for a society for the preservation of large structures – gasholders, chimneys and cooling towers all provide examples of artefacts which represent not only the reality of past industrial enterprise but also the skill and artistry of our forebears. In many cases they are in positions where they could easily be preserved but the transitory thrill of demolition and the desire of the demolition firms to show off their expertise is allowed to outweigh longer-term considerations. And in some areas, such as parts of South Wales, local authorities are concerned to wipe the countryside clear of all those aspects of past industrial activity which they regard in a short-sighted way as evidence of the exploitation of workers by capitalist employers. In Cornwall, china clay heaps have been bulldozed and in the north of England colliery tips are removed, actions which some of our descendants will regret.

While the physical artefacts do not tell the whole story and film and oral history have their part to play, the scale and location of a wide range of industrial and commercial activities and of the communities associated with them can be appreciated only if examples are preserved. Discrimination is of course necessary. We do not want to convert our whole island into an industrial museum and selection is therefore necessary. But we do need to preserve enough so that evidence of the past can be kept alive. The British landscape is a palimpsest which should reflect the whole range of man's activities from the remote past up to the present day.

How to Use This Book

As the Contents page shows, we have divided the area covered by this book, the island of Great Britain (together with the Isle of Man and the Isle of Wight), into seven: south-west England, south-east England, eastern England, midland England, northern England, Wales and Scotland. Within the areas, entries are by county (or region in Scotland). They consist of two types. There are almost 100 main entries which include all the major sites of industrial archaeological importance in Great Britain. Then there is in addition for each county a list of other sites worth visiting. For some counties (or regions) there is no main entry but only a list of subsidiary sites.

Several considerations have been taken into account in choos-

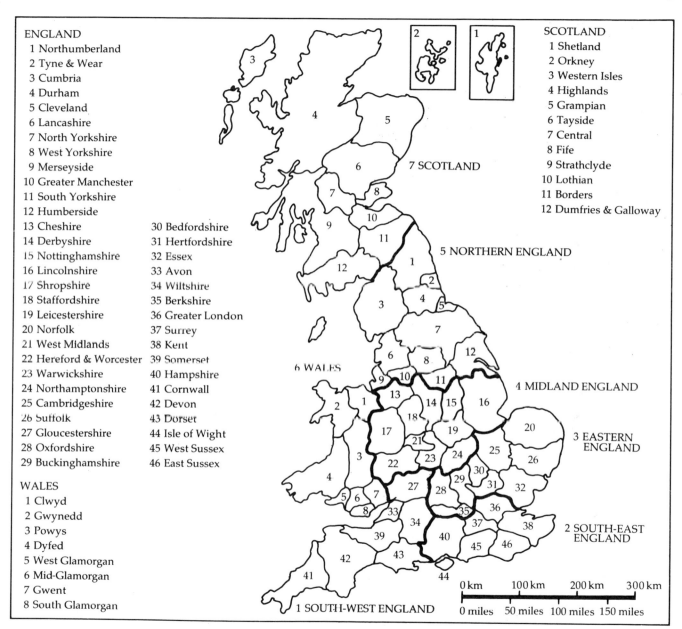

ENGLAND
1 Northumberland
2 Tyne & Wear
3 Cumbria
4 Durham
5 Cleveland
6 Lancashire
7 North Yorkshire
8 West Yorkshire
9 Merseyside
10 Greater Manchester
11 South Yorkshire
12 Humberside
13 Cheshire
14 Derbyshire
15 Nottinghamshire
16 Lincolnshire
17 Shropshire
18 Staffordshire
19 Leicestershire
20 Norfolk
21 West Midlands
22 Hereford & Worcester
23 Warwickshire
24 Northamptonshire
25 Cambridgeshire
26 Suffolk
27 Gloucestershire
28 Oxfordshire
29 Buckinghamshire

30 Bedfordshire
31 Hertfordshire
32 Essex
33 Avon
34 Wiltshire
35 Berkshire
36 Greater London
37 Surrey
38 Kent
39 Somerset
40 Hampshire
41 Cornwall
42 Devon
43 Dorset
44 Isle of Wight
45 West Sussex
46 East Sussex

WALES
1 Clwyd
2 Gwynedd
3 Powys
4 Dyfed
5 West Glamorgan
6 Mid-Glamorgan
7 Gwent
8 South Glamorgan

SCOTLAND
1 Shetland
2 Orkney
3 Western Isles
4 Highlands
5 Grampian
6 Tayside
7 Central
8 Fife
9 Strathclyde
10 Lothian
11 Borders
12 Dumfries & Galloway

5 NORTHERN ENGLAND
6 WALES
4 MIDLAND ENGLAND
3 EASTERN ENGLAND
2 SOUTH-EAST ENGLAND
1 SOUTH-WEST ENGLAND
7 SCOTLAND

0 km 100 km 200 km 300 km
0 miles 50 miles 100 miles 150 miles

ing the sites. First, they have been selected throughout Great Britain so that wherever you are you should be able to find some sites of interest nearby. But, of course, because economic activity has not been evenly distributed throughout the country, there is obviously a greater concentration of sites in some places than in others. Secondly, an effort has been made to select sites by topic so that anyone who visits all the sites in this book will not only have a good appreciation of their geographical distribution, but will also have been made aware of the range of sites which fall within the field of industrial archaeology. Thirdly, as wide a chronological range as possible has been adopted. Some of the sites are of considerable antiquity while others are recent: they range, for example, from a neolithic flint site to a mid-20th-century power station. Finally, the bias of selection has been in favour of main sites which, in the words of the *Michelin Guide*, are worth a detour. This means that open-air museum sites figure prominently because of the range of interest they provide. But this has not been the sole consideration and some single sites of key importance have been included. In other cases, where there is no single outstanding site, a series of linked sites have been described: see, for instance, ironmaking in Cumbria. The great conurbations which have a number of sites of interest present considerable problems, so for Birmingham, Glasgow, Liverpool, London and Manchester, for example, lists of sites have been provided with rather brief descriptions.

If you are touring in a particular county and wish to visit some of the sites of industrial archaeological interest to be found therein, look up the county name in the Contents list (page 5) and turn to the page number given there. All the sites within the county will be described in the following pages. The location of the main sites is indicated on the key maps at the beginning of each section (pages 12, 34, 54, 74, 104, 134 and 160). If you wish to look up one particular site, its page number will be found in the index at the end of the book.

Well-known sites on main routes can be easily found from normal road maps but for others it is advisable to use Ordnance Survey maps. Grid references are provided, keyed to the 1:50,000 (Landranger Series) maps. Normally, six-figure references are given; in certain cases, however, when an area is involved rather than an individual site which can be pin-pointed, a four-figure reference is given.

As those touring a large area may not wish to buy all the relevant Ordnance Survey maps, which have become expensive, good road maps, which are often at a scale of 3 miles to 1 inch or 4 miles to 1 inch, are useful. Many of the sites described in this book are marked on such maps. We would like to stress, however, that Ordnance Survey maps are a good buy if you are touring a fairly small area since they also indicate the where-abouts of other features of interest, such as mills and closed railway lines, which are not shown on the smaller-scale maps.

Many of these sites are operated by public and private museums or by the National Trust, in which case an entry charge is made, while to other sites there is free access. Since charges and opening hours change frequently, no information is given about these. But, in order that readers may check the current position we have given, where possible, the addresses and telephone numbers of sites.

It is no doubt unnecessary to add that visitors should treat sites – some of which are on private property – with respect, but it is advisable to point out that some sites are potentially dangerous and therefore care should be taken in exploring them, particularly with small children.

Through the medium of this book, we hope you will enjoy your exploration of Britain's industrial archaeological heritage.

South-West England

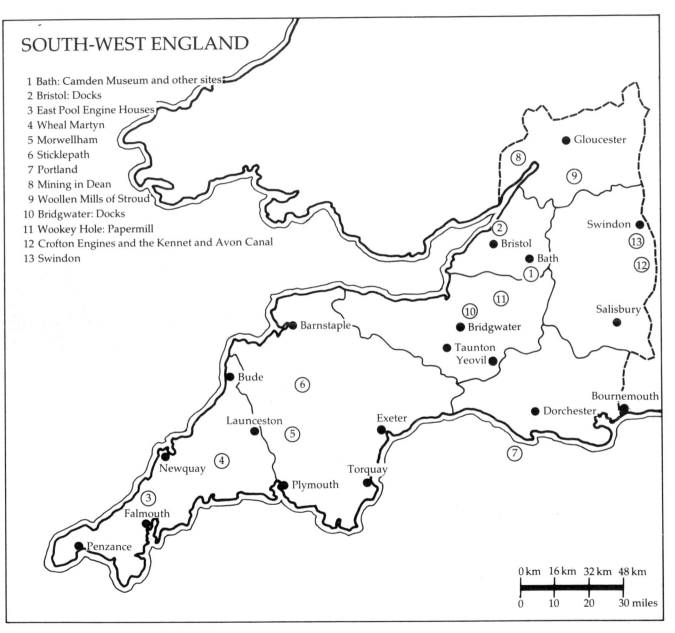

SOUTH-WEST ENGLAND

1 Bath: Camden Museum and other sites
2 Bristol: Docks
3 East Pool Engine Houses
4 Wheal Martyn
5 Morwellham
6 Sticklepath
7 Portland
8 Mining in Dean
9 Woollen Mills of Stroud
10 Bridgwater: Docks
11 Wookey Hole: Papermill
12 Crofton Engines and the Kennet and Avon Canal
13 Swindon

Gloucester
⑧
⑨
Swindon
⑬
Bristol
Bath
①
⑪
⑩
Salisbury
Bridgwater
Taunton
Yeovil
Barnstaple
Bude
⑥
Bournemouth
Dorchester
Launceston
Exeter
⑤
Newquay
⑦
④
Torquay
③
Plymouth
Falmouth
Penzance

0 km	16 km	32 km	48 km
0	10	20	30 miles

AVON

Though there are sites of interest elsewhere, this new county is dominated by its two cities, Bath and Bristol.

Bath: Camden Museum and other sites (172/ST 748 654)

Better known as a Roman town and as a spa, Bath nevertheless had a number of manufacturing industries, of which only one example can be considered here.

The Camden Museum building was originally erected as a real tennis court in 1777 and has subsequently served as a malthouse, pin factory, charity school, light engineering works and luggage factory. It now houses the entire stock-in-trade of J. B. Bowler, a Victorian brass founder, general engineer and aerated water manufacturer, who set up the business in Bath at Corn Street in 1872. The firm operated until 1969, and when the original premises were demolished the contents were transferred to the museum. During almost a century of trading virtually nothing was thrown away so the museum possesses a splendid collection of hand-tools, lathes (in working order), bottles, paper work and many other items reflecting every aspect of the firm's activity. As far as possible the settings re-create the original premises and show in succession: the shop, the general engineering workshop, the office, the pattern shop, the brass foundry, the rough room, the brass finishing shop, the mineral water factory, the essence room, the bottle store, the filling area, and the mineral water office. Two cases contain samples of the bottles used and examples of the calendars given to wholesalers.

Address: Camden Works, Museum of Bath at Work, Julian Road, Bath, Avon BA1 2RH. *Tel.* Bath (0225) 318348.

Victoria Bridge, Victoria Bridge Road (ST 741 650), a 120-foot suspension bridge designed by James Dredge, was built in 1836. It is now restricted to pedestrian use.

Bath is the western terminus of the Kennet and Avon Canal which rises from its junction with the Avon by a flight of six (once seven) locks – a major engineering achievement completed in 1810 – at *Widcombe* (172/ST 755 643–758 646). At the top is the former *Baird Maltings* (c 1850) (172/ST 758 647). For other sections of the Kennet and Avon, see pp. 15, 30, 56.

Bath also bears the marks of the railway. At *Sydney Gardens* (172/ST 758 654) the Western Region main line passes through an elaborate cutting and under a number of masonry and ornamental cast-iron bridges. *Bath Spa Station* (172/ST 753 643) is in Tudor style with curved gables. *Green Park Station* (172/ST 745 647) was built by the Midland Railway in 1874 with an all-over roof. It is now used as a car park.

Bristol: The Docks (172/ST 566 724-590 729)

For a time England's second largest city, Bristol's pre-eminence was largely derived from its position as a port. While the broad outlines of the ancient port can still be traced, its present shape dates from the 19th century when the floating harbour was constructed by William Jessop in the 1800s and improved by Brunel in the 1840s and Howard in the 1870s. A start can be made at *Cumberland Basin* (172/ST 570 723) where the Brunel southern lock and the tubular bridge are notable. From here can be seen the *Clifton suspension bridge* (ST 564 731), a tollbridge designed by Brunel and completed after his death, which is still open to traffic, and the three red-brick Tobacco Bond Warehouses built by the Bristol firm, Cowlin, in 1905–19, early examples of buildings with steel and reinforced concrete frames.

Follow Cumberland Road along the New Cut to the berth of SS *Great Britain*. Floated out in 1843, the first screw-driven, iron-hulled vessel is now back, after an adventurous life, in the dock where she was built. Under reconstruction, *Great Britain* is open to visitors. A walk along Wapping Wharf takes the visitor past the *Fairbairn Steam Crane* built by Stothert & Pitt (Bath) in 1875, now preserved on the wharf by the *Bristol Industrial Museum*, housed in some postwar transit sheds. From here there is a good view up St Augustine's Reach. Immediately opposite is the Bush's tea warehouse built about 1830, now occupied by the Arnolfini Gallery.

When Wapping Road is reached, the Bathurst Basin can be explored. Then follow Midland Wharf and Redcliffe Wharf and cross Redcliffe Bridge and turn along Welsh Back, where the coasters from South Wales once tied up. Here are a number of warehouses in the so-called Bristol Byzantine style, of which the most exotic is the *Old Granary* (Ponton & Gough, 1869), now a jazz club. From Bristol Bridge there is a view up a further reach of the Floating Harbour with Courage's Brewery and the boiler house of the former Counterslip Sugar Refinery on the right.
Addresses: SS *Great Britain*, Great Western Dock, Gas Ferry Road, off Cumberland Road, Bristol, Avon BS1 6UN. *Bristol Industrial Museum*, 'M' Shed, Prince's Wharf, Bristol, Avon BS1 4RN. *Tel.* SS *Great Britain*, Bristol (0272) 20680. *Bristol Industrial Museum*, Bristol (0272) 299771.

There is much else in Bristol but see in particular:
Temple Meads Station (172/ST 595 724), built in 1839–40 as the terminal of the Bristol and Great Western Railway, which has a wooden mock hammer beam roof with a span of 72 feet.

Also Worth Visiting in Avon

Claverton Pumphouse, Ferry Lane (172/ST 791 644). Designed by John Rennie, this pumping house on the Kennet and Avon Canal was built between 1809 and 1813 to raise water from the Avon into the canal. The 24-foot-wide undershot waterwheel, which drives the double beam pumps, can lift 100,000 gallons of water in an hour.

Nearby on the Kennet and Avon Canal is the *Dundas Aqueduct,* Limpley Stoke (172/ST 785 626). At its approach is a wharf with a handcrane made by Acraman of Bristol.

Clevedon Pier (172/ST 400 719). Built in 1867–8, this graceful little pier designed by R. J. Ward and J. W. Grover was used for nearly a century by passenger-carrying paddle steamers. Two spans of the pier collapsed in 1970 but there are still hopes of restoring it. Weston-super-Mare also has a pier, the *Birnbeck Pier* (182/ST 308 624) of 1867, which projects beyond the island which it links with the mainland.

Kelston brass annealing furnaces (172/ST 694 679). These two furnaces, the remains of a substantial brass mill built in the later

18th century, have been incorporated into a marina. Adjacent is a row of workers' cottages.

Priston Mill (172/ST 695 615). A working water-powered cornmill dating from the early 18th century with some machinery from 1850. *Tel.* Bath (0225) 23894.

Saltford, brass battery mill (172/ST 687 670). Plans are in process to restore this mill, which last operated in 1925. Even in its present ruinous condition the layout of the works and the leats which supplied the waterwheels can be discerned.

CORNWALL

The major industrial impact on the county has been made by mining and quarrying though maritime pursuits have also been of importance.

East Pool Mine: Michell's Whim (203/SW 674 416) and Taylor's Shaft Pumping Engine (203/SW 675 419)

One of the most evocative industrial landscapes is that of Cornish engine houses, usually with their chimney stacks rising above

East Pool – Michell's Whim before restoration

the roofless engine house. Perhaps the most atmospheric of these areas is at **Botallack** (203/SX 364 333) where the engine houses are perched near the cliff edge. In the heyday of Cornish mining for tin and copper in the middle of the 19th century, there were hundreds of them; now their number is greatly reduced and even fewer survive intact. By the mid-1920s there were about 20 engines left at work in Cornwall. Further disappearances thereafter led to the formation of the Cornish Engines Preservation Society in 1943, by which time only 12 engines remained, of which seven or eight were working. Today only seven or eight survive, of which the most accessible are the two at East Pool which were taken into the care of the National Trust in 1964. Built by Holman Bros of Camborne, Michell's Whim was the last rotative beam engine to be made in Cornwall. The cylinder is 30 inches in diameter and the piston has an unusually long stroke of 9 feet. The engine was used to haul men and ore up the mineshaft. It worked from 1887 until 1921 when a major fall of rock destroyed the shaft and the old part of the mine was abandoned.

The Cornish pumping engine at Taylor's Shaft nearby was designed by a local engineer and built in 1892 by Harvey's of Hayle. One of the largest pumping engines ever made, its cylinder has a diameter of 90 inches. Originally installed in the Carn Brea Mine, it was brought to East Pool in 1924 where it worked until that mine closed in 1945. It was then employed until 1954 to drain water from the mine to prevent the nearby South Crofty mine being flooded. *Tel.* (National Trust Regional Office) Bodmin (0208) 4284.

Two other beam engines have been preserved by the National Trust, at the **Levant Mine** (203/SW 375 346) and at the **South Crofty Mine**, Pool (203/SW 669 409) but since these mines are still working they can be seen only when visits can be arranged to fit in with normal mine routine. The mine managers should therefore be contacted first. *Tel.* the Manager, Geevor Mine, Pendeen, Penzance (0736) 788662, and the Manager, South Crofty, Camborne (0209) 714821.

In Cornwall the National Trust has also become custodian of **Wheal Coates Engine House**, St Agnes (203/SW 700 501) and of **Wheal Prosper Engine House**, Breage (203/SW 592 272).

Carthew, St Austell: Wheal Martyn Museum, the Cornish China Clay Museum (200/SK 005 555).

Today the major extractive industry in Cornwall is china clay which is obtained by capital-intensive methods by English China Clays. In the St Austell area waste heaps still dominate the

skyline. The economic value of china clay was discovered *c* 1746 by Willliam Cookworthy, a Quaker chemist from Plymouth, who found a small deposit in west Cornwall and then a better supply at St Stephen in Brannel shortly afterwards. Cookworthy was followed by Richard Champion of Bristol and then by the leading Staffordshire potters including Wedgwood, Spode and Minton. From an output of about 2,000 tons in 1800 production has now grown to about 3 million tons a year. And its use has changed. Although known as china clay, porcelain now forms only a small part of the use to which china clay is put. It is used in paper-making, cosmetics, toothpaste, pharmaceuticals and for many other purposes.

As one of the best preserved works from the end of the 19th century, Wheal Martyn was chosen as the site of a museum to portray the history of the china clay industry. The existing pit which was originally established about 1820 by Elias Martyn, a draper from St Austell, was taken over by John Lovering from Elias's son, Richard, about 1880. The works as they exist today probably date from that period. Wheal Martyn continued working until 1931, when the pit was shut, but the works continued to process low-grade clay from other pits in the Trenance valley until 1969.

The reception area is on the ruined remains of the Gomm Clay Works which were in existence before 1884 and closed in the 1920s.

At the museum the visitor can trace the sequence of china clay working. Beside the drive is the (1) 35-foot waterwheel which was used to pump the clay slurry out of the pit. Passing the (2) blacksmith shop, (3) level and (4) incline, one reaches the (5)

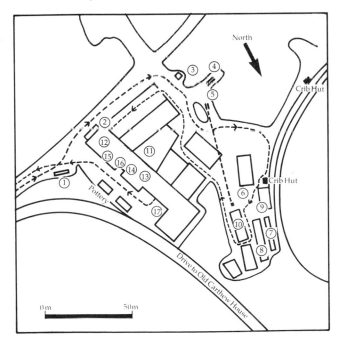

smaller 18-foot waterwheel, now in working order driving the (6) slurry pump. The slurry was then taken to the (7) sand drags and (8) mica drags to remove these waste materials and then to the (9) blueing house where it was screened and dyes were added to counteract any undesirable discoloration. The water was then run off in the (10) settling pits and (11) settling tanks before the clay was dried in a (12) kiln. Then it was stored in the (13) linhay ready for packing in (14) casks or sacks ready to be sent away by (15) wagon, (16) truck or (17) railway, mainly for dispatch by sea from Charlestown, Fowey or Par.

Associated with these works is a pottery and a display area in the linhay.

Address: Wheal Martyn Museum, Carthew, St Austell, Cornwall. *Tel.* St Austell (0726) 850362.

Also Worth Visiting in Cornwall

Camelford, Delabole Quarry (200/SX 075 840). Worked for over 400 years, the 500-foot-deep quarry can be viewed from a platform. Slate-splitting demonstrations are given. *Tel.* Camelford (0840) 212242.

Pendeen, Geevor Mine Museum (203/SW 385 345) includes *tours* of the tin treatment plant on weekdays. *Tel.* Penzance (0736) 788662.

Redruth, Tolgus Tin, Portreath Road (203/SW 692 426). A tin-streaming plant which separates tin from waste. The machinery includes the last working set of Cornish stamps. *Tel.* Redruth (0209) 215171.

St Dominick, Cotehele (201/SX 423 681, 417 681). This National Trust property includes a working watermill with a cider press adjoining, a blacksmith's forge and a wheelwright's and saddler's shops with a sawpit adjacent. On the quay there is an impressive bank of limekilns, the rebuilt Tamar sailing barge *Shamrock* is tied up in one of the docks, and the National Maritime Museum has a small branch museum. *Tel.* St Dominick (0579) 50434.

Saltash, Royal Albert Bridge (201/SX 435 587). Spanning the Tamar, this railway bowstring truss bridge was the last great achievement of Isambard Kingdom Brunel who died, as the bridge proclaims, in 1859. It carries the Western Region main line to Cornwall.

Wendron, Poldark Mine (203/SX 683 316) has a collection of steam engines and other machinery including the exhibits from the former Holman Museum and the Greensplat 30-inch beam engine (*c* 1850), the last beam engine to work commercially in Cornwall. A visit to the mine workings provides a realistic

Morwellham – the great dock with the raised railway system under construction

experience of what a small 19th-century Cornish tin mine was like. *Tel.* Helston (032 65) 3173.

DEVON

Now known for farming and tourism, Devon was once renowned for mining and woollen manufacture.

Morwellham (201/SX 446 697)

Most of the prehistoric and medieval mineral activity was by streaming or shallow digging but in the 18th century the scene in Devon shifted to underground working. The high noon of mining was the first two-thirds of the 19th century when a wide range of metals was produced. The boom in exports of copper and tin led to the development of a number of ports in Devon and Cornwall. Amongst them was Morwellham, virtually at the tidal limit of the Tamar, which became, with the construction of the Tavistock Canal in 1817, an outlet for copper ore and slate. At the height of prosperity for the major complex of mines nearby, Devon Great Consols, between 1848 and 1858, the Tamar valley was Europe's main source of copper and Morwellham with its docks off the Tamar was an extremely busy port. But the period of prosperity was brief. The arrival of the railway at Tavistock in 1859 took away the traffic from the Tavistock Canal which ceased to be a navigable waterway by 1880. Mining declined in the 1870s and 1880s and the pumps of Devon Great Consols stopped in 1901. The port was then abandoned.

Since 1970 the wharves have been cleared, the raised railway system which allowed ore to be tipped directly on the quays has been rebuilt, the docks excavated, buildings have been renovated, and an adit has been opened so that the visitor can now obtain a good impression of this early-19th-century mining port with its associated transport system, industrial housing and limekilns.

Address: Morwellham Quay, near Tavistock, West Devon. *Tel.* Tavistock (0822) 832766.

Finch Foundry – the water-powered tilt hammers and metal-cutting shears

Sticklepath: Finch Foundry (191/SX 641 940)

Agriculture as well as industry required to be serviced by small engineering works. Originally the manor mill grinding corn and later a cloth mill as well, the mill, one of the three at Sticklepath, was converted into an edge-tool factory to make agricultural implements. It was run from 1814 until 1960 by successive members of the Finch family, producing tools such as scythes, billhooks and shovels and hand tools for the china clay and mining industries. At one time it employed as many as 20 men. When it closed the plant rapidly became ruinous but since 1967 it has been restored.

The machinery, powered by water from the Taw, consists of three waterwheels: the first operated a pair of tilt-hammers, together with some ancillary machinery, the second powered a fan from which air was conducted through a system of underground pipes to the various forges, while the third waterwheel drove the grinding mill where the tools were sharpened and finished. Here is a large sandstone grinding wheel whose operation gave rise to the saying 'Keep your nose to the grindstone'.

Upper galleries are devoted to a display of tools made and used at the foundry, drawings, models and pictures illustrating the history of water-power and the history of the works itself which is typical of the small edge-tool works which served agricultural communities.

Address: Finch Foundry, Sticklepath, Okehampton, Devon. *Tel.* Sticklepath (083 784) 352.

Also Worth Visiting in Devon

Dartmouth, Newcomen engine (202/SX 879 515). Used in the Griff Colliery, Nuneaton, this original 1725 Newcomen atmospheric beam engine was re-erected in Coronation Park, Dartmouth to commemorate the 300th anniversary of the birth of Thomas Newcomen, the Dartmouth blacksmith and inventor.

Exeter Maritime Museum, The Quay, Exeter (192/SX 921 921). Housed in early-19th-century warehouses and the canal basin at Exeter, the museum has a wide collection of vessels, including the Brunel Bridgwater dredger. Under the shed of the fish quay is the King's beam, formerly used by customs officials for weighing dutiable goods. *Tel.* Exeter (0392) 58075.

Haytor granite tramway (191/SX 751 778). Built by George Templer and opened in September 1820, this unusual 4-foot 3-inch gauge tramway was used for transporting granite from the Haytor quarries to Ventiford Wharf on the Stover Canal at Teigngrace. The rails were made of granite blocks and the wagons were drawn by horses. The section from the quarry can be traced for about a mile on open moorland.

Ilfracombe, Hele Mill (180/SS 534 475). A restored watermill now operating which may date from the 16th century. It has an early porcelain roller mill and a 1928 diesel engine. *Tel.* Ilfracombe (0271) 63162.

Kingsbridge, William Cookworthy Museum, 108 Fore Street (202/SX 734 446). This museum has displays on the founder of the china clay industry who was born here and the industry itself, and also has a good agricultural gallery with a splendid cider press. *Tel.* Kingsbridge (0548) 3235.

Lynton and Lynmouth Railway (180/SS 721 496). Built to a Swiss design by a local family called Jones in 1890, it is powered by water from the West Lyn. The water is piped to the top station into a tank below one passenger car. The weight of water is sufficient to pull the other car to the top.

Mary Tavy, Wheal Betsey Engine House (191, 201/SX 510 813). The most visible engine house in Devon.

Meldon Viaduct (191/SX 565 924). A 540-foot wrought-iron viaduct, completed in 1874, which carried the railway across the West Okement at a maximum height of 120 feet.

Otterton Mill, Fore Street, Otterton (192/SY 089 852). A restored watermill dating from the 19th century and earlier, it has two wheels in parallel and is again in production. *Tel.* Colaton Raleigh (0395) 68521.

Plymouth: Eddystone Lighthouse, The Hoe (201/SX 478 538). When the present lighthouse was built in 1882, the upper part of the Smeaton lighthouse built in 1759, which was the third lighthouse on the site, was re-erected on the Hoe. See also *St Nicholas Chapel*, Ilfracombe (180/SS 527 429) and *Lundy, Old Light* (180/SS 132 444).

Tiverton, Grand Western Canal (181/SS 963 124). Constructed in 1810–14 as part of a canal intended to link the Bristol and English Channels, this contour canal runs for about 11 miles from the canal basin above Tiverton. The towpath makes a pleasant walk. Pleasure trips can be taken in the summer by narrow boat.

Tiverton Museum, St Andrew Street (181/SS 955 124), is a good example of a local museum with a range of exhibits relating to lace, railways etc. *Tel.* Tiverton (0884) 256295.

Uffculme, Coldharbour Mill (181/ST 163 023). This worsted spinning mill closed in 1981. It is now a museum illustrating the methods of woollen manufacture; the 18-foot iron waterwheel is being restored and a 1910 steam engine is in working condition. *Tel.* Craddock (0884) 40960.

DORSET

Apart from quarrying, Dorset has been remarkably unscarred by industrial activities but Portland and Purbeck are well known for their quarries and there are quarries and clay extraction around Corfe.

Portland: the quarries and other sites (Map 194)

For 400 years quarrying has been carried on here by the open-face system. The evidence of this activity is clear wherever you walk or drive through the isle. Everywhere you can see the stepped quarry faces, piles of stone which has been extracted but not carried away, showing the drill holes by which it was broken from the quarry face, and the remains of cranes for handling the stone. Along the cliffs the quays from which the stone was carried away by sea are visible. Some of the quarrymen's houses date from the late 18th century. There are a number of stone firms still operating.

Durdle Pier (SY 705 718), which has a crane of *c* 1870 by Galpin of Dorchester, is the last surviving 18th-century pier.

The line of the railway, which served the isle from 1865 to 1965, can be seen running alongside the road across the causeway and followed down the east side of the isle. The site of the passenger station, which was demolished in 1969, is now the large roundabout at the southern end of the causeway.

The *merchant's railway incline* with its stone sleepers, opened in 1826 as a mineral railway, runs up from the quay at *Castleton* (SY 686 744).

Portland – quarries and windmill

Two *windmill towers,* one with a little shafting remaining, can be seen south of *Easton* (SY 691 713).

At *Portland Bill*, together with the modern lighthouse and radar station (SY 677 682), there are two disused lighthouses, one in the radio station (SY 677 691) and the other now the Portland Bird Observatory and Field Centre (SY 681 690); a disused coastguard station (SY 676 693); and a triangular sighting point dated 1844 (SY 677 682).

Portland Museum, Wakeham, Easton (SY 695 713) contains material relating to quarrying and railways on the isle and its shipping and the winding mechanism from the old lighthouse.

Also Worth Visiting in Dorset

Bridport, Palmer's Brewery, West Bay Road (193/SY 465 921) is partly thatched and some of its power is still supplied by a waterwheel and a steam engine.

Bulbarrow Hill radio masts (194/ST 777 056, 780 057), four lattice masts of varying heights, are the remains of a World War II wireless station.

Corfe Mullen pumping station (195/SY 974 982) is being restored by the Poole IA Group. There are other pumping stations at *Friar Waddon* (194/SY 652 859) and *Sutton Poyntz* (194/SY 706 840).

Milton Abbas, Brewery Farm Museum (194/ST 804 016). An old farm brewery in which is housed a collection relating to brewing and the history of Milton Abbas, an attractive thatched estate village. *Tel*. Milton Abbas (0258) 880221.

Poole (Map 195). The Quay (SZ 008 903) retains a number of warehouses, the custom house and town beam and the old harbour office. The *Town Cellars,* Thames Street (SZ 008 903) house the maritime museum which illustrates the seaborne trade and shipping of the town; *Scaplens Court Museum,* Sarum Street (SZ 008 904) has displays in a fine 15th-century town house; and the *Guildhall Museum,* Market Street (SZ 009 906), housed in the 18th-century market house and guildhall, portrays the civic and social life of Poole in the 18th and 19th centuries. *Tel*. Poole (0202) 675151.

Weymouth, Harbour (194/SY 680 788). Along the quay are more old warehouses, the custom house and old fish market.

GLOUCESTERSHIRE

This county, sadly truncated by local government reorganization, has two faces: mining west of the Severn and cloth-making in the valleys of the Cotswolds. Water-borne transport along the Severn was also formerly of importance.

Mining and metal-working in Dean: Clearwell Caves and other sites

In Gloucestershire west of the Severn, in the Forest of Dean, iron-mining has been carried on since prehistoric times. Although both mining and iron manufacture have ceased, many signs of these activities can be seen.

Clearwell Caves (162/SO 578 084) are natural caves from which access to the iron lodes could be obtained. How early they were worked is a matter of conjecture but they provide an example of the kind of working carried on before deep mining began in the early 19th century. Known then as Old Ham Mine, it enjoyed an active period between 1846 and 1900 when 62,000 tons of ore were extracted. A further 3,000 tons were obtained during World War I. More recently red ochre for the paint industry was mined.

The Caves are open to the public.

Address: The Rocks, Clearwell Meend, near Coleford, Gloucestershire. *Tel*. Dean (0594) 23700.

Bream, Devil's Chapel Scowles (162/SO 607 046). Another site from which iron ore was won from prehistoric times. The worked-out areas of outcrop are known as 'scowles' and present here and elsewhere in Dean a fantastically contorted but heavily overgrown landscape of pits and intervening pillars. Care should be taken in visiting this site.

Coleford, Whitecliff Furnace (162/SO 568 103). Begun in 1798 and completed in 1806, this is the only coke-fired furnace to survive in Dean. For a time the well-known Scots metallurgist, David Mushet, was connected with it. This furnace, which stands 40 feet high and is 40 feet by 45 feet in plan, is being restored.

Milkwall, Darkhill Furnace (162/SO 590 088). Although the construction of the Severn and Wye Railway destroyed the lower part of this site, the remains of the furnace operated by David Mushet from 1819 till his death in 1847, together with many ancillary buildings, an ore-crushing grindstone and a tramroad with many sleeper blocks in place, can be seen.

Parkend, Blowing Engine House (162/SO 614 082). Built in the early 19th century to provide blast for the furnace and now used as a Field Centre, it is externally complete.

The Woollen Mills of Stroud (Map 162)

The most important industry carried on in Gloucestershire east of the Severn was the woollen industry and its main centre for

Clearwell Caves

several centuries was the Stroud valleys, four of which meet at Stroud: the Painswick and the Slad valleys from the north, the Frome valley from the east and the Nailsworth valley from the south. The combined streams flow westwards towards the Severn. At the height of the industry around 1820, about 200 woollen mills were working; now many have disappeared and only five are making cloth.

A good impression of the scale, type and location of the mills can be obtained by following the Nailsworth valley (A46) from the south and then the Stonehouse valley (A419) west from Stroud.

Starting in the centre of Nailsworth, *Day's Mill* (ST 850 996) can best be seen from the main car park to the west of the A46. A three-storey stone building with a brick projection running from the east end, it has been converted into a shop and art gallery; the inside can be seen during opening hours. *Egypt Mill* (ST 849 999) lies ¼ mile north of Nailsworth. The double millponds have been drained but the openings for the two waterwheels can be seen. A

Nailsworth – Egypt Mill

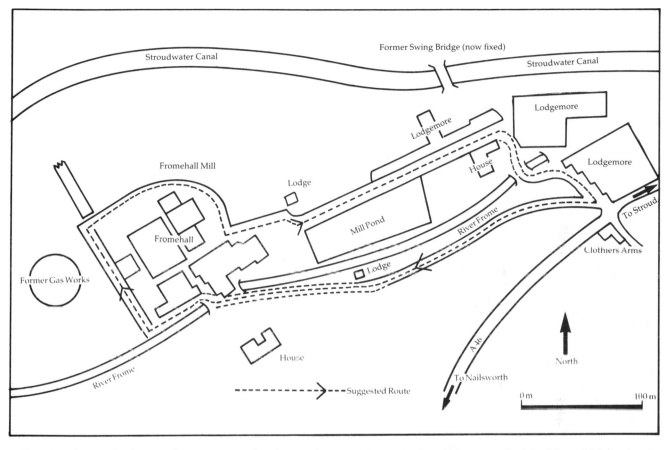

notice at road (attic) level states that it was a medieval cornmill and later became a pre-factory woollen mill. Now an agricultural merchant's, the interior of the building can be inspected when the store is open for business. A handsome clothier's house lies north of the mill. Continuing along the A46, *Dunkirk Mill* (SO 845 005) stands well back from the road on the right and so can easily be missed. A substantial five-storey stone mill, it is one of the finest surviving Cotswold mills. The millpond stretches south almost to Nailsworth; reputedly there are three waterwheels still in place. When a steam engine was installed, the elegant chimney stack was built. The mill buildings are now occupied by a range of small industries. Further along the road is *Merrett's Mill*

(SO 843 014), a late-19th-century brick building which has lost its chimney. The Nailsworth stream then passes under the road and the next sequence of mills is on the left (west) of the road.

Frogmarsh Mill (SO 841 018) lies just off the A46. The three-storey stone mill, like the other mills in the valley originally water-powered, is now a tannery. On the opposite side of the approach road is a circular tower reputed to be either a teazle tower or a drying store. Returning to the A46 and continuing north, just down the next road to the left is *Churches Mill* (SO 843 023), a two-storey building of brick and stone which had two undershot waterwheels. On the main road is *Woodchester Mill* (SO 844 028), a complex of 19th-century buildings, now a piano factory. A little further north is the surviving part of **Rooksmoor Mill** (SO 842 031), a 19th-century flock mill, where mats and cane ware are now made. The saleroom is open to the public. On the outskirts of Stroud is **Lightpill Mill** (SO 840 039) which has a clock in the gable. (The road to the left leads down to Dudbridge which once was a considerable industrial complex with corn and cloth mills, foundries and other works.) Taking the road into Stroud, the **Fromehall Mill** (SO 842 049) can be seen just under half a mile further on down a track opposite a public house, the Clothiers Arms. Park the car on the grass verge just north of the pub and follow the surfaced lane to Fromehall Mill House, now used as offices. From here (see map) a track leads down past the mill and over the Frome. Turn right through Fromehall mill buildings and past the millpond to **Lodgemoor Mill** (SO 845 050), which has a fine 18th-century clothier's house and late-19th-century mill extensions in brick. Cloth is still made here by Strachan & Company and Hunt & Winterbotham. From here, recross the Frome and return to the main road, then turn west towards Ebley on the A419. On this 3-mile stretch a number of the largest Stroud mills are to be found, south of the road. **Ebley Mill** (SO 829 045) was built in 1808–23; the New Mill is a five-storey stone building with a later slate-roofed turret and slender hexagonal chimney which had five waterwheels. It is now occupied by a clothmaker's and a printing firm. Turn left (south) off the A419 – the road crosses the Stroudwater Canal – to reach **Stanley Mill, King Stanley** (SO 812 043), one of the most outstanding mills in the country. The main five-storey block, built in 1812–13, is of brick with ornate windows and of fireproof construction with cast-iron columns. Originally it had five water-wheels but steam power was introduced in 1820. The mill stands on one side of a courtyard which is fronted on the other sides by ancillary buildings. Cloth is still made here.

The tour can of course be followed in the reverse direction with appropriate changes in the instructions: 'on the right' becomes 'on the left', and so on.

More mills can be seen in the Frome, Slad and Painswick valleys and there are some impressive mills in other parts of the county such as **New Mill, Kingswood** (ST 737 930), and **St Mary's Mill, Chalford** (SO 886 021).

Also Worth Visiting in Gloucestershire
Bibury, Arlington Mill (163/SP 113 068). A 17th-century water-mill, once a corn- and fulling mill, it now houses machinery brought from North Cerney, driven by electricity. *Tel.* Bibury (028 574) 368.

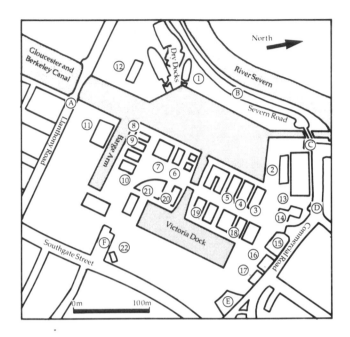

Chalford Round House (163/SO 892 024), a lock-keeper's cottage on the Thames and Severn Canal, stands adjacent to a complex of buildings once associated with the woollen industry. Other features worth visiting on the canal include the west portal of the two-mile tunnel at **Sapperton** (167/SO 944 033), reached by the footpath from the Daneway Inn (167/SO 938 035).

Cheltenham (Map 163) is notable for its ornamental ironwork: cast-iron balconies, porches, Dragon and Onion lamp-posts and hexagonal pillar-boxes.

Gloucester Docks (162/SO 82 18). Here is an important group of industrial buildings whose appearance has changed little for a century. Nearly all parts of the docks can be seen from the vantage points marked on the adjacent map. From A (Llanthony Bridge) there is a view up the main dock basin of 1810 including (12) **Alexandra Warehouse**, (8) and (9) **Biddles Warehouses** facing the Barge Arm in front of which are (10) old bollards, and (11) **Llanthony Warehouse**, built *c* 1870, and down the **Gloucester and Berkeley Canal**. From B (the site of warehouses) and C (the swing bridge above the lock down to the Severn) can be seen (1) the recent pumping house, (2) **North Warehouse** with its inscription at parapet level: 'The Gloucester and Berkeley Canal Company's

Warehouses erected by W. Rees and Son An.º Dom. 1826', (3), (4) and (5), **Robinsons** and **Philpotts** warehouses, and (6) and (7), **Albert Mills** and **Reynolds Mills**, flour mills still in operation. From D (the main Docks entrance) are visible (13) **Tap and drinking fountain** of 1863, (14) **Dock Office**, built *c* 1830, and (15) **City Flour Mills** (Priday Metford), built *c* 1850. On the way to E, go past (16) the classical **Custom House**, and (17) early **19th-century houses**. From E (the car park beside Commercial Road) there is a view of the **Victoria Dock** or Salt Basin of 1847–8 where Droitwich salt was loaded from barges onto schooners and ketches for Ireland and the Continent. The finest of the associated warehouses are (18) **Victoria**, (19) **Britannia** and (20) **Albert**. The **Mayflower**, a 19th-century tug used on the canal, is also visible. From F (off Southgate Street) can be seen (22) the neo-Greek **Weigh-Bridge House**, and (21) the **Mariner's Chapel**. **Bullo Pill** (162/SO 690 099), **Lydney Harbour** (162/SO 633 019–651 014) and **Sharpness Docks** (162/SO 657 022–664 028 and 670 031) are also worth a visit.

Leckhampton Quarries (163/SO 940 180). Now closed, the most active period of quarrying was the mid-19th century. The incline from Tramway Cottage with the stone sleepers still in position can be climbed. At the top are the foundations of the 1921 limekilns and the remains of various tramroads. A spectacular survival of earlier quarrying is the **Devil's Chimney** (SO 947 184) which dates from 1800.

Rodborough, Butterow Tollhouse (162/SO 856 040), a typical two-storey tollhouse with angled front, still has its tollboard intact.

Several *bridges* are worthy of note. *Chepstow Bridge* (162/ST 536 943) is a five-span cast-iron structure designed by John Raistrick and completed in 1816. It still has its orginal lampbrackets. *Mythe Bridge, Tewkesbury* (150/SO 889 337), was designed by Telford in 1826 and built of cast-iron sections by Hazeltine of Shrewsbury. It has a Gothic tollhouse at its eastern end. *Over Bridge* (162/SO 816 196), built by Thomas Telford in 1831, is now bypassed.

SOMERSET

Another recently shrunken county distinguished by mining at either end – on Exmoor and on the Mendips – with market towns and transport centres in between.

Bridgwater Dock Area (Map 182)
Bridgwater has had a varied commercial and industrial past during the last 300 years. Within a small area the remains of a

Bridgwater Docks

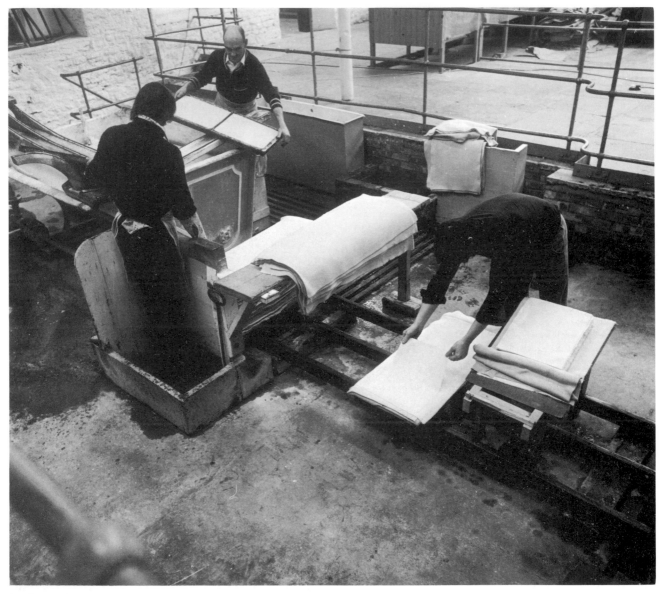

Wookey Hole Papermill

range of activities can be seen. From the Town Bridge walk north along West Quay which has iron bollards made by the local foundry, Culverwell, and a restored crane (ST 300 372). On the left is the red-brick warehouse of Peace Ltd. Continuing along the quay the telescopic bridge (ST 300 374), built for the Bristol and Exeter Railway in 1871, is reached. The bridge's eastern section traversed so as to allow the centre section to roll back, enabling vessels to pass. (The partial demolition by BR in the early 1970s makes interpretation of its function difficult.) The steam engine which was in a small building on the east bank has been removed and the bridge itself has been neglected. North of the bridge on the east bank is the site of Barham's brickworks. One pinnacle (or updraught) kiln survives and other buildings associated with brickmaking but the site is fast falling into decay. Along West Quay is the entrance to the docks (opened in 1841). The two locks of the tidal basin which was scoured by sluices can be seen but the entrance into the river has been blocked. Turn along the tidal basin and cross the bascule bridge which carries the road to Chilton Trinity. On the south side of the inner basin stands Ware's warehouse, a four-storey brick warehouse with stone dressings. On the north side is the Mump – a mound formed by the earth excavated from the inner basin. Walk along the north side of the inner basin. At the far end stands a steam mill (ST 296 375), which used to grind corn and animal feed. In front of the mill leading from the west end of the inner basin is the first lock of the extended length of the Bridgwater and Taunton Canal. The Chilton Trinity road can be reached by skirting the south side of the inner basin. Turn south along the road and at the next corner on the left behind the wall can be seen the site of the glass cone built by the 1st Duke of Chandos in the early 18th century. Turn east into Valetta Place; at the end is West Quay. Turn left and you are back where you started the tour.

Wookey Hole Papermill (182/ST 532 477)

In the past paper-making was a widely-distributed industry, being carried on in various parts of England, of which Somerset was one. Using the clear water of the Axe, a paperworks was established at Wookey Hole in the early 17th century and a watermark was first registered for the Wookey Hole mill in 1783. The mill was rebuilt in the 1850s with a steam engine as well as a Donkin turbine generating 40 horsepower. Offered for sale in 1858, the works was apparently acquired by William Sampson Hodgkinson, the first of the Hodgkinson family who made paper at Wookey Hole until the 1960s. Paper-making has been restarted in the papermill and the sequence of processes can be seen by

visitors. After the tour of the caves, visitors follow the canal which brings water to the papermill. They then pass through the rag boiler room, the vat house, past the heaters and the salle and the drying loft and can see handmade paper, for which there is a growing market, being made by traditional methods.

After the paperworks, other drying lofts in the mill have been restored to house a splendid collection of fairground carvings and relics. Then there is a store of the moulds used for the exhibits at Madame Tussaud's in London, and an archaeological museum.

Address: Wookey Hole Caves Ltd, Wookey Hole, Wells, Somerset BA5 1BB. *Tel.* Wells (0749) 72243.

Also Worth Visiting in Somerset

Allerford, Piles Watermill, Brandish Street (181/SS 905 465). A small cornmill which worked until 1930 and was then used for cider-making until 1940. Owned by the National Trust, it houses an agricultural museum.

Bradford-on-Tone, R. J. Sheppey & Son, Three Bridges (193/ST 178 224). Demonstrations of cider-making and a cider museum. *Tel.* Bradford-on-Tone (082 346) 233.

Charterhouse-on-Mendip, lead workings (172/ST 506 555). Substantial remains of lead-working in the 19th century can be seen in the Blackmoor valley including buddles (ST 504 555) and condensing flues (ST 507 560).

Dunster, a covered *yarn market* in the centre of the village (181/SS 989 438) and a *Mill* (SS 991 434) below the Castle. On a fulling mill site, the present late 17th-century watermill produces flour with recent replacement machinery. *Tel.* Dunster (064 382) 733 or 759.

East Harptree (172/ST 56 55) was a leadmining centre for centuries. The only surviving leadworks chimney on Mendip (183/ST 557 546) marks the site of a 19th-century leadworks.

High Ham, Stembridge Windmill (182/ST 433 305). An early 19th-century mill operated until 1910 and now owned by the National Trust. It is the only surviving thatched mill in the country. *Tel.* Langport (0458) 250818.

Priddy, St Cuthbert's lead smelting works (182, 183/ST 544 505). The last works to operate on the Mendips, closing in 1908; the ruins include the condensing flues.

Shepton Mallet, Anglo-Bavarian Brewery (183/ST 616 437), an impressive four-storey stone building of 1872 now used by a trading company.

Street, C. & J. Clark Ltd Shoe Museum (182/ST 485 368). The museum housed in the original factory has machines, documents and photographs illustrating the history of shoemaking. *Tel.* Street (0458) 3131.

Taunton, British Telecom Museum, 38 North Street (193/ST 227 247). Exhibits illustrate the history of telephone, telegraph and transmission equipment. *Tel.* Taunton (0823) 3391.

WILTSHIRE

A largely agricultural county with cloth-making, brewing and quarrying of some historical significance, its main interest for the industrial archaeologist derives from its position astride the main transport routes between London and the west.

Crofton Beam Engines and the Kennet and Avon Canal (174/SU 262 623)

A problem with canals rising over high ground from which flights of locks descended was to maintain sufficient water in the highest part. The Crofton pumping station was built to keep the top section of the Kennet and Avon supplied with water. The engine house contains two beam engines: that built by Boulton & Watt in 1812 is the oldest working beam engine under steam in the world; the other was built by Harvey's of Hayle (Cornwall) in 1845. With a foreshortened chimney, the engines are now operated by a trust.

Address: Crofton Beam Engines, 273 East Grafton, Burbage, Wiltshire. *Tel.* Marlborough (0672) 870300.

Crofton pump house

The Crofton Engine House is only one of the items of note along the Kennet and Avon in its passage through Wiltshire. Designed and built between 1794 and 1807, by John Rennie, one of the greatest engineers of his time, the canal enters Wiltshire by the **Dundas Aqueduct.** (See above, p. 15)

Avoncliffe Aqueduct (173/ST 805 600) takes the canal across the Avon again.

Bradford-on-Avon wharf and dock (173/ST 825 604) is one of two dry docks on the canal, recently restored.

Devizes (Caen Hill) Locks (173/ST 968 617 – SU 012 617). The canal rises from Semington to Devizes by 29 locks within 2½ miles by 237 feet; 17 of the locks are grouped in one impressive flight at *Caen Hill*. At Devizes there are a number of wharves with warehouses adjacent and at *Devizes Wharf* an iron crane.

At *Honey Street* (173/SU 103 615) there is a wharf and canal community. The canal inn has its original stabling and various other industrial works which grew around the canal's boat-building centre.

At *Burbage Wharf* (174/SU 236 632) is the last wharf crane on the canal.

There are many swing bridges, which turn on ball-bearing races (reputedly the first use of this device), and a number of GWR boundary posts.

At *Wootton Bassett* (173/SU 034 811) there are remains of seven locks of the Wiltshire and Berkshire Canal which linked the Kennet and Avon at Semington with the Thames at Abingdon.

Swindon: Great Western Railway Museum, Railway housing and workshops (173/SU 155 860 – 140 850)

Swindon is essentially a railway town. Accepting the advice of its engineer, Daniel Gooch, that Swindon was the obvious engine-changing point between London and Bristol, the GWR decided to make Swindon the site of its workshops. Although much reduced because of recent changes, the workshops still retain some of their original 1843 buildings.

To house the workers, an estate of houses was constructed from 1845. One of the first Victorian industrial estates, it had 243 houses by 1853. These have been modernized but one (34 Faringdon Road) has been restored and furnished in late-19th-century style and is open to the public. Nearby is the Great Western Railway Museum which was built as a 'model lodging house' in the 1840s. After a number of other uses, including a Wesleyan church, it became a museum in 1962. The main gallery, the Churchward, contains five locomotives (including the *Lode Star*, the *City of Truro* and a replica of the *North Star*) and a number of smaller exhibits; and there are separate rooms devoted to the work of Isambard Kingdom Brunel and Daniel Gooch. *Address:* Faringdon Road, Swindon, Wiltshire. *Tel.* Swindon (0793) 26161 ext. 3131.

The *Mechanics Institution* in the centre of the estate was built in 1853–4 to the design of Edward Roberts and enlarged in 1892. The *hospital* opposite has been converted into a community centre. On the edge of the estate, a *church*, *St Mark's*, was built to the design of Gilbert Scott and partly financed by the railway. The *railway station*, opened in 1842, has been sadly altered.

At *Chippenham* the railway crosses the A420 by an impressive bare round-arched viaduct (173/ST 912 731) built by Brunel in 1839. Further west the railway descends to Bath through the *Box Tunnel*, nearly 2 miles in length with a gradient of 1 in 100, engineered by Brunel in 1841. Its elaborate western portal (173/ST 829 689) can be seen on the left of the A4 as it descends to Box.

Also Worth Visiting in Wiltshire

Apart from the GWR and the Kennet and Avon Canal, the woollen industry provides the major group of survivals.

Bradford-on-Avon, Abbey Mill (173/ST 826 609) rebuilt in 1874; *Greenland Upper Mill* (ST 830 606) and *Kingston Mill* (ST 827 609), now occupied by the Moulton Rubber Company.

Chapmanslade, where some small woollen workshops survive (183/ST 824 478).

Devizes, Anstie's Mill (173/SU 005 615) built in 1785, the earliest woollen factory in Wiltshire.

Malmesbury, Avon Mill (173/ST 936 869), a large L-shaped building, of which part dates from the 1790s.

Trowbridge (Map 173), where there are a number of *clothiers' houses* (The Parade and elsewhere), mill buildings (notably *Ashton Mill* (ST 861 576), *Castle Mill* (ST 855 577) and *Home Mills* (ST 856 579)), most of which are now used for other purposes; and rows of weavers' cottages, particularly at *Newtown* (ST 853 576).

Westbury, Angel Mill and clothworkers' houses in Prospect Square (183/ST 873 512).

Wilton, the carpet factory (184/SU 100 314).

In addition, see:

Wilton Windmill (174/SU 276 617). A tower mill of the 1820s, it is the only working windmill to remain in Wiltshire. It ceased work in the 1920s and has been restored. *Tel.* c/o Marlborough (0672) 870268.

South-East England

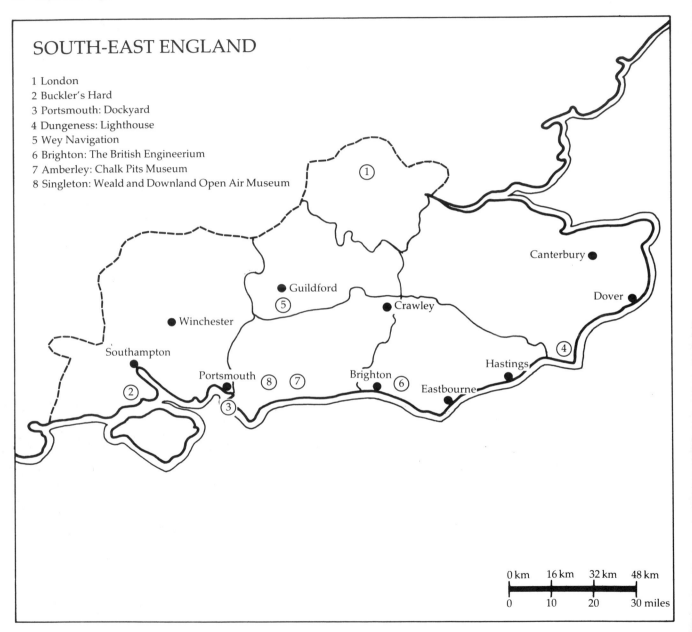

SOUTH-EAST ENGLAND

1 London
2 Buckler's Hard
3 Portsmouth: Dockyard
4 Dungeness: Lighthouse
5 Wey Navigation
6 Brighton: The British Engineerium
7 Amberley: Chalk Pits Museum
8 Singleton: Weald and Downland Open Air Museum

① Guildford
⑤
Crawley
Canterbury
Dover
④
Winchester
Southampton
Portsmouth ⑧ ⑦ Brighton ⑥ Hastings
② ③ Eastbourne

| 0 km | 16 km | 32 km | 48 km |
| 0 | 10 | 20 | 30 miles |

HAMPSHIRE

Hampshire was a mainly agricultural county with brewing and water-powered milling important but it also had two major ports, Southampton and Portsmouth.

Brockenhurst: Buckler's Hard (196/SU 409 001)

In the days of wooden shipping small vessels were built on a convenient beach or river bank. Little was required in the way of capital equipment and the vessels were constructed with the aid of a variety of handtools. Consequently there are few remains to identify particular sites. One such yard, probably the most important of the rural shipbuilding centres in the 18th century, was at Buckler's Hard. Here there was a quay, a hard bank, a co-operative landlord (the Duke of Montague), sheltered but deep water and timber close at hand. The settlement, planned with a street 80 feet wide which proved convenient for the carriage of timber, began with three houses nearest the water on the western edge. Shipbuilding began in the 1740s. In the early 1770s an additional launchway was piled at Buckler's Hard by Henry Adams, the best known of the shipbuilders, to enable larger vessels to be constructed. Most famous of the naval vessels which came from Buckler's Hard was *Agamemnon*, Nelson's favourite ship, launched in 1781. Vessels continued to be built at Buckler's Hard until the early 1950s. A number of houses and two former inns survive of the original settlement. Five buildings are open to the public. The New Inn, at the top of the street, houses the museum containing models and original drawings of ships and material relating to the history of the site. The activities of the Adams family, shipbuilders at Buckler's Hard for more than a century, are well documented. Further down the street are a shipwright's cottage and a labourer's cottage with reconstructed interiors. Then there is a small chapel, formerly a cobbler's shop, in which services have been held since 1885; and

Henry Adams' house, now the Master Builder's House Hotel. The remains of two launchways can be seen at the bottom of the street.

Address: Buckler's Hard Maritime Museum, Buckler's Hard, Brockenhurst, Hampshire. *Tel.* Buckler's Hard (059 063) 203.

Portsmouth Dockyard (196/SU 628 007)

The construction of the great English dockyards starts in the late 17th century. Then works were begun at Chatham, at Plymouth and at Portsmouth. While most of the dockyard at Portsmouth is usually closed to the public, HMS **Victory**, Nelson's flagship at

Trafalgar, can be visited. In the course of restoration to her 1805 condition, *Victory* occupies No. 2 Dock which was constructed in 1802. Built of Portland stone with a bow recess at the landward end and stepped sides, this dock is typical of the six docks at Portsmouth which were made between 1698 and 1803. The basin itself dates from 1691–8 and was enlarged by Bentham in 1795–1801 before the construction of Docks Nos. 1, 2 and 3.

The **Block Mills**, erected in 1802 to house Marc Isambard Brunel's block-making machinery, are of historic importance as the scene of the first application of machine tools to mass production, to make the various types of pulley block required by the Royal Navy. By 1809 the plant had a yearly output of 130,000 blocks. A 74-gun ship of the time required 922 blocks for its rigging. The interior of the building is entirely of wood, so restricting the weight of machines which could be installed on the first floor. It is planned to display some of the Brunel machines in a dockyard museum.

Other buildings of interest include: the *Great Ropery*, a 1,018-foot building which dates from 1775; the *Dockyard Fire Station*, built of corrugated iron on a cast-iron framework, erected in 1843; the *No. 1 Smithery* built to meet the needs of the steam navy in 1852 which has one of the largest foundries in the south of England; the highly decorated *Train Shed* on the South Jetty, built for the convenience of Royalty and others using the branch line from the Harbour Station; the *Chain Testing Shop* of *c* 1850 with its elegant cast-iron columns; and *No. 6 Boathouse*, a massive stone structure of 1843, which houses Brunel's scoring machine.

Address: Portsmouth Royal Naval Museum, HM Naval Base, Portsmouth, Hampshire PO1 3LR. *Tel.* Portsmouth (0705) 822351, ext. 23868.

Also Worth Visiting in Hampshire

Beaulieu, National Motor Museum, Palace House (196/SU 383 029). The major collection of motor vehicles in Britain. *Tel.* Beaulieu (0590) 612345.

Bordon, Headley Watermill (186/SU 812 356). A mill site since the 12th century, this is the last mill in Hampshire to work commercially by waterpower. *Tel.* Bordon (042 03) 2031 in business hours.

Botley, tollhouse (196/SU 509 137), on the A3051, is a two-storey brick building, rectangular in shape with half-hexagonal frontage.

Lymington, salterns (196/SZ 328 940). Embanked pools and three buildings beside Lower Woodside Creek are all that remains of a saltmaking industry, using the sun to evaporate off the water, which has been there from prehistoric times. The 17th and 18th centuries were a period of considerable trade.

Portsmouth, Eastney Pumping Station, Henderson Road, Eastney (196/SZ 674 992). The original pump house of 1868 stands, there is an engine house of 1887 which houses two Watt compound steam engines of that date and in the 1904 pump house are two Crossley gas engines. To complete the sequence there is a diesel engine and two electric pumps of 1922 and 1939. *Tel.* Portsmouth (0705) 737979.

Southampton Docks (196/SU 430 108 etc). Construction began in 1838 and the Princess Alexandra Dock was opened in 1842. Recent changes have involved the alteration or demolition of much of the original work but the Empress Dock (1890) is mostly as built. The piers of the floating dock berth remain while the coal barge dock is now used by timber barges.

Totton, Eling Tidemill (196/SU 365 125). Built on a 15th-century causeway across an inlet of the Test, the present building and machinery date from the 18th and 19th centuries. It has been restored and is open as a museum producing flour. *Tel.* Totton (0703) 869575.

Twyford, Pumping Station (185/SU 493 248) was constructed by the South Hants Water Company in 1898 and extended in 1910. It houses a Hawthorn Davy triple expansion engine. The station had its own quarry and limekilns to produce the lime used as a water softener. Two Ruston diesels of 1935 are housed in an extension to the station. The buildings are in the process of being restored by Southern Water and are not yet open to the public.

Whitchurch Silk Mill (185/SU 463 479). A fine three-storey structure which dates from 1815, it was formerly water-driven but now weaves by electricity. *Tel.* Whitchurch (025 682) 2065.

ISLE OF WIGHT

The Isle of Wight has agriculture, milling and tourism as its main activities.

Bembridge Windmill (196/SZ 639 875). A stone tower mill dating from about 1700. The only remaining windmill on the island, it is owned by the National Trust. *Tel.* Bembridge (098 387) 3654.

Calbourn, Upper Watermill (196/SZ 414 869). Working commercially until recently with a roller plant which last worked in 1955, it now runs in the summer for demonstrations and there is a rural life museum in the grounds.

Carisbrooke Castle donkey wheel (196/SZ 487 877). The well-house and donkey wheel were rebuilt in 1587 over a 161-foot well which was sunk in 1150. The wheel, 15 feet 6 inches in diameter, is operated by donkeys during opening hours. *Tel.* Newport (0983) 523112.

Cowes Maritime Museum, Cowes Library, Beckford Road (196/SZ 496 958), contains a display of relics of the shipbuilding industry in Cowes over the last century. *Tel.* Cowes (0983) 293341. The early port area in Cowes suffered considerable war damage and one of the few survivors is the three-storey stone-built *warehouse* in Medina Road (SZ 498 955).

Carisbrooke – well and donkey wheel

Isle of Wight Steam Railway, The Railway Station, Haven-street (196/SZ 556 898). This 2-mile steam railway has a collection of preserved locomotives, rolling stock and so on. *Tel.* Wootton Bridge (0983) 882204. The most attractive, and little altered, of the island stations is **Shanklin** (196/SZ 581 819).

St Catherine's Point lighthouse (196/SZ 497 754) was built in 1838–40 and reduced from 120 feet to 86 feet in 1875. The lighthouse keepers' houses date from the 1830s and the second two-storey tower was added in 1932. About 1 mile north, on the other side of the main road, is the two-storey circular tower remains of an earlier lighthouse which was begun in 1785 but never finished as it was frequently obscured by mist (SZ 494 773). About 150 yards north-west of this is the medieval pharos attached to St Catherine's Oratory.

Yafford Watermill (196/SZ 446 822). Grinding animal feed until recently, it is now part of a farm park with the wheel and some machinery turned for demonstration. *Tel.* Brighstone (0983) 740610.

Tidemills

Tidemills were an important source of power on the island and at least seven are known to have existed at one time or another: at **St Helen's** (196/SZ 632 887) the dam survives and the shell of the building has been converted into a house; at **Wootton** (196/SZ 547 920), the building can be seen on the bridge; at **East Medina** (196/SZ 508 919) the pool is used as a mooring place and at **West**

Medina (196/SZ 503 914) some machinery survives; at **Yarmouth** (196/SZ 356 894), the three-storey building of 1793 still stands on the dam but the pond is silted up; and at **Freshwater** (196/SZ 348 872) the road to Afton runs along the line of the dam.

KENT

Kent is an agricultural county which also had iron, gunpowder-making and shipbuilding and some important seaports.

Dungeness Lighthouse (189/TR 088 168)
To guide the mariner, the Mediterranean coast came to be lined with lighthouses in the classical period and the Pharos of Alexandria has been regarded as one of the seven wonders of the Ancient World.

After the Roman invasion, Dover became an important port and in the late 1st or early 2nd century a pharos (an octagonal tower 80 feet high and 14 feet square) was erected on the eastern heights overlooking the harbour (179/TR 326 418). One of the most remarkable buildings of Roman Britain, it can still be seen (in a patched-up state) in the grounds of Dover Castle. There are fragmentary remains of a second lighthouse at Dover preserved in the bowels of an abandoned Victorian fort on the western side of Dover.

At Dungeness, set in a ravaged landscape and in the lee of the Dungeness atomic power station, three stages of lighthouse development can be seen. The brick part of the tower of a lighthouse built in 1792 to the design of Samuel Wyatt by William Coke of Holkham now serves as dwellings for the lighthouse keepers. It had a 120-foot wooden tower with a brazier on the top. Alongside is the lighthouse of 1902, a brick tower 140 feet high with 169 steps, which had a light with paraffin vapour burner and weight-driven rotational mechanism. There were additional sector lights half-way up the tower to give warning of the shallows. It ceased to operate in 1961.

Nearby is the concrete tower lighthouse, built in 1965, which replaced it.

Address: Keeper in Charge, Old Lighthouse, Dungeness, Romney Marsh, near Lydd, Kent TN29 9NB. *Tel.* Lydd (0679) 20236.

Also Worth Visiting in Kent

Cranbrook, Union Windmill (188/TQ 779 359). A tall smock mill built in 1814, run by wind until 1954, now milling by electric power. Restored in 1960 by Dutch millwrights, it now has steel sail stocks. *Tel.* Cranbrook (0580) 712312.

Dover, Crabble Watermill (179/TR 297 432). A six-storey mill built in 1812 to supply flour to troops and later to London. Closed in 1890, it has been restored. *Tel.* (Curator, Dover Museum) Dover (0304) 201066.

Dover, Fairbairn jib crane, Wellington Basin (179/TR 319 410). A rare, hand-operated survival of 1868, it could lift 20 tons.

Faversham, Chart Gunpowder Mills (178/TR 010 612). For 300 years Faversham was a major centre of gunpowder manufacture; this works, on the site of the oldest establishment, consisted of two pairs of gunpowder mills, each pair worked in tandem off a single large waterwheel, one of which has been preserved. *Tel.* c/o Faversham (0795) 534542.

Folkestone cliff railway (179/TR 224 355) 180 feet long, has four tracks, the first pair built in 1885 and the second added in 1890. See also the cliff railways at *Broadstairs* (179/TR 397 678) running

through the cliff face from Albion Street down to Viking Bay; *Margate* (179/TR 362 712) from Lower Promenade to the Cliff Top Promenade.

Hythe, Royal Military Canal. Built in 1806 as a defence against invasion by Napoleon, the canal runs from a sluice in the sea wall (189/TR 189 348) to Winchelsea (189/TQ 895 150).

Maidstone, papermills (Map 188). Paper has been an important industry on the Medway and its tributaries. *Hayle Mill* (TQ 756 538) is one of the few still producing handmade paper in a historic building; *Turkey Mill* (TQ 772 555) has a fine 18th-century dry loft.

Meopham Windmill (177/TQ 639 653). An unusual hexagonal smock mill built in 1801. Last worked by wind in 1929, it has been restored to working order. *Tel.* c/o Meopham (0474) 813218 or 812110.

Mersham, Swanton Watermill (189/TR 038 388). Last in business in 1920, it was restored in the 1970s and now grinds local wheat for demonstration. *Tel.* Aldington (023 372) 223 or 01–937 0931 (weekdays).

Sheerness Dockyard (Map 178). Relinquished by the Navy in 1960, it contains a number of interesting naval buildings, particularly the fireproof Archway Block (TQ 911 752) and the iron-frame Boatstore of 1858–60 (TQ 910 753).

Sittingbourne, Dolphin Barge Yard (178/TQ 910 643), a repair facility for Thames barges, is being preserved with a small museum.

Oasthouses are a very characteristic feature of this hop-growing county. Notable ones include: *Chestfield* (179/TR 134 658); *Lamberhurst* (188/TQ 675 355), four dating from 1876; *Pembury* (188/TQ 644 399), and *Sissinghurst* (188/TQ 807 384), at Sissinghurst Castle and now used as tea rooms. The Museum at *Wye Agricultural College*, Court Lodge Farm, Brook, near Ashford (189/TR 066 444) includes an oasthouse which has been fully restored so that the construction and operation are visible.

There are a number of *steam railways* operating in Kent:

Kent and East Sussex Railway, Tenterden Town Station, Tenterden (189/TQ 883 335). *Tel.* Tenterden (058 06) 2943. *Romney, Hythe and Dymchurch Light Railway*, New Romney Station, New Romney (189/TR 074 248), a 14-mile, 15-inch gauge line, is in regular service in summer, *Tel.* New Romney (067 93) 2353. *Sittingbourne and Kemsley Light Railway*, The Wall, Milton Regis, Sittingbourne (178/TQ 905 643), has a 2-foot 6-inch gauge industrial system.

GREATER LONDON (Maps 176, 177)

As the largest British city with a long history of commercial and industrial activity, there is much to be seen. Only a selection of sites can therefore be listed briefly here.

Various kinds of *power* are well represented.
A number of *windmills* survive, of which the best preserved are:

Arkley Mill (TQ 217 953), a restored tarred brick tower mill of about 1800 which worked until 1916 and is now in the garden of a private house.

Brixton Mill, Blenheim Gardens, Lambeth (TQ 305 745), a 48-foot tarred brick tower mill which was restored in 1964 but is at present closed as a result of vandalism.

Croydon, Shirley Mill, Upper Shirley Road (TQ 355 652), a smock mill of about 1855 in the grounds of John Ruskin High School. *Tel.* 01–656 0994.

Keston Mill, Heathfield Road (TQ 415 640), a weatherboarded post mill of about 1716 with a tarred brick roundhouse, in the garden of the Mill House.

Upminster Mill, St Mary's Lane (TQ 556 867). Large white smock mill with cottage and bakery built early in the 19th century and working until World War II. *Tel.* Romford (0708) 44297.

Wimbledon Common Windmill, Windmill Road (TQ 230 725). A hollow post mill of 1817 with a large octagonal roundhouse containing a milling museum. *Tel.* 01–788 7658 or 01–947 2825.

There are a number of *watermills* along the Wandle, including:

Merton Abbey Works, Station Road (TQ 264 698) where a former Liberty's silk printing works established in 1885 in an older building retains a large iron undershot wheel in a wheelhouse.

Morden Hall Park Mills, Morden Hall Road (TQ 262 686), two snuff mills on either side of the river, the one on the east 18th century and the other about 1860. One large undershot wheel survives.

Amongst other *power* sites are:

Three Mills, Bromley-by-Bow (TQ 383 828) were operated by the tide. Two of the three, House Mill (1776) and Clock Mill (1817) remain, the latter turned into offices.

Kew Bridge Pumping Station, Kew Bridge Road, Brentford (TQ 188 780) houses four Cornish beam engines built in 1820–71 to pump water for London. They operated until 1944 and (together with other engines) are back in steam as museum exhibits.

Fulham Gasworks, Sands End Lane, Michael Road (TQ 260 768) has the oldest surviving gasholder (*c* 1830) and one with some of the finest ironwork. See also the impressive group of gasholders at Goods Way, *King's Cross* (TQ 300 833), dating from 1868–74, repainted in their original colours.

East Greenwich Gasworks (TQ 393 794), 1892, has two large holders, one of which is said to be the largest in the world.

Battersea Power Station, Cringle Street, Nine Elms Lane (TQ 290 775) was built by Sir Giles Gilbert Scott in 1934 and extended in 1954; this cathedral of power is now obsolete.

The drainage of London is a major example of *public services.*

Abbey Mills Pumping Station (TQ 388 832) was built in Gothic

Kew Bridge pumping station

style in 1865–8 to house eight beam engines to pump sewage as part of Sir Joseph Bazalgette's scheme for the drainage of London.

The Embankment (TQ 303 798 – 317 808) provides a cover for the lower interceptor sewer (and for the Underground) built by Sir Joseph Bazalgette in 1864–70 through which sewage flows by gravity to the Abbey Mills Pumping Station. Along the Embankment are elaborate dolphin lamp standards and benches with cast-iron ends. There is a memorial to Bazalgette near Charing Cross bridge, the two brick piers of which are the remains of Brunel's suspension footbridge, the Hungerford Bridge, 1841–5. Across the river at the south end of Westminster Bridge can be seen the South Bank Lion which originally was on the site of the Lion Brewery nearby. It was made in 1837 of Coade Stone, an artificial stone designed to withstand London's corrosive air.

Many forms of *transport* can be seen.

Regent's Canal, 1812–20, can be followed from Little Venice, Blomfield Road, Paddington (TQ 262 818) to Limehouse Dock, Narrow Street, E14 (TQ 363 810).

St Pancras station

The Roundhouse, Camden Town

Grand Union Canal was built between 1794 and 1801 from Brentford to the Midlands. See in particular at Hanwell a flight of six locks behind the hospital (TQ 146 797) and the unusual Three Bridges aqueduct at Windmill Lane (TQ 143 797) where road, rail and canal cross.

Surrey Iron Railway ran from Wandsworth to Croydon with an extension to Merstham, 1801–46. There are relaid sections of the track in the grounds of Wallington Public Library, **Shotfield** (176, 187/TQ 288 637), where there is also a copy of a tollboard, and **Purley** Rotary Field (176, 187/TQ 316 622). Parts of the original track survive outside the Joliffe Arms Hotel, **Hooley** (187/TQ 290 542) and the route of the railway can be walked.

Railway stations: King's Cross (TQ 303 830), built 1850–2 by William and Lewis Cubitt; **Paddington** (TQ 266 813), built by I. K. Brunel and M. Digby-Wyatt in 1855; **St Pancras** (TQ 301 828), designed by W. H. Barlow and built 1868–74; and **Liverpool Street** (TQ 333 817), built in 1872–5, all have splendid overall train sheds. Each is fronted by a hotel: King's Cross by the functional Great Northern, Paddington by the Great Western Royal in French Baroque style, St Pancras by the Midland Grand, Gilbert Scott's Gothic profusion of 1873–6, and Liverpool Street by the turreted and gabled Great Eastern Hotel.

London Bridge-Deptford viaduct (TQ 334 798–373 774), 3¾ miles long with 878 arches, is claimed to be the longest brick structure in the world.

Camden Town Roundhouse, Chalk Farm Road (TQ 283 843). This stabling for at least 20 locomotives, built in 1847 for the LNWR, is now a theatre. *Tel.* 01–267 2564.

Wharncliffe viaduct, adjacent to Uxbridge Road, Hanwell (TQ 150 804). Built of yellow brick in 1836–7 by I. K. Brunel to carry the GWR over the Brent, it is 900 feet long with eight arches and the massive square pillar piers are hollow to lessen the load of the structure. It was widened in 1874.

Tower Bridge (TQ 337 802). Opened in 1894, this bascule bridge spanning the Thames is a familiar landmark. Now electrically operated, two of the steam engines have been preserved. *Tel.* 01–407 0922.

Thames Tunnel. Built by Marc Brunel in 1825–43 between Rotherhithe and Wapping, it was used as a pedestrian tunnel until taken over by the Underground railway in 1869. The original access shafts at Rotherhithe (now a pumping station) and Wapping (the entrance to the Underground) survive while the engine house in St Marychurch Street, Rotherhithe (TQ 352 798) has been restored.

Kingsway Tramway Tunnel (TQ 305 817), an underpass opened in 1906 to take trams from Waterloo Bridge to Theobalds Road, is now partly used for motor vehicles but the disused Theobalds Road end can be seen.

London Transport Museum, Covent Garden (TQ 305 812) has a comprehensive collection of road and rail vehicles, including

St Katharine's Docks

Bollard, St Katharine's Docks

many working exhibits, which, together with maps, historical posters, photographs and audio-visual displays, chronicle 200 years of public transport in London. *Tel.* 01–379 6344.

St Katharine's Docks (TQ 339 805) were built by Thomas Telford in 1825–8 and covered an area of 23 acres. Most of the surrounding warehouses have been demolished but one of the later ones has been renovated and a few of the original dock fittings survive. In the East Basin is the Maritime Trust's Historic Ship Collection including the *Kathleen and May* topsail schooner, the *Lydia Eva* herring drifter, the *Nore* lightship and the *Cambria* Thames barge. *Tel.* 01–481 0043.

Riverside Warehouses, Wapping High Street and Wapping Wall (TQ 342 802, 353 805) are a typical 19th-century dockside development with five- to seven-storey warehouses lining both sides of the street.

Croydon airport terminal and traffic control building, Purley Way (TQ 311 636) is one of the few monuments connected with air travel. Built 1927–8, the severely functional building was the largest in the world at that time. The airport closed in 1959. The control tower, terminal, two hangars and the hotel now form part of an industrial estate.

Distribution and services are exemplified by the following.

Covent Garden Market (TQ 303 808). Formerly the major English wholesale market for fruit and vegetables, it now houses a variety of shops and eating places. The Floral Hall was reputedly constructed from parts of the Crystal Palace when it was dismantled in Hyde Park after the Great Exhibition.

Smithfield Meat Market (TQ 318 817), built 1867–8, has a fine cast-iron interior.

James Smith & Sons umbrella shop, 32 New Oxford Street (TQ 301 815) is a splendid example of a Victorian shop front.

George Inn, Borough High Street, Southwark (TQ 327 801). Only one side of this, the last remaining galleried inn in London, survives. It was famous as a coaching terminus in the 18th and 19th centuries.

Comparatively little is preserved of *manufacturing industry.*

Fulham Pottery, 210 New King's Road (TQ 244 761) was founded in the late 17th century; a 19th-century bottle oven remains beside a modern building. See also a tile kiln in the yard at Hippodrome Mews, Walmer Road, *Kensington* (TQ 242 805).

Whitbread's Brewery, Chigwell Street, Barbican (TQ 326 819) retains some 18th-century buildings. The Porter Tun Room (John Smeaton, 1784) has the second largest timber roof in Europe. It

James Smith & Sons umbrella shop

Battersea Power Station

was one of the first sites in London to adopt steam power on a large scale. See also Truman's *Eagle Brewery*, Brick Lane, Spitalfields (TQ 338 820) which dates from 1756 (Wilkes Street façade) and 1837, and the *Ram Brewery*, Wandsworth High Street (TQ 256 747) where traditional ales are still made using steam engines, probably the last working commercially in Britain.

Kirkaldy Experimenting and Testing Works, 99 Southwark Street (TQ 318 804). David Kirkaldy moved to these custom-built premises in 1873. His special testing machine which takes up almost the whole ground floor was used to test all kinds of construction materials. At present it can only be viewed externally but part of the building is to be converted to a museum.

Spitalfields silk-weavers' houses are distinguishable by their attic rooms with large windows to provide maximum light. An outstanding example is at 14 Fournier Street (TQ 338 818) but a number can be seen in this area.

Working class housing can be seen in many places in central London: off Charing Cross Road, off New Oxford Street (Model Dwellings for Families by Henry Roberts, 1849), off Kingsway and elsewhere.

Science Museum, Exhibition Road SW7 (TQ 268 794). Its collections began in 1857 and it became a separate museum in 1909. The major museum illustrating the range of British achievements in science and industry, its exhibits (original equipment, copies and models) include a range of power units (stationary and moving), manufacturing industry, hand and machine tools, building construction, etc. *Tel.* 01–589 3456.

SURREY

Surrey is a county notable for service industries, canals and railways.

River Wey & Godalming Navigation (Maps 176, 186)
Before the improvement of the roads carried out by the turnpike trusts from the late 17th century, water transport was important, particularly for the carriage of agricultural products and heavy goods. The first stage of improvement affected the rivers. The lower part of the River Wey was made navigable for barges in 1653 when 15 miles of navigation between Weybridge and Guildford were created by the construction of 12 locks and the

Barges unload at Coxes Lock Mill, Addlestone

digging of 10 miles of artificial channel. In 1763 the navigation was extended a further 4 miles upstream to Godalming. In the early 19th century it had an active trade, particularly in agricultural produce, but traffic declined once the railway had reached Guildford in 1845. Some commercial traffic continued until 1958. In 1964 the Wey Navigation was given to the National Trust and in 1968 the Godalming Navigation was also handed over.

The entrance to the canal from the Thames at **Weybridge** (Thames Lock) is by a single wide-beam wooden gate (176/TQ 073 655); there is a simple lock-keeper's cottage here. Alongside **Coxes Lock** at **Addlestone** (176/TQ 061 641) is the 18th-century office building of Allied Mills and a seven-storey 19th-century eastern block with a gabled attic. There is a water turbine here. At **Pyrford** the wheel pits of Newall Mill can be seen (186/TQ 040 574). **Walsham Gates** (186, 187/TQ 050 578), a flood lock, is one of the few turf-sided locks left: it has peg-and-hole paddles, as has the Worsfold Gates at **Send** (186/TQ 016 557), also a flood lock. In both cases the gates are normally left open.

At **Guildford** there is a fine range of three- and four-storey warehouses (186/SU 992 497) and an 18th-century wooden treadmill crane (SU 994 495). The treadwheel is 20 feet in diameter and 4 feet wide. On **Dapdune Wharf** (SU 993 503) there are the remains of a boatbuilding and repair yard for the Wey Navigation with cottages, boat shed, forge and hand-operated crane.

Stonebridge Wharf (186/SU 998 464) was the entrance to the now derelict Wey and Arun Canal. A little further along the canal the piers of the demolished bridge of the Guildford–Horsham railway line can be seen (TQ 001 462).

Address: River Wey and Godalming Navigation, Dapdune Lea, Wharf Road, Guildford, Surrey GU1 4RR. *Tel.* Guildford (0483) 61389.

Other features on the Wey and Arun Canal (Map 186), opened in 1816, are the **Gosden Aqueduct** (TQ 007 456) which is dry; **Birtley Wharf, Bramley** (TQ 018 435) which is still in water; **Run Common Wharf, Stanley Green** (TQ 033 419) where the canal crosses the Cranleigh–Bramley road (dry); and **Elmford Wharf** (TQ 039 390) at the summit of the canal.

Some remains of the other Surrey canal, the **Basingstoke Canal** (opened in 1796), are of interest: **Woodham Locks, Byfleet** (186-187/TQ 033 609–052 618), a set of five locks; **Framley Locks, Purbright** (186/SU 911 566–944 569), a derelict set of 14 locks giving a 91-foot rise which runs parallel to the former L&SWR (now SR) Southampton line; and, at **Frimley Green**, an aqueduct which carries the canal over the railway (186/SU 893 565).

Also Worth Visiting in Surrey

Betchworth, Dorking Greystone Lime company, Station Road (187/TQ 208 514). Extensive chalk quarries with a number of limekilns, railway tracks and so on are visible from footpaths in the area.

Claygate telegraph tower (187/TQ 158 647). A three-storey Semaphore House with flat roof, one of a series of Admiralty stations for relaying messages between London and Portsmouth *c.* 1823–8. Others survive at **Cobham** (187/TQ 089 585), Chately Heath (five storeys); and **Guildford** (186/TQ 002 492), 39 Pewley Hill.

Cranleigh, Swallow's Tile Works, Brookhurst Hill (187/TQ 076 393). A local tile works with five small kilns, established in 1894.

East Clandon, icehouse, Hatchlands (187/TQ 067 519). A fine small domed icehouse on National Trust property. *Tel.* Guildford (0483) 222787.

Edenbridge, Haxsted Watermill Museum (187/TQ 418 455). A 17th- and 18th-century mill which last worked in 1949 and has been extensively restored and works for demonstrations. It also houses an exhibition on the Wealden iron industry. *Tel.* Edenbridge (0732) 862914.

Esher, mileposts (Map 176). Most striking is a 3-foot stone cylinder outside the Orleans Arms in Portsmouth Road (TQ 147 655). Others can be found between 24 and 26 Milbourne Lane (TQ 142 640), in Claremont Park (TQ 134 630) and in the south side of the cutting on the A3 just south-west of Claremont House (TQ 127 629).

Godalming, water tower, Frith Hill Road (186/SU 969 447). Late

19th-century. There are also water towers at *Busbridge* (186/SU 987 428), and *Gravelly Hill, Caterham* (187/TQ 337 533).

Outwood Windmill (187/TQ 327 456). The oldest working windmill in the country, it was built in the mid-17th century. *Tel.* Smallfield (034 284) 3438.

Reigate Heath Windmill (187/TQ 234 502). A mid-18th-century post mill with roundhouse which was converted to a chapel in 1880.

Shalford Watermill (186/TQ 002 477). A timber-framed and tile-hung mill with a low breastshot wheel which now belongs to the National Trust. *Tel.* Guildford (0483) 61617.

Staines, West Station, Wraysbury Road (176/TQ 033 718). An unusual example of a private house (*c* 1820) converted to a station (1885). See also *West Ewell Station*, Chessington Road (176, 187/TQ 214 627); *Baynards Station, Rudgwick* (187/TQ 076 351) (disused).

Walton-on-Thames, bridge and tollhouse (176/TQ 093 665). An iron bridge of 1863–4 on the brick-built arched approaches and parapets of the original tollbridge of 1759. From the north bank the brick and tile tollhouse can be seen.

Coal duty boundary posts (see below, p. 64) exist in various parts of the county, for example ½ mile east of *Sunbury* lock (176/TQ 116 689); *Esher* (Map 176), Lower Green Road (TQ 139 657) and near 100 Douglas Road (TQ 140 658); *Whyteleafe* (Map 187) ¼ mile south of the station (TQ 340 581) and Stuart Road (TQ 353 570).

EAST SUSSEX

East Sussex is a mainly agricultural county with a few remains of the early iron industry.

Brighton: The British Engineerium (198/TQ 285 066)

Water is a basic need. To supply the growing demand for water of expanding Brighton and Hove, the Goldstone Pumping Station was opened in 1866. It started with a Woolf Compound condensing beam engine built by Easton & Amos (Southwick Street, London). In 1876 a second engine, by Eastons & Anderson, was added at the opposite end of the boiler house which contained three Lancashire boilers supplying each engine. The engines could pump respectively up to 130,000 and 150,000 gallons of water from 160-foot-deep wells. In 1934 the six boilers were replaced by four new Lancashire boilers and by the 1940s

the changeover to electric pumping was under way and the earlier engine was disused. In 1952 No. 2 engine was stopped but kept on standby until 1954. The engine and boiler houses then stood disused for 20 years until in 1974, after attempts to demolish them had been defeated, the British Engineerium was founded as a centre for the history of engineering. Restoration began the following year. Two of the boilers have been put back into steam to power No. 2 engine. The coal store of 1875 now houses a large number of contemporary full-size and model steam engines and Victorian inventions, illustrating the main aspects of engineering development. The centrepiece of this gallery is a 90-hp Corliss horizontal engine which gained first prize at the Paris International Exhibition of 1889 and then generated electricity at a hospital at Brévauner, near Paris. Brought to the Engineerium, it was restored in 1975–6.

The workshop of 1875, where many of the exhibits have been restored, has original – as well as modern – machine tools, driven by line-shafting and belts from a single-cylinder horizontal steam engine of 1862.

There is also a collection of road locomotives and fire engines. *Address:* The British Engineerium, Nevill Road, Hove, East Sussex BN3 7QA. *Tel.* Brighton (0273) 559583.

Also Worth Visiting in East Sussex

Ashburnham Brickworks (199/TQ 684 161). A double kiln, the covered firing area and outbuildings remain.

Battle Railway Station (199/TQ 755 155), a fine example of a Victorian country station designed by William Tress in the Gothic style in 1852. The *hospital* (TQ 731 159) built in 1841 as a workhouse and the *tollhouse* (TQ 738 160) are also worth noticing.

Beachy Head, Belle Tout Lighthouse (199/TV 563 955), built by Stephenson in 1831. Since it was replaced by the present lighthouse its lantern has been removed and it has been converted into a dwelling.

Brighton, Volk's Electric Railway (198/TQ 316 038–332 034). Opened in 1883, it was the first such tramway in Britain; it runs from the Aquarium to Black Rock along Brighton front. The *West Pier* (TQ 303 037) was built in 1866 and extended in 1893; the *Palace Pier* (TQ 314 037) was built 1891–9. *Brighton Railway Station* (TQ 310 049) has a splendid train shed built in 1893.

Burwash, Bateman's Watermill (199/TQ 670 236). In the grounds of an ironmaster's house of 1634 which was later inhabited by Rudyard Kipling. The flour mill dating from 1750 and the turbine which Kipling used to generate electricity have

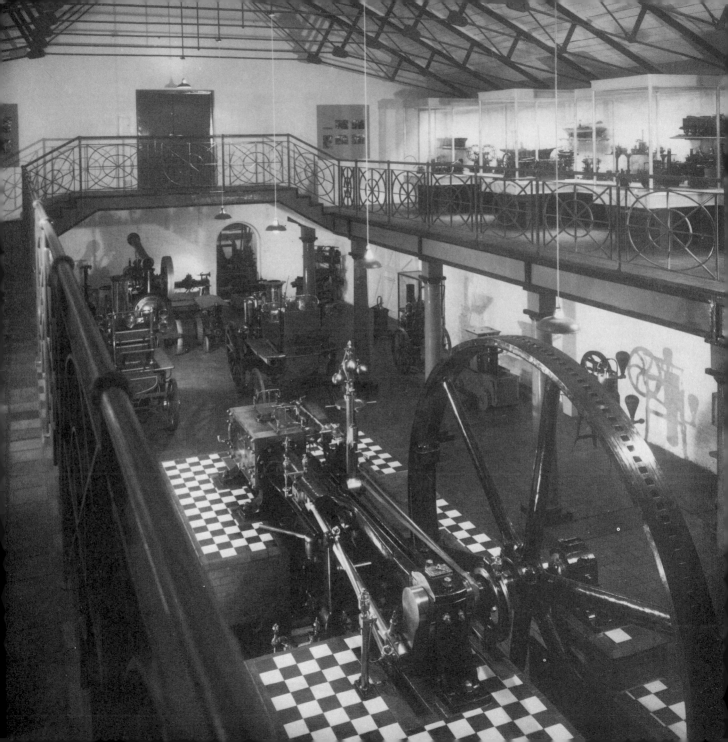

been restored and are open as part of the property which is owned by the National Trust. *Tel.* Burwash (0435) 882302.

Hastings, net shops (199/TQ 827 094). About 40 two- or three-storeyed wood structures used for storing nets and fishing gear since the 16th century still remain. *East Hill Lift* (TQ 828 096), built in 1900–3, was originally water-balance operated, now electrified. *West Hill Lift* (TQ 822 095), built in 1890, runs through a natural cave in the rock. First operated by a gas engine, it is now electrically powered. *Hastings Pier* (199/TQ 811 091) was built 1869–72 and modernized in the 1930s.

Hove, West Blatchington Windmill, Holmes Avenue (198/TQ 279 068). A hexagonal wooden smock mill on a 3-storey flint and brick base built about 1820 and last used commercially in 1906. It is now being restored. *Tel.* c/o Brighton (0273) 734476/776017.

Lewes, Harvey's Brewery (198/TQ 419 103) is an impressive group of buildings. *Ashcombe tollhouse* (TQ 389 093), a circular single-storey brick building with a domed roof, is clearly visible on the south side of the Lewes bypass.

Nutley Windmill (198/TQ 451 291). A probably 17th-century open trestle mill, it went out of use early in the century but has been fully restored. *Tel.* c/o Uckfield (0825) 2969 or Mayfield (0435) 873367.

Polegate Windmill (199/TQ 582 041). Early-19th-century brick tower mill last worked in 1943 and now restored. *Tel.* c/o Polegate (032 12) 4763.

Sheffield Park Railway Station (198/TQ 403 237). The southern terminus of the Bluebell Line which runs to Horsted Keynes. There is a collection of historic locomotives and rolling stock and a regular steam service is run in the summer. *Tel.* Newick (082 572) 2370.

Stanmer (Map 198). A *donkey wheel* can be seen in the corner of the churchyard in Stanmer Park (TQ 336 096) and a *horse-gin* next to Stanmer House (TQ 336 095).

Upper Dicker, Michelham Priory Watermill (199/TQ 557 093). The mill, which produces flour, is part of a complex including the priory buildings, a barn, forge and wheelwright's shop. *Tel.* Hailsham (0323) 844224.

Wadhurst Church, iron grave slabs (188/TQ 641 319). Dating from 1617–1771, the 30 cast-iron slabs in the floor of the chancel, nave and aisles form a fine collection of one product of the Wealden iron industry. Cast-iron slabs or gravestones can also be seen at *Burwash* (199/TQ 677 247), *Rotherfield* (199/TQ 556 297), *Salehurst* (199/TQ 749 243) and *Sedlescombe* (199/TQ 777 188).

Wych Cross, Pippingford furnace (187/TQ 450 316). Two early-18th-century furnaces and a gun-casting pit have been excavated

and are being preserved. Scarletts iron furnace at *Cowden* (187/TQ 443 401) has been excavated and preserved by the present owner.

'Bow bells' milestones, so called because they bear a string of five bells below a bow of ribbon and the Pelham Buckle, survive at mile intervals along the A22 from Lingfield (Surrey) to Hailsham. The first in East Sussex is at *Forest Row* (187/TQ 426 353) and the last is at *Hailsham* (199/TQ 586 084); miles 33, 47 and 55 are modern replacements as are the ones along the B2104 between Hailsham and Langney. A second series, without the Pelham Buckle, exists along the A26 from *Uckfield* (198/TQ 475 193) to *Lewes* (TQ 425 116).

WEST SUSSEX

West Sussex is a mainly agricultural county but transport also provides some sites of interest.

Amberley: Chalk Pits Museum (197/TQ 028 118)

Extractive industries supplying stone, minerals, clay and lime continued to be important. The old Amberley chalk pits operated from the 18th century, and were at one time one of the largest lime-burning complexes in existence. Their 36 acres provide the site for this museum which the visitor approaches along a path which follows the private railway line which formerly linked the limepits to the main line. The warehouse sheds are now used as a bookshop. Next are the two kilns built in 1870 with a grinding wheel and locomotive shed adjacent. Continuing on the right, there are the blacksmith's shop and the bagmender's and cobbler's shop. On the left, the former office buildings house an office display, canal, railway and other exhibits while next door is the cinema in what used to be the granary and hay loft where a slide presentation introduces the site. Nearby is the omnibus garage and roads exhibit, the municipal engine house in which is installed a 30-hp Robey semi-diesel engine from Littlehampton sewage station and the shed which houses a number of small stationary engines. Further into the chalk pits there is the waterpump house which provided water from a well for use in the quarry and the massive bank of Belgian or de Wit kilns built in 1904 which originally had 18 chambers. Beyond these kilns is a brickyard drying shed brought from Nightingale's Brickworks at Petersfield and the industrial railway and tunnel which has track and several locomotives. The tunnel, now blocked, formerly linked this quarry with another on the other side of the hill. Finally, above kiln 2 near the entrance is a shed housing a collection of radio equipment.

Immediately adjacent to the Pits is the main railway line from Arundel to London with a typical Victorian country station, Amberley, a canal cut used in the working days of the Wey and Arun Canal and a wharf on the river Arun. Houghton Bridge nearby is a 19th-century industrial settlement.

Address: Chalk Pits Museum, Houghton Bridge, Amberley, Arundel, West Sussex. *Tel.* Bury (079 881) 370.

Singleton: Weald and Downland Museum (197/SU 875 129)
Some buildings can be preserved on site; others have to be moved to ensure their continuing existence. Formed to rescue good examples of vernacular buildings, the Weald and Down-

land Museum was first opened to the public in 1971. On this site at Singleton a number of buildings have been re-erected. Of particular interest to the industrial archaeologist are the Lurgashall watermill removed from its original site north of Midhurst; a drainage windmill from Pevensey; the Beeding toll cottage; a donkey wheel from Patching, east of Arundel, where the gin worked a three-throw pump; a 10-foot-diameter treadwheel from Catherington, north of Portsmouth; and the Southwater forge. There is also a display of charcoal burning and a sawpit. A variety of vernacular dwellings – the 14th-century Winkhurst House, the 15th-century Bayleaf Farmhouse, a granary from Littlehampton – have been re-erected on this part of the West Dean estate, and a number of cattle sheds in some of which are smaller displays including a cider press. In the centre of the site an urban group is being assembled to form a market square,

Chalk Pits Museum – de Wit kilns

Weald and Downland Museum – Titchfield Market Hall

including the Titchfield Market Hall, Crawley Hall and Lavant House.
Address: Weald and Downland Open Air Museum, Singleton, near Chichester, West Sussex. *Tel.* Singleton (024 363) 348.

Also Worth Visiting in West Sussex

Balcombe, Ouse Viaduct (198/TQ 323 278) was built in 1839–41 to carry the London–Brighton line across the Ouse valley at a height of 96 feet; it is 1,475 feet long. Another notable viaduct is at *East Grinstead*, Imberhorne (187/TQ 383 378), west of the town.

Bognor Regis, Ice House (197/SZ 936 995). Was built for the Hotham Park estate about 1792.

Duncton, limekiln (197/SU 961 163), a large mid-19th-century triple kiln. See also the three kilns at *Washington* (198/SU 119 123).

Ford, Airfield (197/SU 989 029). Opened in 1918 as a training field for the Royal Flying Corps, it was used during World War II by the RAF and RN. It is now disused but three hangars survive on what is now mainly an industrial estate.

Henfield, Woods Watermill (198/TQ 218 138). An 18th-century mill with a waterwheel of 1854, it has been restored to working order and houses a wildlife and countryside exhibition. *Tel.* Henfield (0273) 492630 or Haywards Heath (0444) 413678.

Lindfield, horse-gin house (198/TQ 347 254). Nearby at Old Place (198/TQ 349 259) the iron cage of the horse-gin above a well is visible from the land behind the church.

Petworth, Burton Watermill (197/SU 978 180) is powered by a water turbine of about 1920. *Tel.* Sutton (079 87) 293.

Petworth, Coultershaw water-powered beam pump (197/SU 973 194). A three-throw pump driven by a breastshot waterwheel which pumped water from the River Rother to Petworth from 1784 to the 1950s. It now pumps water to a fountain. *Tel.* Chichester (0243) 786044.

St Leonard's Forest, hammer-ponds (198/TQ 213 292 and 219 289), associated with forges which operated from the mid-16th to mid-17th century. See also the hammer-ponds at *Slaugham* (198/TQ 249 280), which served a furnace operating 1574–*c* 1653, and *Crabtree* (198/TQ 229 251).

Shipley, King's Windmill (198/TQ 143 218). Built in the late 19th century and once owned by Hilaire Belloc, it has been restored to working order in his memory.

The *piers* at *Bognor Regis* (197/SZ 934 987), built in 1865 and now badly ruined, and at *Worthing* (198/TQ 149 023), built in 1862, are worth seeing.

Weald and Downland Museum – Catherington treadwheel

Eastern England

EASTERN ENGLAND

1 Biggleswade: Shuttleworth Collection
2 Leighton Buzzard: Narrow Gauge Railway
3 Stretham: Old Engine
4 Southend: Pier
5 Harwich: Crane and Navigation Lights
6 **Weeting: Grime's Graves**
7 Fakenham: Gasworks
8 Stowmarket: Museum of East Anglian Life
9 Woodbridge: Tidemill

Fakenham ⑦

Kings Lynn

Norwich

③ ⑥ Thetford

Ely

Cambridge

⑧

Ipswich ⑨

Bedford

① Harwich ⑤

② Luton

Aylesbury Colchester

Oxford ④

Reading

0 km 16 km 32 km 48 km

0 10 20 30 miles

BEDFORDSHIRE

This largely agricultural county has some items of transport interest, including aviation.

Old Warden Aerodrome: Shuttleworth Collection (153/TL 150 448)
The first flying machines took off from grass airfields. Not many still exist but Old Warden Aerodrome provides an example. Here is also to be found the Shuttleworth Collection of historic aeroplanes. The collection is divided into four main groups:

1 Flying machines before World War I including the Blériot Type XI of 1909, a Blackburn of 1912 and a replica Avro Triplane IV of 1910.
2 Aeroplanes used in World War I: the Avro 504K, the Sopwith Pup (1916) and the Bristol F2b Fighter (1917), the most effective fighting aircraft of the war.
3 Private and sporting aeroplanes between the wars, including the DH 60 Moth, the Granger Archaeopteryx, the DH 88 Comet and the Percival Gull and many others.
4 Aircraft used by the Flying Services since 1918: the Avro Tutor, Hawker Tomtit, Hawker Hind, Gloster Gladiator (the last RAF biplane fighter), examples of the two famous British World War II fighters – the Hawker Hurricane and Supermarine Spitfire (both based at Duxford) – the Avro Anson and more recent trainers such as the DH Tiger Moth and Chipmunk, the Miles Magister and the Percival Provost.

There are also some engines and miscellaneous items of equipment in the collection which, while concentrating on small aircraft, provides a valuable perspective of the development of airborne flight in an authentic setting.
Address: The Shuttleworth Collection, Old Warden Aerodrome, near Biggleswade, Bedfordshire. *Tel.* Northill (076 727) 288.

Nearby at Cardington are the ***Airship Hangars*** (153/TL 082 468). The earlier hangar was built in 1917 as part of the Royal Airship Works. It was extended in 1927 and a second built to house the R100 and R101 but the crash of the latter brought Britain's airship era to an end.

Leighton Buzzard Narrow Gauge Railway (165/SP 928 241)
Narrow gauge railways used to be employed in many parts of the country for industrial purposes. At Leighton Buzzard a 3½-mile line was built in 1919 to link the sand quarries with the main line because of the increased road traffic during World War I when the demand for Bedfordshire sand grew markedly as cheap supplies of Belgian sand were no longer available. The 2-foot-gauge line was built in two parts: a main line from the Billington Road and then a number of spurs owned by the individual companies leading to the quarries. After 1955 the sand was increasingly carried by road transport and in 1969 British Rail closed the interchange sidings.

The railway was taken over by the Leighton Buzzard Narrow Gauge Railway Society which runs passenger trains on Sundays during the summer from Pages Park on the Billington Road to Vandyke Road. The line was originally worked by two Hudswell-Clarke 0–6–0 tank engines but because they proved unsatisfactory they were replaced by petrol-engined Simplex locomotives. Since its formation the Railway Society has acquired a number of steam and diesel narrow-gauge locomotives from elsewhere, including *Chaloner* built by de Winton in 1877. It now has a fleet of 17 locomotives. The railway workshops are at the former Stonehenge brickworks.

The route of the line provides a sight of the Marley Tile Works, the Redland Tile Works and several quarries. Marley's Bank, with a gradient of 1 in 25, is one of the steepest sections of railway line in Britain worked by adhesion alone.
Address: Pages Park Station, Billington Road, Leighton Buzzard, Bedfordshire. *Tel.* Leighton Buzzard (0525) 373888.

Pixie crosses a footpath on the Clipstone Estate

Also Worth Visiting in Bedfordshire

Bedford, Great Ouse Lock (153/TL 055 495), the furthest upstream lock of the Ouse Navigation established in the late 17th century, and the rest of the navigation have been restored.

Stevington Windmill (153/SP 992 528). Late-18th-century post mill with a roundhouse added later. It has been restored to working order. *Tel.* Oakley (023 02) 2184 or (County Hall) Bedford (0234) 63222.

Stewartby Brickworks and Housing (153/TL 02 42). One of the major industries in Bedfordshire is brickmaking and the Stewartby Works of the London Brick Company is claimed to be the largest brickworks in the world. From 1926 a 'garden village' with houses, schools and a village hall was built for the brickworkers. The village was named after the then chairman of the company.

Willington dovecote and stables (153/TL 107 499). Now owned by the National Trust, this 16th-century stone dovecote with stepped gables was built by Sir John Gostwick, Cardinal Wolsey's Master of the Horse. The stables opposite date from the same period. *Tel.* c/o Bedford (0234) 771745.

BERKSHIRE

This mainly agricultural county has no major industrial sites. Those which exist are largely concerned with agricultural processing or the extractive industries or transport across the county. The following sites are worth a visit:

Bradfield College (175/SU 603 725), a largely purpose-built school, has the shell of a small gasworks in attractive diamond brickwork, now converted to a house.

Chaddleworth, Woolley Park (174/SU 410 802) has an 18th-century horse-driven cornmill with an 18-foot spur wheel powered by two horses.

Eastbury, old forge (174/SU 347 773). Housed in a 1½-storey 19th-century building, it has two hearths and two anvils. The blacksmith is mainly employed in shoeing racehorses.

Newbury (Map 174). *Phoenix Brewery*, Bartholemew Street (SU 469 667), a classical brewery behind the inn and brewer's house, has been converted to an architect's office. *Newbury Museum* (SU 473 671) is housed in the 17th-century Cloth Hall and Cornmarket which stood alongside the early Kennet Navigation. *Tel.* Newbury (0635) 42400.

Reading (Map 175) has a number of buildings of interest. See, for example, the *Brewery* in East Street (SU 718 731), now disused, which viewed from the east has a mounting series of slate roofs and a large roof-top water tank; the Victorian Gothic brick *sewage pumping station* of *c* 1865 alongside the Canal (SU 725 735) which now houses electric pumps with fine switchgear; and *Rosehill Water Tower* (SU 722 745), built of concrete *c* 1935.

The Kennet and Avon Canal runs through Berkshire and includes 21 locks which raise boats 134 feet. *Sheffield Lock* (175/SU 649 708), an early-type lock, has timber and turf sides. A wooden swing bridge built over the canal *c* 1810 survives at *Woolhampton* (174/SU 573 666).

Brunel's Great Western Railway crossed the county later and there are two of his bridges of note. The *Maidenhead Bridge* (175/SU 902 810) of 1838, over the Thames, has two of the largest and flattest arches ever built in brickwork. With a span of 128 feet and a rise of only 24 feet 3 inches to the crown, it was confidently predicted at the time that it would immediately collapse. At *Windsor* (175/SU 961 773), a bowstring bridge of 1847–9 carries the Slough and Windsor branch over the Thames. Originally the approaches were of timber and the girder was supported on cast-iron cylindrical piers, but all this has been replaced by arcaded brick abutments. At *Windsor and Eton Central Railway Station* (175/SU 967 769) Madame Tussaud's have developed an exhibition on 'Royalty & railways' based on the royal waiting room. *Tel.* Windsor (075 35) 60655. At *Windsor Riverside* (175/SU 968 772) the station and royal waiting room was designed by Sir William Tite in 1851; it has a Tudor bay window and a turret; the range of doors on the south side allowed mounted troopers to assemble on the platform. The railway stations at *Mortimer* (175/SU 672 641), *Reading* (175/SU 715 738) and *Slough* (175/SU 979 802) – where half the former stables of the railway hotel survive – are also noteworthy.

BUCKINGHAMSHIRE

Buckinghamshire is a county whose main sites are related to agricultural processing or transport.

Bletchley, Denbigh Hall Bridge (152/SP 863 353), an original LNWR bridge carrying the line over the A5 road. Between April and September 1838 trains from Euston terminated here, passengers being conveyed by horse-drawn coach to Rugby for trains to Birmingham (Curzon Street).

Brill Windmill (164/SP 652 142). A late 17th-century post mill which was restored in 1948. *Tel.* Brill (0844) 237557.

High Wycombe, Wycombe Chair and Local History Museum, Castle Hill, Priory Avenue (175/SU 868 932). The chair-making industry of the Chilterns has been centred on High Wycombe for over 200 years. This museum illustrates the history and design of the English country chair and in particular the development of the Windsor chair. There are also displays of lace-making and other aspects of local history. *Tel.* High Wycombe (0494) 23879.

Ivinghoe, Ford End Watermill, Ford End Farm (165/SP 941 166). A small three-storey mill with an overshot waterwheel. *Tel.* c/o Cheddington (0296) 668939.

Ivinghoe, Pitstone Windmill (165/SP 945 157). A restored post mill with brick roundhouse, possibly built in the early 17th century, owned by the National Trust. *Tel.* c/o Cheddington (0296) 668227.

Lacey Green Windmill (165/SP 819 008). Restored smock mill of the mid-17th century, thought to be the oldest surviving example in Britain. *Tel.* c/o Princes Risborough (084 44) 4954 or Bourne End (062 85) 23444.

Marsworth locks, Grand Union Canal (165/SP 905 143–930 138). The Grand Union (Grand Junction) Canal descends by a flight of

Arch of chairs at High Wycombe to celebrate the visit of the Prince of Wales in 1880

seven locks down the Tring cutting through the Chilterns at this point, a fall of 42 feet. The locks were constructed by William Jessop in 1792. A towpath runs along the canal and is accessible from a number of the side roads which cross it. Further north at *Wolverton* (152/SP 801 418), a 100-foot iron trough aqueduct carries the canal over the Ouse. Built in 1809–11 to replace an earlier masonry aqueduct, the high embankment on either side is pierced by 'cattle creeps', small accommodation tunnels.

Newport Pagnell, cast-iron bridge (152/SP 878 438). Built in 1810, this is one of the oldest such bridges in daily use. Said to be inspired by Paine's bridge at Sunderland, no longer extant, it was cast by Walker's of Rotherham.

Quainton Windmill (165/SP 746 203). Brick tower mill built in the early 1830s and operated until the turn of the century. *Tel.* Quainton (029 675) 372.

Wolverton, railway viaduct and housing (152/SP 815 422). The six-arch viaduct, which carries the Midland Region (formerly London and Birmingham railway) over the Ouse, was built in 1838. Just south is the railway town built to house the workers at the railway engineering works.

CAMBRIDGESHIRE

Cambridgeshire, a low-lying agricultural area requiring drainage, has engineering in Peterborough and brickmaking nearby.

Stretham Old Engine (154/TL 515 728)

For centuries men tried to drain the Fens. Some success was achieved by Vermuyden in the early 17th century and more determined attempts were made later in the century to drain Waterbeach Level with the use of windmills; further progress was made in the following century. With the high price of corn during the Napoleonic Wars, John Smeaton recommended the installation of a steam engine in 1813. Eventually his recommendation was accepted and the Stretham Engine was built in 1831. The beam engine was made by the Butterley Company;

originally rated at 105 hp, the reboring of the valves in 1909 increased its efficiency. Steam was supplied by two Lancashire boilers which were replaced in 1871; a third was added in 1847 and replaced in 1878. The engine drove a scoopwheel 37 feet in diameter and 2 feet 5 inches wide which could raise 30 tons of water each revolution with its 48 ladles. In 1925 the steam engine, which was last used in 1941, was replaced by a Mirrless diesel four-cylinder engine of 137 kw, one of the few air-blast diesels still to be seen, driving a Gwynnes pump; this remains on standby. The Stretham Old Engine has now been restored by a trust.

Address: Stretham Engine, Stretham, Ely, Cambridgeshire. *Tel.* Stretham (035 389) 236.

There is another pumping station, *Fleam Dyke pumping station*, at Fulbourn (154/TL 539 548) which pumps water to supply Cambridge.

Also Worth Visiting in Cambridgeshire

Bourn Windmill, Caxton Road (153/TL 312 580). An open trestle post mill with a typical medieval-style straight gable, it is possibly the oldest surviving windmill in the country. There was a record of a mill on the site in 1636 and it was last worked in 1927.

Cambridge, Cheddars Lane Sewage Pumping Engine (154/TL 465 593). Built in 1894 and powered by two Hathorn, Davy differential 80-hp tandem compound steam engines, supplemented from 1909 by a pair of 94-hp gas engines and from 1937 by a 114-hp electric motor. The site is being developed as the Cambridge Museum of Technology.

Cambridge Station (154/TL 462 573) was built in 1845 in Italianate style. It has a single mainline platform for both up and down lines, the longest platform in the world – 1650 feet. See also the Jacobean style *Wansford Station* (142/TL 093 980), headquarters of the Nene Valley Steam Railway; and *Lord's Bridge Station, Barton* (154/TL 395 545), the best preserved station on the now disused LNWR branch to Cambridge of 1862.

Duxford, Imperial War Museum Airfield (154/TL 460 460). At this military airfield which still has some 1914–18 hangars there is a collection of civil as well as military aircraft, tanks, naval patrol boats etc. *Tel.* Cambridge (0223) 833963.

Ely, Wicken Fen Pumping Mill (154/TL 563 707). An early 20th-century small-scale smock mill built for pumping purposes, now preserved by the National Trust in a nature reserve. *Tel.* Ely (0353) 720274.

Great Chishill Windmill (154/TL 413 388). An open trestle post mill last worked in 1951 and restored in the 1960s.

Cambridge – Cheddars Lane pumping station

Lode Watermill, Anglesey Abbey, Lode (154/TL 520 625). An 18th-century mill last worked in 1910, now being restored for the National Trust. *Tel.* Cambridge (0223) 811643.

Over Windmill, Longstanton Road (154/TL 381 689). A mid-19th-century tower mill last worked about 1929, now restored. *Tel.* Swavesey (0954) 30742.

Peterborough, Star Pressed Brickworks, Dogsthorpe (142/TF 204 022). One of the oldest brickworks still in operation, it has two 16-chamber Hoffman kilns (*c* 1900), brick presses, originally steam-driven, with disused engine house and chimney and an aerial ropeway (*c* 1925).

St Neots, Paine's Brewery, Market Place (153/TL 182 602). The 18th-century office frontage was the Bull Inn; the tall brewing block was rebuilt after a fire in 1906 and other buildings date from the 1870s. *Paine's Maltings* in Bedford Street (153/TL 185 606) is a three-storey ornate red-brick Victorian Gothic building with a large square kiln at one end; nearby (153/TL 184 601) can be seen a tall red-brick chimney with the name 'Paines' in white brick which was preserved when its malt-extract factory burnt down in the 1950s. At the other end of the street, *Paine's Flour Mill* (153/TL 184 606) matches the maltings in even grander Victorian style.

Soham, Downfield Windmill Fordham Road (154/TL 609 717). A tower mill converted in 1887 from a smock mill. Last in business in the late 1950s, it is now producing flour again. *Tel.* c/o Leicester (0533) 707625.

Swaffam Bulbeck, Commercial End (154/TL 55 63). The remains of an early 19th-century trading centre based around a wharf on the now silted up Swaffam Bulbeck lode with merchants' houses, granary, salt store, maltings, brewhouse, warehouses and so on.

Thornhaugh, Sacrewell Watermill, Sacrewell Farm (142/TF 078 001). A mid-18th-century complex of three-storey mill of 1755 with an 1860s pitchback wheel, granaries and miller's house. *Tel.* c/o Stamford (0780) 782222.

Wisbech (Map 143) was an important market town and river port which has retained some fine *warehousing*, for example in North Street (TF 461 097) and on New Quay (TF 462 097). *Elgood's Brewery*, North Brink (TF 455 092) has an attractive late-18th-century frontage with later buildings behind. To the south-west of the town is a fine pair of drainage beam-engine houses, *Waldersea* (TF 433 062) of 1832 on the south bank of the Nene, and *North Side* (TF 430 063) of 1878 opposite.

'Trinity Hall' milestones, a famous series erected in 1729–33 from Cambridge along the old London Road (B1368) for 16 miles, pre-date turnpike milestones and are probably the oldest surviv-

ing series. The first is in Trumpington Road, *Cambridge* (154/TL 452 569). Particularly notable ones can be seen at *Melbourn* (154/TL 408 430), which is larger and more elaborate than the others, and *Great Chishill* (154/TL 404 414), which has a later cast-iron plate added.

ESSEX

This agricultural county has processing trades, maltings and engineering works together with holiday resorts along the coast.

Southend Pier (178/TQ 885 850)

One way in which the Victorians went on holiday was by paddle-steamers which called at piers specially constructed at seaside resorts. Many were actively used until 1939 but with the virtual disappearance of such steamers – the *Waverley* which operates from the Clyde is almost the last of the line – their number has sadly diminished. The most famous of these piers is also the longest, the 1¼-mile cast-iron pier at Southend-on-Sea, erected in 1889 by Arral Bros of Glasgow to the designs of James Brunless. It replaced the earlier wooden pier of 1830 which was extended in 1846 to the same point as the present pier. As the pier was so long a double-track electric 3-feet 6-inch railway, built by the Southend Local Board Crompton Electric Railway, used to run the length of the pier. Built in 1927, the Prince George extensions of the pier are of concrete. Because it has been damaged by fire and storm in recent years, maintenance is expensive and as a result its future is in doubt. But while it exists it is well worth a visit.

Address: Foreshore Office, Eastern Esplanade, Southend-on-Sea, Essex. *Tel.* Southend (0702) 611880.

Other piers in Essex exist at *Clacton-on-Sea* (169/TM 177 143) and *Walton-on-the-Naze* (169/TM 264 215).

Harwich: Crane and Navigation Lights (Map 169)

Increasing traffic and heavier loads carried by sea required better facilities. The *Harwich Treadwheel Crane* (TM 263 324), an improved form of cargo-handling, was built in 1667 on the site of the Naval Yard and was moved to its present site on Harwich Green, on a slight eminence where once stood 'Queen's Mount Battery', about 1932. Each of the two treadwheels is 16 feet in diameter and 3 feet 10 inches wide. Made of oak, the wheels are spaced 4 feet apart on a common axle 13½ inches in diameter. The crane was operated by men walking on the interior of the

wheels, working on the same principle as donkey wheels. A hazard was the absence of any form of brake. The crane head consists of a horizontal beam fitted with a pulley; the jib projects 17 feet 10 inches. The original boarded roof has been replaced by pantiles.

The *High and Low Lighthouses* (TM 262 325 and 263 326) nearby were built in 1818 under the supervision of John Rennie to replace earlier wooden towers. In 1836 the lights were acquired by Trinity House but became redundant in 1863 because of the changing course of the channel. The High Lighthouse is a 90-foot nine-sided tower of grey gault brick which has been a residence since 1909. The Low Lighthouse is a 45-foot-high ten-sided tower of brick. The ground floor has a projecting canopy to provide a public shelter. Both were sold to Harwich Council in 1909 but the Low Lighthouse was repossessed by Trinity House in 1970 and is now used as a pilot signal station.

The High and Low Lighthouses are 150 yards apart and were leading lights. When one light could be seen above the other the vessel approaching Harwich was on the correct course.

The new navigation light towers built in 1862 can also be seen. The shore light is mounted on a 50-foot tower while the offshore light is smaller and supported by two V-shaped legs. Both lights are in a poor condition and have also been superseded.

In Harwich (Map 169) see: *St Nicholas Church* (169/TM 262 327) which has interior slender columns, gallery and window tracery all of cast iron made locally; the *Electric Palace*, Kings Quay Street (TM 262 328), one of the earliest purpose-built cinemas, which has recently been restored; the *Town Hall* (TM 260 329) on

Harwich – treadwheel crane

The Quay built as a hotel for the Great Eastern Railway in 1864; and 1 and 2 *Custom House* (TM 259 327) (off West Street), houses converted into a Custom House about 1798 and used as such until 1935.

Also Worth Visiting in Essex

Aythorpe Roding Windmill (167/TL 590 152). A large post mill with roundhouse constructed about 1760, last used about 1932. *Tel.* Chelmsford (0245) 67222.

Chappel railway viaduct (168/TL 897 284) was built in 1847–8 to carry the Colchester, Stour Valley, Sudbury and Halstead Railway across the River Colne. It is 80 feet high and 1,066 feet long, with 32 arches each with a span of 30 feet. It is still used by trains between Marks Tey and Sudbury. At the north end of the viaduct is *Chappel and Wakes Colne Station*, the headquarters of the Stour Valley Preservation Centre which has a number of steam locomotives and historical rolling stock. *Tel.* Earls Colne (078 75) 2903. There is also an impressive railway viaduct in *Chelmsford* (167/TL 702 067) which opened in 1843 to carry the Eastern Counties Railway over the Can and into the station. Built on a curve, it has 51 30-foot arches (27 of which are 'closed' and used industrially) and is half a mile long in total.

Chelmer and Blackwater Navigation, running nearly 14 miles from Springfield Basin, Chelmsford (167/TL 714 067) to Heybridge Basin, near Maldon (168/TL 872 068), opened in June 1797 and closed in March 1972 but it has been partly reopened since 1975 for recreational use. It has 12 locks, including a sea lock, and five original bridges.

Colchester, Bourne Watermill, Bourne Road (168/TM 005 238). A 16th-century fishing lodge subsequently converted to a mill, now owned by the National Trust.

Halstead, Townford Silk Mill (168/TL 813 304) was converted from a cornmill in 1825 by Samuel Courtauld. In 1844 it was fitted with a beam engine. The three-storey weatherboarded and slated mill across the Colne has two long window ranges typical of textile mills. It is now a store. Halstead was the scene of the early growth of the Courtauld Company and its influence can be seen in many ways.

Mistley Maltings (168/TM 109 319, 117 320). The old maltings, adjacent to Mistley High Street, were erected 1807–28 and are characteristic of their age, being of two storeys and manually operated with small anthracite-fired drying kilns with perforated tile floors, open steeping tanks and narrow tile-surfaced germinating floors. These can be contrasted to the late-19th-century five- and eight-storey maltings nearby which include huge kilns with wire mesh floors, mechanical rakes and wide germinating floors.

Rayleigh Windmill (178/TQ 809 915). A brick tower mill built about 1790, now used as a museum by the Rayleigh and District Antiquarian and Natural History Society. *Tel.* c/o Rayleigh (0268) 776627 or 740447.

Stansted Mountfitchet Windmill (167/TL 510 248). A tower mill built in 1787, retaining all its machinery. *Tel.* c/o Bishop's Stortford (0279) 813159.

Thaxted, John Webb's Windmill (167/TL 609 309). A brick tower built in 1804. The ground floor contains a rural museum. *Tel.* c/o Thaxted (0371) 830366.

Watertowers are characteristic of the flat Essex countryside. The most famous landmark in *Colchester* is 'Jumbo', a 105-foot-high brick watertower built in 1882 on Balkerne Hill (168/TL 993 252). A red-brick castellated tower of 1872 can be seen in *Epping* (167/TL 457 018). Examples of late-19th-century 'wheel' pumps for village water supply can be seen at *Clavering* (167/TL 478 323), on Hill Green; *Goldhanger* (168/TL 904 088); *Peldon* (168/TL 990 164); and *Steeple* (168/TL 936 029). Examples of more common types of pump can be seen in many places: *Bradwell-on-Sea* (168/TM 004 071); *Earls Colne* (168/TL 863 286); *Rayleigh* (178/TQ 807 907) in the High Street; *Ridgewell* (155/TL 737 408); and *Southminster* (168/TQ 964 995).

HERTFORDSHIRE

Hertfordshire has been a mainly agricultural county geared to supplying London; thus its sites are largely concerned with agricultural processing and transport.

Ayot Green, Tollhouse (166/TL 223 130) is the only one surviving in the county and is atypical, being built *c* 1728, a half-timbered brick cottage, before tollhouse design had become largely standardized.

The Grand Junction (Grand Union) Canal passed through Hertfordshire and its most spectacular section is the cutting 1½ miles north-east of *Tring* (165/SP 948 120–933 137). Built in 1800, it carries the canal for 1½ miles at 382 feet above sea level through the Chiltern escarpment. About a mile south, on the A41, is *Cow Roast Lock* (SP 959 103), 328 feet above sea level, and the side road crossing the canal here leads to *Dudswell Wharf* (SP 966 097) where a warehouse remains. A number of early bridges survive on the canal, the most attractive being that carrying the approach road to The Grove (166/TQ 087 988), outside *Watford.*

Hatfield, Mill Green Watermill, Old Mill House and Mill, Mill Green (166/TL 240 097). A 17th-century building with machinery of the 18th and 19th centuries, it last worked in 1911 and is now being restored. *Tel.* Hatfield (070 72) 71362.

London Colney, De Havilland Mosquito Museum, Salisbury Hall (166/TL 195 028). The birthplace of the De Havilland Mosquito, the museum contains the first Mosquito, a much later Mosquito, a Vampire and a Venom together with 800 scale models illustrating the history of aviation. *Tel.* Bowmansgreen (0727) 23274.

St Albans, Kingsbury Watermill Museum (166/TL 138 075). A 16th-century building altered in the 18th century which worked until the 1960s and has now been restored with displays of milling machinery and dairying and farming implements. *Tel.* St Albans (0727) 59880.

Welwyn viaduct (166/TL 245 147) was built in 1848–50 of local blue brick to carry the Great Northern Railway about 90 feet above the River Maron. Over 1,600 feet long, it has 40 arches of an average span of 40 feet. Two later seven-arch brick viaducts can be seen on the loop line from Stevenage at *Cuffley* (166/TL 306 017), 1910, and over the B158 and the River Lea south of *Hertford* (166/TL 320 113), 1920.

London Coal Duty Boundary Markers were erected in the mid-19th century along railways, waterways and roads in a 20-mile radius from the GPO in St Martin's-le-Grand in central London to delineate the area within which the City of London could levy duty on incoming coal. There are 44 of these in Hertfordshire, the most striking of which is the 12-foot-high stone obelisk alongside the railway at *Brookmans Park* (166/TL 243 028). Close by, another four can be seen: at the south end of Water Lane, *North Mimms* (TL 250 031), and in *Potters Bar* on the A1000, and in Church Road (TL 260 021) and in Hawkshead Road (TL 257 025).

Maltings are one of the most characteristic buildings in the county and can be found in many towns, often now used for other purposes. Good examples can be seen at *Baldock* (166/TL 246 337); *Bishop's Stortford* (167/eg TL 491 206); *Hertford*, in West Street (166/TL 320 120); and *Ware* (166/eg TL 360 140).

NORFOLK

Norfolk is an agricultural county with associated industries.

Weeting, Grime's Graves (144/TL 817 898)

Inevitably, industrial archaeology concentrates on the past 200 years but it does have a wider time-span and can bring prehistoric activities within its scope. One example is provided by tin streaming; another is the winning of flints, which were used by prehistoric man to provide the cutting edge of tools such as axes and knives and for arrowheads. At first, flints could be picked up on the surface of the ground but larger and better quality flints

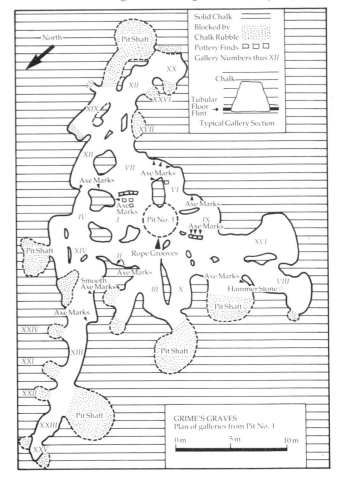

Map by courtesy of Her Majesty's Stationery Office

Grimes Graves – aerial view

were later obtained by mining. From about 2000 B.C., flint-knappers dug shallow pits to obtain them in the band of chalk which runs from southern England through East Anglia. One such site, known as Grime's Graves, is in Norfolk. Covering an area of 34 acres, the site is pockmarked with nearly 400 craters, filled-in pits from which the flint has been extracted. From these pits miners worked out through a complex of galleries to obtain the 'floor-stone'. One of these shafts, Pit 1, has been excavated. Visitors can climb down a ladder to the bottom of the shaft and see the galleries (now illuminated) from which the flints were won.

The name Grime's Graves was given to the site before the Norman Conquest: Grime is another name for Woden, chief of the Anglo-Saxon gods, and 'graves' means 'holes' or 'hollows'.

For information, *Tel.* Thetford (0842) 810656.

Fakenham Gasworks (132/TF 919 293)

Originally, many towns had their own gasworks but during the last century most have disappeared. The gasworks at Fakenham, which ceased production in 1965, is the last English example of a small horizontal retort hand-fired gasworks. Originally built in 1825, the present retort house dates from 1846 when street gas lighting was introduced into the town. Though most of the plant is 20th-century, it is a good example of the small 19th-century gasworks. Gas was produced in a retort house which consisted of producer beds below with horizontal retorts above. Coke was burnt in the producer beds with a limited air supply to produce carbon monoxide which then rose around the retorts which were charged with coal, and burned to produce the heat needed to drive off the gas and other volatile constituents from the coal. These gaseous products were drawn from the retorts along pipes by an exhauster – a kind of fan – to a condenser where they cooled and much of the tar and ammonia condensed out. Next the gas passed through a Livesey washer which removed the remaining tar and ammonia and then through purifiers which removed the final impurity, sulphuretted hydrogen. From there the gas passed through the station meter, to measure the volume of production, into the gasholders from which it was distributed

to the consumers. The retort beds at Fakenham were rebuilt in 1907 and 1910 and the exhausters and purifiers about the same time. The station meter and Livesey washer date from the 1920s while the present condenser was installed in 1953. The earlier of two gasholders, a cast-iron single lift holder dated 1888, remains while a riveted steel one of 1924 has been demolished. Adjacent are offices containing all the testing equipment and a showroom. The works is virtually complete, including tools and minor equipment, and has a small collection of early gas meters. Attempts are being made to preserve the site and open it to the public.

Also Worth Visiting in Norfolk

Berney Arms Drainage Windmill (134/TG 465 051) is accessible by train from Norwich or Great Yarmouth to Berney Arms Station, by boat from Great Yarmouth, or by a 3-mile walk from Halvergate across the marshes for which an ordnance survey map is advised. A seven-storey tarred tower mill which originally ground cement clinker, it was used for drainage purposes until 1948. It is now fully restored and houses an exhibition on windmills. *Tel.* c/o Cambridge (0223) 358911 ext. 2295.

Coltishall limekiln (134/TG 269 202) is a very fine example of a typical underground East Anglian kiln with an unusual pointed arched roof to the chamber.

Denver Windmill (143/TF 605 013). A large mill of 1835 recently restored, retaining most of its machinery. *Tel.* c/o Downham Market (0366) 382285.

Great Bircham Windmill (132/TF 760 327). A 52-foot tarred brick tower mill of 1846 with an earlier bakery. *Tel.* Syderstone (048 523) 393.

Great Yarmouth (Map 134) retains much from its role as a commercial and fishing port. For example: the 1907 *crane* on South Quay (TG 523 072) on the site of the Elizabethan town crane; the survivor of four *Customs posts* on Hall Quay (TG 523 074) which marked the limits of the legal quays; a number of *fish-curing houses* – Trinity Place (TG 527 069), Blackfriars Road (TG 527 070), Admiralty Road (TG 527 060), Sutton Road and Middle Road East (TG 526 062) – some still in use; the *Fish Wharf* (TG 525 059) and a fish warehouse nearby in Battery Road (TG 529 058); and a rare thatched *icehouse* by Haven Bridge (TG 521 074). A monument to Great Yarmouth's modern role as a resort is the *Docwras Peppermint Rock Factory*, Regent Road (TG 526 076).

Gressenhall, Museum of Rural Life, Beech House, Gressenhall, Dereham NR20 4DR (132/TF 974 170). Displays of Norfolk farming, rural people, crafts and industries, including a fine collection of internal combustion engines, in a 1777 workhouse. *Tel.* Dereham (0362) 860563.

Gunton Sawmill (133/TG 224 335). A thatched water-powered sawmill with a unique vertical sawframe driven by two iron pitchback wheels supplied by water from an ornamental lake. It is now being restored. *Tel.* c/o Norwich (0603) 61122 ext. 5224.

Holkham Hall Estate (Map 132) is the prime example of a self-sufficient agricultural estate: the estate works at Longlands Farm (TF 880 400) included a foundry, forge, sawmill; the Great Barn (TF 890 414) of 1778, scene of the famous Coke sheep shearings; icehouse (TF 882 427); a mid-19th century brick gasworks retort house (TF 878 431); Peterstone brickworks (TF 862 428); limekiln (TF 869 436). *Tel.* Fakenham (0328) 710374.

Horsey Wind Pump (134/TG 457 221). A brick tower drainage mill last worked by wind in the 1940s, now maintained by the National Trust. *Tel.* (National Trust Regional Office) Aylsham (026 373) 3471. Other drainage mills open to the public in summer months are *Stracey Arms Wind Pump* (134/TG 442 090); and *Thurne Dyke Wind Pump* (134/TG 401 159). A number of small wind pumps can be seen including *St Olaves* (134/TM 457 997); *Starston* (156/TM 232 844); and *Upton* (134/TG 404 132).

King's Lynn (Map 132) is an ancient port which retains some trade. *Hampton Court*, Nelson Street (TF 617 197) is a merchants' hall with a late-14th-century warehouse on the west side; the half-timbered *Hanseatic Warehouse* in St Margaret's Lane (TF 617 198) dates from c 1475 and *Clifton House*, Queen Street (TF 616 199) has a 15th-century brick merchant's tower with a view down the river; 16th-century and later warehouses can be seen at *Marriott's Barn*, South Quay (TF 616 198), *Fermoy Centre*, King Street (TF 615 203) and in King's Staithe Lane (TF 616 200); the Wren-style *Custom House* on Purfleet Quay (TF 616 200) is 17th-century; *Alexandra Dock* (TF 615 207) dates from 1869 and *Bentinck Dock* (TF 617 210) from 1883.

Ludham, Boardman's Wind Pump (134/TG 370 192). A small-scale open-framed wind pump, the only trestle mill left with a turbine, restored in 1981. *Tel.* c/o Norwich (0603) 61122 ext. 5224.

Melton Constable (Map 133) was developed as a railway town by the Midland & Great Northern Railway, 1885–1910. The locomotive works (TG 043 330) are now disused; there is railway housing (TG 045 330), a school and institute.

North Walsham & Dilham Canal (Map 133). A two-storey warehouse remains at Royston Staithe (TG 297 314) at the *North Walsham* end of the canal. A bridge and the remains of a builder's yard survive at the staithe at *Dilham* (TG 333 255). At

Honing there is a bridge and milestone (TG 328 273) and a lock nearby (TG 331 270) and Briggate lock and bridge (TG 315 275).

Norwich (Map 134). *Coslany Bridge* (TG 227 088) of 1804 is one of the earliest surviving iron bridges. See also *Station Road Bridge* (TG 226 093), 1882, and *Foundry Bridge* (TG 238 085), 1880s. *Pank's Showroom*, Castle Hill (TG 233 083) is a remarkable cast-iron and glass-fronted structure of about 1868. The *Bridewell Museum*, Bridewell Alley (TG 230 087), between St Andrew Street and Bedford Street, is a medieval merchant's house, later a bridewell and now housing displays of local industries. *Tel.* Norwich (0603) 22233 ext. 700. Nearby at 3 Bridewell Alley is *Colman's Mustard Museum*. *Tel.* Norwich (0603) 27889. The *Strangers Hall Museum of Domestic Life*, Charing Cross (TG 228 088) includes shop signs and transport. *Tel.* Norwich (0603) 22233 ext. 645.

Sheringham Lifeboat (133/TG 157 436), on the Front, is a rare example of a rowing lifeboat, built in 1894 for a private lifeboat company. See also at *Gorleston* (Map 134) *Storm House* (TG 530 036), the headquarters of another life-saving and salvage association, now a café; and two *lifeboat houses* (TG 530 040), one the RNLI house of 1883 and the other that of the Gorleston Volunteers.

Stalham staithe (133, 134/TG 373 246) is a wherry port with early-19th-century granary, warehouse and storehouses.

Sutton Windmill (134/TG 396 239). The tallest tower mill still standing in Britain at about 80 feet, it ceased work in the early 1940s and is now being restored. *Tel.* Stalham (0692) 81195. See also 19th-century tower mills at *Billingford* (156/TM 167 786); and *Wicklewood* (144/TG 077 027). *Tel.* c/o Norwich (0603) 61122 ext. 5224.

Thursford Green, Thursford Collection (132/TF 978 345) has a collection of traction engines, fairground equipment and mechanical organs. *Tel.* Thursford (032 877) 238 or Fakenham (0328) 3836. See also *Bressingham Steam Museum* (144/TM 080 807). *Tel.* Bressingham (037 988) 386; and *Strumpshaw Steam Museum*, Strumpshaw Hall (134/TG 348 067). *Tel.* Norwich (0603) 36782.

Wolferton Railway Station (132/TF 660 286) is the station for the Sandringham Estate. The 1868 royal waiting room is now a museum. *Tel.* Dersingham (0485) 40674. See also *Sheringham Station* (133/TG 157 430), headquarters of the North Norfolk Railway which runs steam services from April to October. *Tel.* Sheringham (0263) 822045.

OXFORDSHIRE

Oxfordshire is a mainly rural county although brickmaking and the woollen industry have a long history here.

Chipping Norton, Bliss Tweed Mill (164/SP 293 268). A most impressive four-storey mill with an unusual domed chimney. Designed by George Woodhouse and built in 1872 on the site of an earlier watermill, it is now disused.

Cogges, Manor Farm Museum (164/SP 362 096). A re-creation of a prosperous Edwardian Oxfordshire farm which has a medieval core and some buildings of the 17th–18th centuries. *Tel.* Witney (0993) 72602.

Didcot, Engine Shed (174/SU 525 906). Entered through Didcot station, it contains a large collection of GWR locomotives and rolling stock. *Tel.* Maidenhead (0628) 31767.

Garford, Venn Watermill (164/SU 430 949). A rural cornmill built about 1800 on an ancient site, it last worked about 1940 and is now being restored.

Henley, Nettlebed brick kiln (175/SU 703 863). A conical 17th-century kiln, 30 feet high with a diameter tapering from 20 feet at the base to 3 feet at the top.

Hook Norton Brewery (151/SP 349 332). A fantasy collection of buildings erected in 1900 by William Bradford which house a small brewery.

Mapledurham Watermill (175/SU 669 768). An 18th-century and earlier mill in the grounds of Mapledurham House restored to working order and producing wholemeal flour. *Tel.* Kidmore End (0734) 723350.

Minster Lovell, Chartist village (164/SP 31 10). A settlement was established here by the Chartist Land Company in 1847. Though most are considerably altered, 62 of the original 78 cottages survive.

Oxford, British Telecom Museum, 35 Speedwell Street (164/SP 514 058). Founded in 1963, it has a range of early telephone equipment. *Tel.* Oxford (0865) 46601.

Oxford, Rewley Road Station (164/SP 506 063), the former terminus of the Buckinghamshire Railway, is now a tyre depot. It was built in 1851 by the contractors Fox Henderson & Company, who built the Crystal Palace, using some of the same prefabricated components.

Oxford Canal (Map 164) begins near Oxford station (SP 508 064) and has a fine series of bridges within the city: red-brick ones (for example, SP 494 098, 495 096, 504 073), three counterweighted wooden draw bridges (for example, SP 502 088), and a cast-iron roving bridge at Isis Lock (SP 506 066). Nearby is the 1850 swing bridge (SP 506 066) which carried the Buckinghamshire Railway over the Sheepwash Channel of the Thames. Following the canal north for about 7 miles, Thrupp is an attractive canalside settlement (SP 480 158).

Rotherfield Greys, Greys Court (175/SU 724 834). The grounds of this National Trust house contain a 16th-century donkey-powered wheel which was used to draw water from a well and supplied water to the house until World War I, and a horse-engine from Shabden Court, Surrey, in which two horses drove two pumps in a well. *Tel.* Rotherfield Greys (049 17) 529.

Witney, blanket factories (164/SP 355 103). *Early's Mill,* Mill Street, includes an early 19th-century mill beside the river; *Smith's Mill,* Bridge Street, dates from *c* 1900.

Woodstock, Combe Sawmill (164/SP 418 150). An estate sawmill, joinery and smithy built in 1852 with a watermill and a steam engine.

SUFFOLK

Suffolk is an agricultural county with maltings and mills.

Stowmarket: Museum of East Anglian Life (155/TM 048 585)
Industrial archaeology, despite its name, is concerned with country crafts as well as urban industries. Some aspects of the craft of a largely rural county are preserved at Stowmarket. Alton Mill, an 18th-century watermill, together with the millhouse (which has a privy originally flushed by a sluice from the millpond) and cart lodge have been moved here from Tattingstone, near Ipswich. A pond has been made to enable the overshot wheel to be operated. Nearby at the end of the lane which leads from the main display is the mid-19th-century Eastbridge windpump. A smock drainage windpump, the last of a group of four on the Minsmere level (near Leiston), it worked until 1939. Nearer the entrance is the timber-framed 19th-century smithy from Grundisburgh (about 20 miles from Stowmarket) which is complete with blacksmith's tools. It was the workplace until 1968 of Frederick Joseph Crapnell, the last blacksmith there. In the museum buildings the workshops of three rural craftsmen, a wheelwright, a saddler and a rakemaker, have been erected. There is also the reconstruction of a village store. In the Engine Room is displayed a range of engines, the largest of which is the steam engine from a mill at Wickham Market, together with ropemaking and other equipment. Three barns house a selection of farm carts, vehicles, drills, threshing machines and other agricultural implements. On summer Sundays there are demonstrations of rural crafts such as sheep-shearing, lace-making and corn-dolly-making.
Address: Museum of East Anglian Life, Abbot's Hall, Stowmarket, Suffolk IP14 1DL. *Tel.* Stowmarket (0449) 612229.

Woodbridge Tidemill (169/TM 275 487)
Power from the tides is something sought in our own time, so far

Museum of East Anglian Life – Eastbridge windpump

without success. But our ancestors harnessed the power of the sea with tidemills; there were once about 200 tidemills working in Great Britain. The earliest English mill was reputedly at Dover by 1086. The site at Woodbridge dates from 1170 though the present mill, partially constructed from ships' timbers, was built in 1793 and worked until 1957. It was then operated by diesel motor until 1967. Restoration has recently taken place and the mill is again in working order. The principle of operation was for the incoming tide to be impounded in a pond whose gates shut when the tide began to ebb. The waterwheel, which was normally undershot or low breastshot, was turned by the release of impounded water. The mill thus had two periods of operation, changing each day with the tides, during 24 hours. The 18-foot-diameter wheel at Woodbridge, which is at the end of the building, drives four pairs of stones. Unfortunately when the mill was not working the pond was sold off for a marina but a small pond has been made so that the mill can be operated for demonstration purposes. The mill has three storeys and a further two floors in the mansard roof. There is a lucam on the quay side of the building.
Address: Warden, 17 Clare Avenue, Woodbridge, Suffolk. *Tel.* Woodbridge (039 43) 2048.

Also Worth Visiting in Suffolk

Brent Eleigh, cast-iron road bridge (155/TL 934 483). An early example of 1813, now bypassed. This may be compared with the late example of *c* 1870 at *Bures* (155/TL 906 340).

Bungay, Staithe (156/TM 343 898). A group of warehouses etc., at the head of the Waveney Navigation.

Debenham, Cyder House, Aspall Hall (156/TM 170 653). A stone apple-crusher of 1728 and a wooden press of 1729 are preserved on the premises where cider is still made with modern machinery. *Tel.* Debenham (0728) 860510.

Easton, crinkle-crankle wall (156/TM 282 586). These walls were built with undulating curves and no buttresses and are a Suffolk speciality. Another fine example can be seen at *Eye* (156/TM 143 741) in Lambeth Street.

Felixstowe, Dock & Railway Company offices (169/TM 280 329). The only original building to survive, the two-storey timber structure with slate roof was built in Swiss chalet style *c* 1880. Nearby (TM 281 332), the only 19th-century commercial building to remain in the largely modernized docks is this six-storey red-brick *roller mill. Felixstowe Town railway station* (TM 303 352) has some fine cast-iron work of 1897.

Herringfleet drainage windmill (134/TM 466 976). A tarred weatherboard smock mill of 1830 – but typical of an earlier

pattern – which drove a scoopwheel. The last in the Fens, it remains in working order and is occasionally operated. *Tel.* c/o Ipswich (0473) 55801.

Ipswich Docks (Map 169) developed from 1882 on the site of the medieval quay and are surrounded by mainly 19th-century buildings. Of most interest are *Isaac Lord's Warehouse* (TM 169 441), stretching from Fore Street, where the buildings may be 15th century, through to Common Quay, with additional buildings added in each century up to the 19th; and the 1844 classical style *Custom House* in Key Street (TM 166 441).

Leiston, Garrett's Engineering Works (156/TM 444 625). This firm, whose modern works is on the edge of the town, was established here in 1778. Most of the old site is in ruins but a notable survival, for which there are plans for a museum, is the timber and iron 'Long Shop', an erecting shop of 1853.

Lowestoft (Map 134) became a port in the 19th century with the creation of the harbour as part of the construction of the Norwich & Lowestoft Navigation in 1827–33. Engineered by William Cubitt, Lake Lothing was linked with the sea to the east and with Oulton Broad to the west and a protective breakwater was constructed at the mouth of the new channel. The harbour was improved in the late 1840s by Sir Morton Peto when he brought the railway to the town and created a new resort. The town is still a fishing port. The *fishing harbour* (TM 550 927), at the mouth of Lake Lothing, was expanded in 1883–1903. A number of *fish-curing houses* survive (small compared with those at Yarmouth), particularly in Raglan Road (TM 547 931), off Cambridge Road (TM 548 940), Norwich Road (TM 541 933) and Raglan Street (TM 546 934).

Pakenham Watermill (155/TL 937 695). A late-18th-century building on the site of a Tudor mill, it last worked commercially in 1974 and has been restored. *Tel.* c/o Lavenham (0787) 247179 or Bury St Edmunds (0284) 3506. Nearby is a working windmill.

Saxstead Green Windmill (156/TM 253 645). A tall post mill with roundhouse dating from the 18th century and later raised in height. *Tel.* Earl Soham (072 882) 346.

South Cove, Cove Bottom brickworks (156/TM 494 798). A remarkable survival of a small 19th-century brickworks still working. See also the brickworks at *Aldeburgh* (156/TM 451 570) and *Hoxne* (156/TM 176 766).

Sudbury, Navigation warehouses, Quay Lane (155/TL 873 408). A fine red-brick building of 1791 at the head of the Stour Navigation, now converted to a theatre, and a smaller similar building of the 1800s.

Thorpeness Windmill (156/TM 467 598). A post mill with a

Woodbridge tidemill

roundhouse built in 1824 as a cornmill, moved to its present site in the early 1920s and converted to pump water for the village supply. It now contains an exhibition of local history. *Tel.* (Suffolk County Planning Officer) Ipswich (0473) 55801.

Woodbridge, Buttrams Windmill, Burkitt Road (169/TM 264 493). A six-storey tower mill built in 1835 and last worked in 1928, it is maintained by the county. *Tel.* c/o Ipswich (0473) 55801.

Railways were once more numerous in Suffolk than they are now and a number of notable buildings survive. For example: the Jacobean crossing cottages at *Great Barton* (155/TL 907 651); the Renaissance station and fine skew-arch bridge in Out Northgate, *Bury St Edmunds* (155/TL 853 652); the station and associated buildings at *Darsham* (156/TM 404 697); the station and Railway Inn at *Finningham* (155/TM 062 677); the large but remote Raydon Wood station at *Raydon* (155/TM 061 404); the elaborate Jacobean station at *Somerleyton* (134/TM 480 965); the Jacobean station of 1846 at *Stowmarket* (155/TM 051 589); and, to compare with the last, a small station in the same series at *Thurston* (155/TL 918 650).

Various forms of road transport can be seen at the *East Anglia Transport Museum*, Chapel Road, Carlton Colville (134/TM 515 901). *Tel.* c/o Ubbeston (098 683) 398.

Maltings are a characteristic building in this agricultural county and particularly notable examples can be seen at *Beccles* (134, 156/TM 426 904), Gosford Road; *Bungay* (156/TM 341 897); *Bures* (155/TL 907 341); *Bury St Edmunds* (Map 155), Bridewell Lane and College Street (TL 855 638), Southgate Street (TL 860 636), off Fornham Road (TL 852 653), Northgate Street (TL 854 651) and Mildenhall Road (TL 849 663); *Halesworth* (156/TM 388 777); *Ipswich* (Map 169), Key Street (TM 166 440), New Cut West and Dock Street (TM 167 437) and Princes Street (TM 157 440); *Long Melford* (155/TL 859 443); *Newmarket* (154/TL 643 640), Fordham Road; *Oulton Broad* (134/TM 518 929); *Snape* (156/TM 393 574); and *Stowmarket* (Map 155), Station Road and Creeting Road (TM 051 588), off Ipswich Street (TM 053 582) and Bury Road (TM 047 590).

Midland England

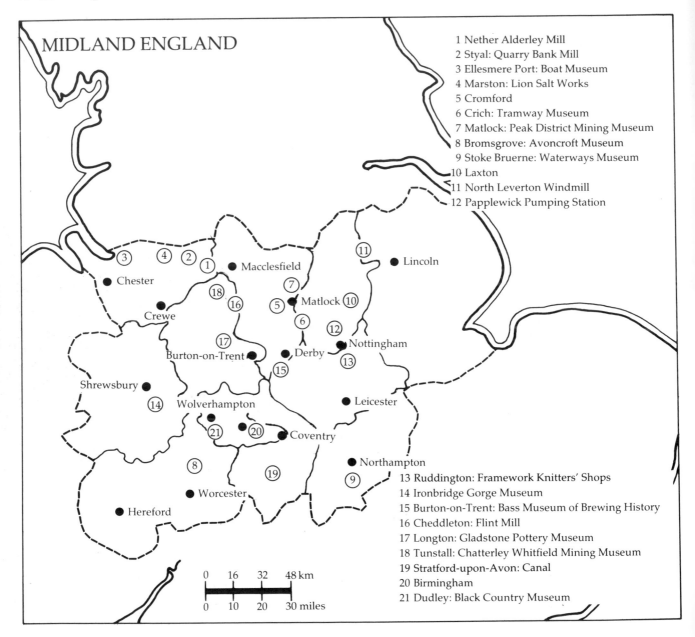

MIDLAND ENGLAND

1 Nether Alderley Mill
2 Styal: Quarry Bank Mill
3 Ellesmere Port: Boat Museum
4 Marston: Lion Salt Works
5 Cromford
6 Crich: Tramway Museum
7 Matlock: Peak District Mining Museum
8 Bromsgrove: Avoncroft Museum
9 Stoke Bruerne: Waterways Museum
10 Laxton
11 North Leverton Windmill
12 Papplewick Pumping Station

13 Ruddington: Framework Knitters' Shops
14 Ironbridge Gorge Museum
15 Burton-on-Trent: Bass Museum of Brewing History
16 Cheddleton: Flint Mill
17 Longton: Gladstone Pottery Museum
18 Tunstall: Chatterley Whitfield Mining Museum
19 Stratford-upon-Avon: Canal
20 Birmingham
21 Dudley: Black Country Museum

CHESHIRE

A county of varied activity: agriculture, salt and textiles, important for transport too.

Nether Alderley Mill (118/SJ 844 763)

Without bread man cannot live. So a basic element in any community was a means of producing flour. The Domesday Book reveals that by the Norman Conquest there were a considerable number of watermills in England producing flour and their number increased in the 12th and 13th centuries with the growth of population. Of the many which trace their origin to this period, Nether Alderley, whose existence was first mentioned in 1290, provides an example. Little is known of this early mill but the present low stone building with its stone-flagged roof (with four dormer windows) reaching almost to ground level, first mentioned in 1591, continued in operation until 1939. Shortly after that date it became derelict but after World War II it was given to the National Trust and has now been restored.

Nether Alderley is a fairly typical water-powered cornmill. From the millpond the water flows to drive two overshot waterwheels (12 feet in diameter and 3 feet wide with a capacity of 8 hp each) in tandem, an unusual arrangement. The 16th-century machinery has long since been replaced and the present set of equipment – probably the third – dates from 1850 and later. The sequence of milling operations is assisted by gravity. From

the garner or bin floor the grain is fed to the stone floor where it is ground and the flour is collected below on the sack floor. Below in the basement is the pit wheel whose power is transmitted upwards by gearing and shafting to the two pairs of French burr stones, the sack hoist and the meal sifter.

At one time it was sometimes necessary to dry grain before grinding and the drying kiln here should be noted, but it long ago became uneconomic to dry grain and the kiln probably went out of use 90–100 years ago. Nowadays only dry grain is purchased for grinding.

Address: Nether Alderley Mill, Congleton Road, Alderley Edge, Cheshire. *Tel.* Wilmslow (0625) 531510.

Styal: Quarry Bank Mill (109/SJ 835 829)

One of the essential elements of the British Industrial Revolution was the shift from domestic to factory manufacture in the textile industry. Quarry Bank Mill is an early example of the large cotton factory, located in a somewhat isolated situation in the valley of the Bollin to employ water power. Built by Samuel Greg in 1784, its 100-hp waterwheel 32 feet in diameter, installed in 1819, was later replaced by a turbine. Though there were later additions, the red-brick main building of the mill, with its central pediment and clock surmounted by a bellcote, looks today as it did in the 1830s. Here Samuel Greg initially employed pauper apprentices to spin cotton and adults to weave. The sequence of cotton cloth manufacture can be traced in the mill's exhibits. In 1855 the mill contained 5,952 throstle spindles, 5,184 mule spindles and 305 looms. Also to be seen is the manager's office, the counting house and the enormous wheel chamber, at present containing a turbine and in which it is hoped to install what is thought to be the most powerful waterwheel still surviving in England. Linked with the mill were the Apprentice House dating largely 1790–1831 and the houses (for example, Oak Cottages 1820–5), the school (1823), the shop and the chapel (1823) built for the cotton workers. The leat running from the mill pool can also be traced. The mill ceased production in 1959.

Quarry Bank Mill and the nearby village of Styal are one of the best preserved factory colonies in Britain.

Address: Quarry Bank Mill, Styal, Wilmslow, Cheshire SK9 4LA. *Tel.* Wilmslow (0625) 527468.

Ellesmere Port: The Boat Museum (117/SJ 405 773)

Industrial archaeology is not only concerned with buildings and other fixed structures; it also includes within its scope moving items, such as boats, railway locomotives, cars and trucks, and aircraft. Ellesmere Port is the home of a Boat Museum which has a collection of the craft of Britain's canals and rivers which includes icebreakers, a weedcutter, a Worsley mine boat, a tunnel tug, the last wooden Mersey flat, a range of powered and unpowered boats, narrow and wide, and the former ICI Weaver packet *Cuddington*. The 30 boats represent the largest collection of inland navigation craft afloat in Europe. In a museum building there are displays which tell the story of British canals and their craft. This site at Ellesmere Port is at the junction of the Shropshire Canal, which drops down the hillside by a flight of locks, and the Manchester Ship Canal, built in 1866 to enable sea-going vessels to reach the centre of the cotton industry. There were some splendid warehouses built by Thomas Telford on what was virtually an island. Unfortunately most of them have gone but a few survive together with a pump house (1874), complete with four steam engines, one of which has been restored to working order, the tollhouse and other buildings. There are also the remains of Porters Row, canal housing built in

1833. At the entrance into the river there is a lighthouse.
Address: The Boat Museum, Dock Yard Road, Ellesmere Port, South Wirral, Cheshire L65 4EF. *Tel.* Liverpool (051) 355 1876.

Marston: Lion Salt Works (118/SJ 671 755)
Since Roman times salt has been produced in Cheshire by the open-pan method of evaporation. Engaged in the salt business since 1721, the Thompson family moved to Marston in 1842.

Most salt is now produced in vacuum chambers and the Lion Works is the last of the older type of salt works where brine is pumped from the local salt beds and reduced to crystals by boiling in open pans. The works consists of an untidy group of wooden and brick buildings. Brine is pumped up about 150 feet by a horizontal steam engine into the large brine tank at the rate of 3,000 gallons per hour, from which it is distributed by gravity feed to each working salt pan. One of the salt pans, No. 3, has been restored to its condition *c* 1900. While the pans then were riveted and heated by a hand-fired coal fire, the more modern pans are welded and fired by oil. As the salt crystallizes it falls to the bottom of the pans and is then raked to the side and shovelled into tubs to form 14-lb blocks of salt. It is then taken away to be dried slowly, cut and wrapped. In the smithy, which has the original punching and shearing machine and steam engine, repairs and maintenance were carried out. Adjacent is the Trent and Mersey Canal which now stands above the surrounding landscape devastated by subsidence with large flashes – water-filled depressions – interrupting communication. The canal was used by the Thompson family to dispatch their salt. Trips are now run from Wincham Wharf, Northwich, to the works, which also had its private railway line linking up with the national network; but it now distributes its salt by road.

Address: Lion Salt Works, Marston, Northwich, Cheshire. *Tel.* Northwich (0606) 2066.

The Salt Museum, Weaver Hall, London Road, Northwich (118/SJ 658 732). This museum has displays illustrating the historical development of the industry from Roman times to the present day with particular emphasis on its heyday in the 19th century.

Also Worth Visiting in Cheshire

Anderton canal lift (118/SJ 647 753). Built in 1875, this unique and impressive canal lift – the only one in Britain – is used to transfer vessels in water-filled tanks between the Trent and Mersey Canal and the River Weaver 50 feet below.

Bunbury Watermill (117/SJ 573 581). A brick-built cornmill of about 1850 on an earlier site, it ceased working after flooding in 1960 but has now been restored. *Tel.* (North West Water Authority) Liverpool (051) 327 1275.

Chester, Railway Station (117/SJ 413 669). A two-storey brick Italianate station built in 1847–8 for the Chester & Crewe, Chester & Birkenhead and Chester & Holyhead Railways. The main front is over 1,000 feet long and originally had a single 750-feet-long platform. To the north is the Goods Station and opposite the splendid Queen Hotel of 1859–60.

Crewe railway housing and workshops (118/SJ 705 555). A railway town begun in 1843 to house the workshops and workers of the Grand Junction Railway. Though many houses have been cleared, some good examples of 19th-century industrial housing remain.

Farndon, Stretton Watermill (117/SJ 454 530). An early 17th-century cornmill with two waterwheels powering 18th- and 19th-century machinery which ended work in 1959. It has been restored. *Tel.* (County Museums Service) Northwich (0606) 41331

Nantwich, Churches Mansion (118/SJ 650 524). A typical Elizabethan merchant's half-timbered house, now a restaurant. *Tel.* Nantwich (0270) 65933.

Warrington Transporter Bridge (108/SJ 596 876). Built in 1913–14 to provide communication across a loop of the Mersey, but no longer in use.

DERBYSHIRE

Leadmining, textiles and transport (road, canal and rail) provide the main sites of interest.

Cromford trail (Map 119)

A key development in the British Industrial Revolution was the shift of manufacture from the home to the factory, a development which can be seen at Cromford, which was one of the early centres of the new factory-housed cotton industry. Begin your tour at:

Cromford Mill (SK 298 569). A three-storey stone building, the

Old Mill was built by Sir Richard Arkwright in the 1770s and was the first successful water-powered cotton mill. After cotton manufacture ceased the factory had a number of other uses. It is now in process of restoration as a museum. *Tel.* Wirksworth (062 982) 4297. The works got its water partly from the Bonsall Stream and partly from the Cromford Mear Sough, a stream draining a mine. The water is brought to the mill by a cast-iron aqueduct which crosses Mill Lane. On the south side of the road is the mill manager's house and further to the east is the drive to Rock House built as a residence by Sir Richard Arkwright.

Continue along Mill Lane to reach: *Cromford Wharf*, the terminus of the Cromford Canal, 14½ miles in length, built in 1793 to provide a link with the Trent and Mersey Canal. Warehouses and the former counting house survive around the basin and cottages; the former smithy and a sawpit can be seen across the yard. As the supply of water for the canal proved inadequate, the *Leawood pumping station* was built in 1849, 2 miles southeast of Cromford, to pump water from the River Derwent. The beam engine by Graham & Company, installed in a tall gritstone building with an imposing 95-foot chimney, has been restored to working order. Nearby is the *Wigwell aqueduct*, 200 yards long and 30 feet high, built by William Jessop. Return to Cromford Wharf along the canal. If Mill Lane is taken to the left it passes the church built by Sir Richard and, after crossing the 15th-century bridge, reaches the entrance lodge to *Willersley Castle*, his later

residence. Return along Mill Lane towards Cromford and take the drive to the right just past the church which leads to the A6 then turn north along the A6 to reach:

Masson Mill, a six-storey brick building erected by Arkwright in 1783–4. It is now flanked by modern extensions to the north and south. Still in use, it is occupied by English Sewing Cotton Ltd. Return south by the main road to Cromford Market Place and turn right past the Greyhound Inn. Continue until North Street is reached on the left.

Industrial housing: to provide for his workers Arkwright built a number of houses. The finest examples, two rows of two-storey houses built about 1777, are in North Street. At the end are the school and schoolhouses also built by Arkwright. Further up Cromford Hill, in Bedehouse Lane are the Bedehouses or Alms-houses, built in the late 17th century. Still further up the hill is Black Rock and in the fields the scattered heaps of old leadmine workings. Return to the centre of Cromford down Cromford Hill.

Other cotton mills with associated housing can be seen at *Belper,* particularly *North Mill* (119/SK 345 481) and *North Row* (SK 348 478); *Calver, Calver Mill* (128/SK 248 745); *Cressbrook, Cressbrook Mill* (SK 173 726); *Darley Abbey, Mill and Library* (128/SK 354 386); and *Glossop, Cotton Mill* (110/SK 029 924).

Crich: Tramway Museum (119/SK 351 544)

One of the more ephemeral methods of urban transport has been the tram. Introduced into Britain in the 1860s, the early trams were horse-drawn but from the 1890s electric traction developed and tramways spread rapidly. By the 1920s there were some 14,000 tramcars in operation in Britain but the development of the motor bus and the private car reduced their numbers and now only in Blackpool are tramcars still in operation.

In a disused quarry at Crich on part of the route of a former narrow gauge mineral railway, 1 mile of standard gauge track has been laid down on which are run a number of trams from various parts of Britain (and a few from overseas). The collection of trams in operation and awaiting restoration, built between 1873 and 1953, now numbers about 50.

At the terminus is being constructed the kind of street scene which would have formed the surroundings of an urban tramway about 1910. It includes the façade of the Derby Assembly Rooms (1763–74), gaslights from Oldham and a cast-iron tram shelter from Birmingham.

At the Wakebridge halt there is a replica of a leadmine.
Address: Tramway Museum, Crich, Matlock, Derbyshire BE4 5DP. *Tel.* Ambergate (077 385) 2565.

Leadmining in the Peak District

Before the Roman occupation lead ore was possibly worked in the Peak District and it was certainly worked by the Romans themselves. Working continued subsequently and the heyday of leadmining occurred between 1700 and 1800. The introduction of steam power greatly facilitated the draining of mines but required capital, with the result that the industry was carried on by larger mining companies in the first half of the 19th century. After 1860 the industry rapidly declined. Some idea of the history of the industry can be obtained from displays in the *Peak District Mining Museum* (119/SK 293 581) housed in the Pavilion in the centre of Matlock Bath which has an 1819 waterpressure engine as centrepiece.

Address: Peak District Mining Museum, Matlock Bath, Derbyshire. *Tel.* Matlock (0629) 3834.

The most impressive surface remains of a 19th-century lead-mine are to be seen at *Magpie Mine, Sheldon* (119/SK 172 682) with its engine house of 1869–70 and chimney of 1840, two winding houses, a boiler house, agent's house and smithy. A general impression of the site can be obtained from the road.

Ashover, Stone Edge chimney and smelt mill (119/SK 334 670). Claimed to be the oldest industrial chimney in the world, it was used for smelting lead until about 1870. The cupola nearby dates from about 1811 and remains of condensing flues, furnaces and water channels can also be seen.

Castleton, Odin Mine crushing circle (110/SK 135 835), completed in 1823, is the most intact remaining crushing circle in Derbyshire. It has an iron track 18 feet 2 inches in diameter and 15 inches wide and a gritstone wheel crusher about 5 feet 10 inches in diameter and 12 inches wide.

Goodluck Mine, Via Gellia (119/SK 270 565) is a good example of a small-scale drift leadmine dating from the 1830s. On the surface are examples of tools, implements and artefacts which have been found in the mine during restoration, as well as other displays. Visitors, who are advised to wear stout footwear, can also go underground on a guided tour. For admission contact R. Amner, 58 Foljambe Avenue, Walton, Chesterfield. *Tel.* Chesterfield (0246) 72375.

Holme Bank chert mine, Bakewell (119/SK 216 691) was first opened in 1767, reputedly by Josiah Wedgwood. The mine had a number of owners and was eventually acquired in the 1920s by Captain H. Davey-Thornhill. It was operated until 1960 when water problems and lack of sales for the outmoded grinding process forced its closure. Worked on a longwall face, it contains some 6 miles of tunnel in an area ½ mile by ¾ mile. For information contact Colin Laidler, 9 Peakland View, Darley Dale, Matlock, Derbyshire. *Tel.* Darley Dale (062 983) 4658 (evenings).

Speedwell Mine, Castleton (110/SK 139 827). Mining started here in 1771 when an attempt was made to intersect the main lead veins. However, little lead was found and mining was discontinued about 1814. In the course of stream-mining caves were struck and so a canal tunnel was cut for boats for the haulage of ore and waste rock. Tourists may travel by boat through the first part of the canal to Bottomless Pit, a large natural cavern. *Tel.* Hope Valley (0433) 20512.

Wirksworth Moot Hall (119/SK 288 541) is the meeting place of the Barmote Court which still meets twice a year. The building is decorated with carvings symbolic of the leadmining industry.

Also Worth Visiting in Derbyshire
Cromford Station House, iron footbridge and east side waiting room (119/SK 303 575) were built in French style for the Midland Railway in 1850–60.

Dale Abbey, Cat & Fiddle Windmill (129/SK 438 398). A late 18th-century post mill with a roundhouse added in 1844. *Tel.* Darley Dale (062 983) 4374.

Derby Industrial Museum, The Silk Mill, off Full Street, Derby (128/SK 356 364). Housed in the Silk Mill constructed on the foundation arches of the mill built for Thomas Lombe in 1717–21 and rebuilt in 1910, the museum contains a collection of Rolls-Royce engines and displays illustrating the history of Derbyshire industries. *Tel.* Derby (0332) 31111.

Elvaston Castle Country Park Museum (129/SK 406 330). Displays include a gas engine house, rack saw bench, blacksmith's, plumber's, joiner's, wheelwright's, saddler's and cobbler's shops and a collection of horse-drawn vehicles, agricultural machinery and hand-tools. *Tel.* Derby (0332) 71342.

Heage, Morley Park Furnaces (119/SK 380 492). A pair of masonry furnaces, 36 feet high, built 1780 and 1818. Visible from the A61.

High Peak Trail (119/SK 313 560). This footpath follows the course of the Cromford and High Peak Railway, opened 1830–1 between Cromford and Dowlow, near Buxton. Its finest single monument is:

Middleton Top Winding Engine, Wirksworth (119/SK 275 552). Built in the 1820s, the Cromford and High Peak Railway was intended for horse operation but because some of the hills were too steep winding engines were installed. The only survivor is this 1829 double single-cylinder beam engine built by the Butterley Company. *Tel.* Wirksworth (062 982) 3204.

Rowsley, Caudwell's Watermill (119/SK 255 657). A water-powered roller mill of 1874 which illustrates the changed technology that swept away the earlier small mills grinding by stones. *Tel.* Darley Dale (062 983) 4374.

Shardlow (129/SK 443 304). A splendid inland canal port with warehouses and shops dating from the 18th century on the Trent and Mersey Canal.

HEREFORD AND WORCESTER

Hereford and Worcester, a new administrative county, is largely agricultural with some small-scale industry and some transport sites.

Avoncroft Museum of Buildings (139/SO 952 684)
Preservation is one of the functions of industrial archaeology. This museum was born after the failure of efforts to prevent the destruction of the 15th-century Merchant's House in Bromsgrove. The timbers were saved and the building was re-erected here in 1967. Other buildings and structures have followed, including the roof timbers of the Guesten Hall, Worcester; the cruck-framed barn from Cholstrey (Herefordshire), a local granary, and the String of Horses – a large Elizabethan private house – from Shrewsbury which now serves as the reception building.

The Danzey Green (originally Botley) post mill from near Tanworth-in-Arden was built about 1826 but was disused by 1895. Now restored, it has a full-time miller. The chainshop, which has 14 hearths, belonged to Jones & Lloyd of Colley Gate, Cradley while the smaller nail workshop came from Sidemoor, Bromsgrove. Both are complete with tools and equipment. Demonstrations of chainmaking are held. The entrance building is the octagonal counting house from Bromsgrove Cattle Market used from 1853 to the late 1960s as the Auction Cash Office and for other purposes. The 19th-century rack saw from the Heber Percy estate is housed in a separate building; Forge Cottage provides accommodation for the Area Museum Service, and there are some wagons in the Wagon Shed.
Address: Avoncroft Museum of Buildings, Stoke Heath, Bromsgrove, Hereford and Worcester. *Tel.* Bromsgrove (0527) 31886 or 31363.

Also Worth Visiting in Hereford and Worcester
Bewdley Museum, Load Street, Bewdley (138/SO 787 753). Housed in the 18th-century butchers' shambles, there are dis-

plays of a number of local crafts: charcoal-burning, rope-making, coopery, etc, and a reconstruction of a foundry. *Tel.* Bewdley (0299) 403573.

Hereford, Broomy Hill Pumping Station, the Herefordshire Waterworks Museum (149/SO 497 393) houses the oldest vertical triple expansion engine in Great Britain and the only two-cylinder vertical condensing pumping engine, both built by Worth Mackenzie. *Tel.* c/o Hereford (0432) 4104.

Hereford, Museum of Cider, 21 Ryelands Street (149/SO 502 399) tells the story of Herefordshire farm cider-making and has a 1920s cider factory, vat house and cooper's shop. *Tel.* Hereford (0432) 54207.

Mortimers Cross, Lucton Watermill (149/SO 426 638). An 18th-century mill with an undershot waterwheel which produced animal food until the 1940s. *Tel.* c/o Wolverhampton (0902) 765105.

Newnham Watermill, Mill Lane, Newnham Bridge (138/SO 644 688). Built about 1700 with an undershot waterwheel, it worked commercially until 1953. *Tel.* Newnham Bridge (058 479) 445.

Redditch, Forge Mills Needle Nuseum, 275 Bromsgrove Road

Avoncroft – the 19th century rack saw on its original site near Warwick

Leicester – old Fish Market

(139/SP 045 685). A 16th-century forge mill site converted to needlemaking in the 1730s, it was in operation until 1958. The scouring and polishing machinery was water-driven. *Tel.* Redditch (0527) 62509.

Severn Valley Railway (138/SO 715 927–793 754). This standard-gauge steam railway runs the 12½ miles from Bridgnorth to Bewdley, for much of the way close to the Severn. *Tel.* Bewdley (0299) 403816.

Stourport, canal basins (138/SO 810 710) provide the links between the Staffordshire and Worcestershire Canal and the River Severn. Note the Tontine Hotel, *c* 1770, built by the canal company; the clock warehouse, *c* 1812; and the York Street lock tollhouse of 1853.

Tardebigge, canal locks and engine house (139/SO 990 689–150/SO 934 644). Opened in 1815, this flight of 30 locks on the Worcester and Birmingham Canal raises the canal by a total height of 217 feet. Nearby is the engine house (now converted into a nightclub) which housed the engine which operated the pumps to raise the water up the flight again. From the top lock the canal runs level through four tunnels to Gas Street, Birmingham.

LEICESTERSHIRE

The east of the county is predominantly agricultural while coalmining and textiles are the most important industries in the west and north. Sites of interest include the following:

Ashby-de-la-Zouch Station (128/SK 355 163), built in 1849 in classical style with an impressive façade.

Bagworth Station (140/SK 442 093), built in the style of a tollhouse on the Leicestershire and Swannington Railway.

Castle Donington, Donington Collection (129/SK 446 275), has over 70 single-seater racing cars, a similar number of Leyland historic vehicles and racing motorcycles. *Tel.* Derby (0332) 810048.

Foxton, canal incline and locks (141/SP 691 897). A flight of 10 staircase locks built on the Grand Union Canal in 1810–12 with their associated side ponds and lock-keeper's cottage at the summit. Because the locks were narrow and their use time-consuming, a steam-powered inclined plane was constructed alongside in 1898–1900, the canal barges being raised or lowered floating in wheeled tanks in five minutes instead of 70 minutes using the locks. But its use proved uneconomic; it ceased

operation in 1911 and was dismantled in 1920. While the locks are still in use, the inclined plane is overgrown.

In **Leicester** (Map 140) see:

Leicester Museum of Technology, Abbey Pumping Station, Corporation Road (SK 589 067). This former sewage works pumping station was built in 1891 to house four Woolf beam engines. One of the original 12 Lancashire boilers has also been preserved. The boiler house has been converted into a transport gallery. There is also a knitting gallery, a display of stationary engines and fire engines, and a unique steam shovel. *Tel.* Leicester (0533) 61330.

East Midlands Gas Museum (The John Doran Museum), Aylestone Road, Leicester (SK 581 024). The only permanent museum devoted entirely to the history of the gas industry, the collection is housed in part of the original Aylestone Road gasworks. Among the more important exhibits are a gas engine and a working gas radio. *Tel.* Leicester (0533) 549414, ext. 2192.

Leicester has two notable railway stations: *London Road* (SK 594 040), built by the Midland Railway in 1892, and the disused *Central Station* (SK 581 047), built by the Grand Central in 1899.

Old Fish Market (SK 587 043) of 1877 is an outstanding example of a cast-iron structure.

Loughborough: Great Central Station, Main Line Railway Trust (129/SK 544 205) operates a regular weekend service of steam-hauled trains on 5 miles of old LNER track via Quorn and Woodhouse to Rothley. *Tel.* Loughborough (0509) 30726 and 216433.

LINCOLNSHIRE

Lincolnshire is a county of wind- and water-mills with some ports and waterways.

Alford Windmill, East Street (122/TF 457 766). A six-storeyed five-sailed tower mill with four pairs of stones, built in 1813 and worked until 1955. *Tel.* Kirton Lindsey (0652) 648382.

Alvingham Watermill (113/TF 365 914). A late 18th-century mill with a breastshot waterwheel, last worked in 1950. *Tel.* South Cockerington (050 782) 544.

Boston (Map 131): sites include 18th-century *warehouses* in South Street along the Witham (TF 330 430), a *granary* beside the *Dock* (TF 332 431), *Van Smirren's Warehouse* (TF 327 438) on

Doughty Quay and the cast-iron *Hospital Bridge* (TF 331 449) and stone *Bargate Bridge* (TF 332 446), both designed by John Rennie.

Burgh le Marsh, Dobson's Windmill, High Street (122/TF 503 649). A tarred brick tower mill with five sails built about 1833 and last worked in 1947. *Tel.* Skegness (0754) 810281.

Heckington Windmill (130/TF 145 436). The only remaining eight-sail mill in England, built in 1830 but with earlier machinery transferred to it after damage at the end of the 19th century. *Tel.* Sleaford (0529) 60241.

Lincoln, Museum of Lincolnshire Life, Old Barracks, Burton

Dogdyke Pumping Station – 1856 Bradley & Craven beam engine

Road (121/SK 973 722), has a growing industrial section including steam, oil and gasfired engines, etc. *Tel.* Lincoln (0522) 28448.

New Bolingbroke (122/TF 308 579) is a new settlement of the 1820s intended to be a market town. A basin for water traffic and a crescent of shops remain.

Sibsey, Trader Windmill (122/TF 345 510). A brick tower mill with six sails built in 1877 on the site of an earlier post mill. *Tel.* c/o Wolverhampton (0902) 765105.

Skegness, remains of pier (122/TF 572 634). Built in 1881, 1,800 feet in length, it was the fourth longest pier in Britain. Several sections of it were destroyed in storms in January 1978.

Sleaford Maltings (130/TF 075 452). With eight massive blocks flanking a central engine house of 1903, this is one of the largest maltings ever built in England. It is now used for other purposes. The early 19th-century *gas works* (130/TF 076 464) is also worth noting.

Stamford, Brewery Museum, All Saints' Brewery, All Saints' Street (141/TF 028 071). Established by Samuel Smith's in Melbourn's brewery, Scotgate, the brewery, which operated until 1974, still contains much of its 19th-century equipment with the original steam engine. *Tel.* Stamford (0780) 52186.

Tattershall, Dogdyke Pumping Station (122/TF 206 558) contains a 16-hp beam engine of 1855 coupled to a 28-foot scoop wheel, and the Ruston diesel and Gwynnes centrifugal pump which replaced them in 1940. There is another marsh pumping station beside the Welland at *Pinchbeck* (131/TF 261 261).

Notable stations in the county include: *Alford Station* (122/TF 445 755), built by the East Lincolnshire Railway in Tudor-Gothic style in 1854; *St Mark's Station, Lincoln* (121/SK 972 707), which was built by the Midland Railway in 1846 with a fine classical façade and portico and has opposite an unusual octagonal signal box; and *Water Street Station, Stamford* (141/TF 038 069), built in the style of an Elizabethan manor house and now converted to other uses.

NORTHAMPTONSHIRE

Northamptonshire is important for its shoe industry (of which there is very little surviving evidence), for quarrying and for transport.

Stoke Bruerne: Waterways Museum (152/SP 745 500)

The East Midlands was almost at the hub of the English canal system which played an important part in the transport of

industrial products from the early 18th century until the later 19th. Created by British Waterways Board at a wharf on the Grand Union Canal, the locks, the hump-backed bridge, the canalside inn and the grain warehouse which houses a collection of relics of 200 years of canal history form a picturesque complex. One of the double-locks has been converted to house a barge-weighing machine and there are various canal boats on display. In the museum is a full-sized replica of a narrow boat cabin. Just to the north is the Blisworth tunnel (SP 729 529–739 503), at 3,056 yards the longest single-bore canal tunnel in Britain still in regular use. Begun in 1794, its construction caused great difficulties. For several years a double track horse tramway ran over the hill from Blisworth Wharf to Stoke Bruerne until the tunnel was completed in March 1805.

Address: Waterways Museum, Stoke Bruerne, Near Towcester, Northamptonshire. *Tel.* Roade (0604) 862229.

Also Worth Visiting in Northamptonshire
Braunston (Map 152) is a canal settlement at the junction of the Grand Union and Oxford Canals. About 400 yards west of the bridge carrying the A45 over the canal are twin cast-iron roving bridges at the junction of the 'old' and 'new' lines of the Oxford Canal (SP 532 660). To the east is a canal tollhouse (SP 538 658) and another cast-iron roving bridge over what was the original course of the Oxford Canal and is now a marina. Further east at Little Braunston (SP 545 660) is Braunston bottom lock with boat-building sheds and a boat-gauging dock (now a dry dock for boat maintenance) on the north side of the canal, while on the

south is the later engine house which was used to pump water from the reservoirs below the bottom lock to the top lock.

Hunsbury Hill Ironstone Trail (152/SP 738 584). The remains of extensive quarries and tramway cuttings dating from 1873 to 1921. Part is used by the **Northamptonshire Ironstone Railway Trust** which has a collection of locomotives and rolling stock used in the industry.

Irchester Country Park (152/SP 91 66). Now a pleasant area of forest walks and picnic meadows, evidence of the 'hill and dale' back-filling of open-cast ironstone workings can still be seen in the area.

Kettering, Timpsons Shoe Factory, Bath Road (141/SP 870 799). Built in the 1920s, this large concrete factory with very large windows epitomizes industrial architecture of its time.

Kilsby Railway Tunnel was built with considerable difficulty for the London and Birmingham Railway, opened in 1838. The monumental architecture of the portals can be seen at the southern entrance (152/SP 578 698), and one of the two 60-feet-diameter ventilation shafts is situated on the north of the A5 (140/SP 569 708).

Little Billing, Billing Mill (152/SP 813 610). A museum of milling in a restored cornmill, access is through the Billing Aquadrome. *Tel.* Northampton (0604) 408181.

Northampton, Central Museum, Guildhall Road (152/SP 755 604). The Boot and Shoe room has a cobbler's shop, a number of older footwear machines and a large collection of footwear. *Tel.* Northampton (0604) 34881 ext. 392.

Northampton, Footshape Boot Works, Barrack Road (152/SP 753 619), was built in 1913 for the Barratt brothers who had pioneered in this country the system of supplying boots through the post. This probably represents the peak of development of the show frontage with the title of the factory carried in stone letters as balustrading to an imposing three-storey office block fronting the working area located mainly under clerestory roofs.

Northampton, Manfield Building, Campbell Square (152/SP 755 609). Erected in 1857 of brick and stucco by Moses P. Manfield and extended westwards in the 1880s, these were the first large premises to be erected by a Northampton shoe manufacturer, ostensibly as a warehouse but having three storeys together with a row of 'half-windows' at pavement level, an arrangement often quoted as typical of Northampton shoe factories. See in contrast the single-storey *Manfield Factory* of 1890–2 in Wellingborough Road (SP 771 613).

Sudborough tollhouse (141/SP 971 822), on the A6116. An early circular tollhouse of 1660 with a conical roof.

Railway monuments worth seeing include: *Kettering Station* (141/SP 864 780) of 1857 which has good decorative ironwork; *Oundle Station* (141/TL 046 890) of 1845, designed by W. Livock in neo-Tudor style and now much neglected.

NOTTINGHAMSHIRE

Nottinghamshire is distinguished for agriculture, mining and framework knitting. It is also of interest for transport and water supply.

Laxton Open Field Village (120/SK 720 670)

Although there are remnants of open-field cultivation at Braunton (north Devon), Rhosilli (Gower), the Isle of Axholm and elsewhere, Laxton is the last open-field village in England. We do not know how this system – where the arable cultivation was carried on in large fields without hedges or other enclosures –

began but it was a form of husbandry which dominated the landscape of Midland England for over a thousand years. As happened elsewhere, the nucleated village settlement at Laxton is surrounded by three fields of more than 250 acres each, the West Field, the Mill Field and the South Field, with the arable land cultivated in strips. There is also common pasture for grazing. While agriculture is carried on at Laxton in something like the same way it has been carried on for centuries, inevitably there has been adaptation to changing conditions of market and technique. In fact the landscape of Laxton includes the results of enclosure by agreement, enclosures under the authority of an Act of Parliament and of a comprehensive consolidation of stripholdings for greater efficiency. In 1951 on the death of the 6th Lord Manners, Laxton was acquired by the Ministry of Agriculture in order 'to preserve the open fields [and] to help tenants to meet the demands of the future'. In 1981 the ownership of the village was transferred to the Crown Estate Commissioners. Not an economic proposition in modern conditions, Laxton is the nearest approach to the historical self-governing farming community which remains in England, providing a visual demonstration of the traditional way of farming in the Midland plain.

North Leverton 'Subscription' Windmill (120/SK 776 820)
A later introduction into Britain than the watermill, the windmill was usually built in places where water power was not easily available though infrequently it was used to supplement water power. Windmills were most commonly used for grinding corn but they were also employed for other purposes such as sawmilling, drainage, etc. They began to be built in England in the 12th century and their numbers spread until by 1800 there were something like 10,000. They were of three types: the post mill, where the whole body of the mill turned on a central post in order that the sails should catch the wind most effectively; the smock mill, usually timbered, which took its name from its shape; and the tower mill. In these latter two cases the cap could be moved to turn the sails into the wind.

Erected in 1813, North Leverton Mill, run by a group of farmers, is the last windmill in commercial operation in England. A three-storeyed mill built of brick and coated with tar to keep out the weather, it has an ogee-shaped cap typical of the East Midland mills. The cap has a fantail – a device designed to keep the sails automatically in the eye of the wind. The sails are patent sails with shutters or flaps whose angle can be altered to take account of the strength of the wind. From the second floor (the granary floor), the grain flows to one of three sets of stones on

the first floor where it is milled and then to the ground floor where it is stored. Adjacent to the mill is a warehouse and the miller's cottage.

Address: North Leverton Windmill, North Leverton, Nottinghamshire. *Tel.* Retford (0777) 6599.

Papplewick Pumping Station (120/SK 584 522)
One of the essentials of urban development is a supply of fresh water for drinking, washing and cooking. Until the early 19th

receive water from the Bestwood station in 1880. Later, to enable the water resources of the area to be better exploited, a well and pumping station were also constructed. Opened in 1884, the Papplewick Pumping Station, an ornate Victorian engine house, is equipped with two single-cylinder beam engines built by James Watt & Company in 1884. The engines were powered from steam provided by six hand-fed, coal-fired Lancashire boilers. The interior of the engine house is elaborately decorated and has stained-glass windows. The station closed in 1969 when the beam engines were replaced by electric pumps; it is now in the care of a charitable trust which has brought back the blacksmith's shop into operation as well as restoring the engines to working order.

Address: Papplewick Pumping Station, off Longdale Lane, Ravenshead, Nottingham NG15 9AJ. *Tel.* (Custodian) Nottingham (0602) 632938.

Ruddington: Framework Knitters' Shops (129/SK 571 328)
Nottinghamshire was the birthplace of the machine-made hosiery industry employing the stocking frame, invented by William Lee of Calverton in 1589. Originally a domestic industry, the manufacture was carried on in workshops in back gardens or yards by 1800. The characteristic long windows lighting the frame shops can still be seen in some parts of the East Midlands. At Ruddington, in a group of four cottages and two workshops and outhouses (a purpose-built 'traditional type' complex erected in 1829), changing displays illustrate both the development of framework knitting and its regional history. In one workshop there are 15 hand frames, winding wheels and allied equipment

century most of Nottingham's water came from the River Leen but this became increasingly polluted and about 1830 a waterworks was built at Basford from which water was pumped by the Castle Pumping Station. In 1857 the Bagthorpe works at Basford was opened from which 2 million gallons a day were pumped from the new red sandstone beds to Nottingham by three beam engines, one of which has now been re-erected in the Nottingham Industrial Museum at Wollaton Park. A further pumping station was built at Bestwood in 1871 (the engines were scrapped in 1968). A covered reservoir was constructed at Papplewick to

Ruddington – restored workshop interior

which provide some evidence of the way in which this small-scale hosiery industry, made redundant by the development of power-driven factory manufacture, was carried on. Two of the four cottages have been restored to indicate the living conditions of a framework knitter *c* 1850 and of a hosier *c* 1900.
Address: Joint Hon. Secretaries: The Vicarage, 2 Peacock Close, Ruddington, Nottingham NG11 6JF; or Long Acre, Old Road, Ruddington. *Tel.* Nottingham (0602) 212116 or 213287.

There is also a framework knitters' museum in Main Street, **Calverton** (129/SK 618 492). *Tel.* Woodborough (060 744) 2836;

and other framework knitters' workshops in **Hucknall** (129/SK 538 488) and **Keyworth** (129/SK 613 303). Framework knitters' houses can also be seen in Leicestershire at **Kegworth** (129/SK 488 267) behind the Britannia Inn; and in **Wigston** (140/SP 608 991); and Atkins framework knitters' shop at **Hinckley** (140/SP 425 941).

Also Worth Visiting in Nottinghamshire

Awsworth, Bennerley Viaduct (129/SK 471 437–476 441). Threatened with demolition, the 1879 viaduct, 484 yards long with 15 piers, is one of the two great surviving iron viaducts in the country. It carried the Great Northern Railway across the Erewash.

Beeston, textile mills (129/SK 53 36). There are a number of impressive mills, particularly the Anglo-Scotian of the 1870s and Swiss Mills of 1886, along Wollaton Road.

Bestwood, vertical colliery winding engine (120/SK 549 501). A unique engine built in 1873. *Tel.* Mansfield (0623) 823148.

Lound Hall National Coalmining Museum (120/SK 700 730). The National Coal Board collection of mining machinery, steam winding-engines, locomotives, miners' tools and the headgear from Brinsley Colliery. It has simulated underground galleries almost 2 miles in length. *Tel.* Mansfield (0623) 860728.

Nottingham Industrial Museum, Wollaton Park (129/SK 531 394). An annexe to Wollaton Hall, it includes a beam engine from the Basford Water Works and a horse gin. *Tel.* Nottingham (0602) 284602.

Nottingham, Morton Clayton Canal Warehouse Museum, Canal Street (129/SK 575 394). A museum of the history of the River Trent and canal transport located in a warehouse into which an arm of the canal runs. *Tel.* Nottingham (0602) 284602.

Ollerton Watermill (120/SK 653 674). An 18th-century mill with later alterations, the wheel and sluice dating from 1830, it is now in working order. *Tel.* Mansfield (0623) 822469.

Three *stations* of note are the single-storey **Castle Station, Newark** (121/SK 796 543), built by the Midland Railway in 1846; the **Midland Station, Nottingham** (129/SK 576 393), rebuilt in 1904; and **Worksop Station** (120/SK 586 797), built in 1850.

SHROPSHIRE

Shropshire is the cradle of the Industrial Revolution: ironmaking, leadmining and pottery as well as road, rail and canal sites are of interest.

Ironbridge Gorge Museum (127/SJ 672 034)
A key place in the British Industrial Revolution is held by a small area in the valley of the Severn. Here iron was first successfully smelted using coal – a key technological breakthrough – and the first cast-iron bridge in the world was made. Other aspects of the early Industrial Revolution can also be seen here either in their original locations or, in some cases, brought here from elsewhere. Because there is so much to be seen and because the museum provides good information material, it is necessary here to do little more than list what can be seen.

Coalbrookdale Furnace, where Abraham Darby perfected the smelting of iron with coke in 1709, is rightly the starting point, with the Great Warehouse now housing a museum of iron. The Elton Collection is also on display nearby. In *Coalbrookdale* are a number of houses including Rosehill House, Carpenter's Row, and Rose Cottages.

On the bank of the River Severn is the *Severn Warehouse* built by the Coalbrookdale Company in the 1840s with a wharf adjacent which now houses an interpretive exhibition of the Gorge. Further down the river is the *Iron Bridge* itself, the first iron bridge in the world, cast at Coalbrookdale in 1779 and now restored. Continuing on the B4373, on the left are the *Bedlam Furnaces*, constructed in 1757, now being excavated. Across the river is *Maw's Tile Works*, now a part of the Museum. Continuing on the B4373, the road crosses the *Hay inclined plane* by which barges were transferred from the upper to the lower levels of the Shropshire Canal and the *Tar tunnel*, a source of natural bitumen in the 18th century.

Then we come to the *Coalport China Works* where china was made from the 18th century until 1926.

On the plateau above the river is the *Blists Hill Open Air Museum*, in the 19th century an active industrial area but derelict by 1950. Here along the Shropshire Canal there are blast furnaces, the beam engines David and Sampson, a mine, a brick and tile works, an adit, a fireclay mine with steam winding-engine, a printing shop and a Telford tollhouse.

There is no other site in the country where examples of so many industrial developments which helped to make Britain the first industrial nation can be seen.

Address: Ironbridge Gorge Museum Trust, Ironbridge, Telford, Shropshire TF8 7AW. *Tel.* weekdays: Ironbridge (095 245) 3522, weekends: Telford (0952) 586309.

Also Worth Visiting in Shropshire
Bridgnorth, Castle Hill funicular railway (138/SO 717 929).

Opened in 1892, it was originally hydraulically operated but is now electrically powered. *Tel.* Bridgnorth (074 62) 2052.

Longdon-on-Tern Aqueduct (127/SJ 617 156). This, the first substantial cast-iron aqueduct, built by Telford in 1795 to carry the Shrewsbury Canal across the River Tern, can be seen from the road.

Munsterley, Snailbeach leadmines (126/SJ 375 022). One of the first English leadmines, it was worked from Roman times but especially during 1784–1911. Remains include engine houses, dressing sheds, boiler house, smelting flue chimney, shafts, reservoirs and railway track.

Shrewsbury, Coleham Pumping Station (126/SJ 496 121) contains two Woolf compound beam engines used for sewage pumping 1900–70. *Tel.* Shrewsbury (0743) 54811.

STAFFORDSHIRE

Staffordshire has had a wide range of industries including mining, brewing and pottery. It is crossed by a number of canals, railways and roads.

Burton-on-Trent: Bass Museum of Brewing History (128/SK 247 234)
In previous centuries brewing was very much a local activity and many towns had their own breweries, some of which survive though generally used for other purposes. The construction of canals enabled some concentration to take place but it was the coming of the railway which led to the rise of Burton-on-Trent as a centre of the brewing industry. Its natural advantage was a good supply of suitable water.

Opened in 1977, the Bass Museum occupies a converted 19th-century building which was formerly the central joiner's shop on the Bass brewery site at Burton and so it benefits from the activity, sounds and, not least, the smells of a working plant. The main exhibition is on the first floor and traces the development of brewing, where William Bass began operation in 1777, from the Middle Ages. On the second floor an exhibition traces the history of the transportation of beer from the 18th century to the present day. On the ground floor there is an exhibit concerned with the water supply which includes two restored pumps. Opposite the museum building is a 250-hp horizontal compound steam engine built by Robey of Lincoln in 1905 and a five-barrel model brewhouse from the Cape Hill Brewery, Smethwick; and nearer the entrance is a reconstructed ale bank which houses the Bass No. 9 locomotive (saddle-tank built in 1901) and the directors' coach.

Address: Bass Museum, Horninglow Street, Burton-on-Trent, Staffordshire. *Tel.* Burton-on-Trent (0283) 45301 or 42031.

Brewing is now a highly concentrated industry, but where breweries still exist visits can be usually be arranged.

Cheddleton: Cheddleton Flint Mill (118/SJ 972 526)

One of the constituents of pottery is flint which, it was dis-covered in the 17th century, when added to clay made it significantly whiter and gave it strength. This additive was adopted in the Potteries. Flint was not available locally but was brought from the coastal chalk outcrops of southern England or at a later date from the coasts of Belgium and northern France. Before being added to the clay body the flints were first calcined in a kiln, making them easier to grind.

At Cheddleton there exists a small industrial complex by the side of the Caldon Canal, which was linked via the Trent and

Bass Museum – Robey steam engine

waterwheel, fed by a leat from the River Churnet. The North Mill, built *c* 1720, is powered by a 22-foot-diameter low breast wheel and has a 14-foot diameter pan. It has been restored to its early-19th-century state while the South Mill, earlier a cornmill, retains its original machinery and has a wheel 20 feet 5 inches in diameter. After grinding with water the slurry was run into settling tanks from which the surplus clear water was drawn off. The slop flint is then pumped to the slip drying kiln from which the flint is removed in blocks or 'cake'. It is then ready for dispatch to the potters. The flint mill ceased operation in 1963.

Address: Cheddleton Flint Mill, Cheadle Road, Cheddleton, near Leek, Staffordshire.

Mersey Canal to the River Weaver and so to Runcorn, the port to which the flints were carried by ship from southern England, Belgium or France.

The flints were unloaded by crane at Cheddleton and stored in the open. When required they were taken to kilns, which were top-loaded like limekilns. From the bottom of the kiln the calcined flints were then taken by wagon on a cast-iron plateway to one of the mills where they were ground in the pan driven by a

Longton: Gladstone Pottery Museum (118/SJ 914 433)
Evidence of pottery-making is fast disappearing but at Longton, one of the six towns of Arnold Bennett's Potteries, a typical works has been preserved. Though china was made on the site from about 1787, the present buildings date from about 1856 and take their name from a Mr Gladstone of the late 19th century. It remained a typical unmodernized medium-size potbank until it closed in the mid-1960s.

Four bottle ovens dominate the courtyard round which the manufacture was organized. The steam engine in the engine house provided power to drive the machinery in the sliphouse from which the clay was taken to the workshops where throwing and slipcasting took place. Upstairs was the mouldmaking department. Before being fired the pottery was placed in fireproof containers known as saggars which were piled up in the kilns for firing. Thus the sequence of processes can be followed.

The museum also has exhibition galleries which tell of the rise of the Staffordshire potteries and the use of clay as a building material and houses displays of ceramic tiles and ceramic sanitary ware.
Address: Gladstone Pottery Museum, Uttoxeter Road, Longton, Stoke-on-Trent, Staffordshire. *Tel.* Stoke-on-Trent (0782) 319232 or 311378.

Other Sites Related to the Pottery Industry:
The Etruscan Bone and Flint Mill, Hanley (118/SJ 872 478) processed material (like Cheddleton) for the pottery industry. It stands by the Trent and Mersey Canal.

There are a number of potteries along the Trent and Mersey Canal including a group, the *Longport Potteries*, Burslem (118/SJ 857 494); *Twyford's Works*, Cliffvale, Hanley (SJ 873 464), which produced sanitary ware; and *Josiah Wedgwood's Etruria Works*, Stoke-on-Trent (118/SJ 867 475), the site to which the firm moved from Burslem.

Tunstall: Chatterley Whitfield Mining Museum (118/SJ 885 534)
Coal was one of the major elements in the British Industrial Revolution but since it has lost its dominant position in the energy field and production has contracted, pits have closed, headgear has been removed and tips have been contoured and grassed over. Before everything goes, Chatterley Whitfield colliery, one of the first in Britain from which an annual output of 1 million tons of coal was once obtained, has been opened to the public. Coal was collected from various outcrops in north Staffordshire from the 13th century but mining developed in the area

of the Potteries in the 18th century to fire bottle kilns, power steam engines and smelt iron ore. Production expanded in the 19th century and continued at Chatterley Whitfield until 1977.

The museum has an exhibition area on the surface and some of the plant, including a 1914 horizontal two-cylinder steam winding-engine by Worsley Mesnes. But the main feature is a series of displays in the Holly Lane seam 700 feet below ground which show the various stages in the development of mining technology from hand working to modern machine coal extraction. Though the cramped conditions of earlier types of working (unsuitable for museum purposes) and the noise, dust and activity are missing, the descent in the lift and the walk along the galleries, wearing protective helmets and lamps with experienced miners as guides, provides a real sense of what life in a coalmine was like.
Address: Chatterley Whitfield Mining Museum, Tunstall, Stoke-on-Trent, Staffordshire ST6 8UN. *Tel.* Stoke-on-Trent (0782) 813337.

Also Worth Visiting in Staffordshire
Froghall limekilns (119/SK 027 476). An extensive bank of limekilns at the terminus of the Caldon Canal.

Kidsgrove, Harecastle tunnel north entrances, (118/SJ 837 541). Portals of canal tunnels on the Trent and Mersey Canal constructed by Brindley (1766–77) with a towpath, and by Telford (1825–7) with a towpath. Before Telford's tunnel, horses worked over the top of Harecastle Hill along Boathouse Lane, which can still be followed.

Leek, Brindley Watermill, Mill Street (118/SJ 974 571). Used for cornmilling from about 1752 and latterly for sawmilling until 1940, it is now restored to cornmilling with displays of millwrighting in the adjacent James Brindley Museum. *Tel.* Leek (0538) 384195.

Sandon Station (127/SJ 947 293) was built in 1848 in Jacobean style with a large covered porch; it is now closed.

Stoke-on-Trent railway station and hotel (118/SJ 879 456). The station (1848) has three Dutch-style Jacobean gables with a single-storey colonnade, faced by the North Stafford Hotel designed as a Jacobean manor house with flanking buildings.

WARWICKSHIRE

Warwickshire is now a mainly agricultural county crossed by canals and railways.

Chatterley Whitfield Mining Museum

Stratford-upon-Avon Canal

To improve the facilities for the transport of heavy goods, canals were constructed to supplement river navigation. Some were built quickly; others, like the Stratford-upon-Avon Canal which was started in 1793 and not completed until 1816, more slowly. This canal was never a commercial success, particularly because the Worcester–Birmingham canal, opened in the previous year, offered an alternative route. It was sold to a railway company in 1856 and remained in railway ownership for a century. Then because of the cost of repairs to a road bridge, the Warwickshire County Council applied to close the canal. This was successfully opposed and the canal was restored by voluntary effort. The southern section, 13½ miles in length from the canal basin in *Stratford* (151/SP 204 548) to the Kingswood Junction at *Lapwood* (139/SP 187 708), was vested in the National Trust in 1960 – a pleasant and eventful length of canal with 36 locks and three iron aqueducts: at Bearley (151/SP 162 608) 475 feet long; Wootton Wawen (SP 159 629) and Yarningale (SP 184 664). It is crossed by

29 cantilevered cast-iron bridges and 11 others. Another distinctive feature is a number of barrel-roofed cottages along the canal, which can be seen at Preston Bagot, Lawsonford and Kingswood.

Also Worth Visiting in Warwickshire

Chesterton Windmill (151/SP 348 594). An unusual mid-17th-century stone mill with four windows above six arches on piers. It worked until 1910 and was restored in 1971. *Tel.* Warwick (0926) 43431.

Great Alne Watermill (150/SP 123 589). Built about 1800 on an earlier site, it now grinds flour by the power of a water turbine installed in 1904. *Tel.* Great Alne (078 981) 341.

Stratford-upon-Avon and Moreton-in-the-Marsh tramway (151/SP 205 547). A horse wagon is preserved in Stratford Gardens near the former tramway brick viaduct of eight arches over the Avon. Nearby is a cottage called Tramway House. Opened in September 1826, the route of the tramway can be followed for most of its way.

Warwick, Gasworks, Saltisford (151/SP 278 653). The façade, including two octagonal towers which contained the gasholders, dates from 1822.

WEST MIDLANDS

West Midlands is a new county, highly urbanized, which brings together Birmingham and the Black Country.

Birmingham

Birmingham, the major conurbation in the Midlands, was once the centre for a wide range of small industries, many of which have gone. But there are a number of sites of interest of which only a small selection can be noted here.

Due to its extensive network of *canals,* Birmingham is sometimes called the Venice of England; see especially *Gas Street Canal Basin* (139/SP 062 866), the terminus of the Birmingham and Worcester Canal and the Birmingham Canal. *Brindley Walk and Farmer's Bridge Locks* (139/SP 060 870), restored in 1969; the basin has two preserved canal cranes and there are 13 locks on the Birmingham and Fareley Canal here.

Curzon Street Station (139/SP 078 871). The northern counterpart to the demolished Euston Arch, designed by Hardwick as the terminus of the London and Birmingham Railway. It became a goods depot in 1854.

Gun Barrel Proof House, Banbury Street (139/SP 078 866). Built in 1813, this two-storey brick building has an impressive insignia over the portico and testing shops behind.

Bournville, model housing and factories (139/SP 048 810). Built by Cadbury Brothers from 1879 to 1914.

Smith Field Market, Jamaica Row (139/SP 074 865). Built in 1883 as a commodity market; with fine cast-iron work.

Birmingham Museum of Science and Industry, Newhall Street, Birmingham B3 1RZ (139/SP 065 873). Although devoted to the activities of the industrial Midlands, the museum is not restricted to local products. The prime exhibits include a large collection of stationary steam and hot air engines, which are regularly operated, railway locomotives (including the *City of Birmingham*), road vehicles, aircraft (a Spitfire Mark IX and a Hurricane Mark IV), automatic production machines and machine tools, mechanical musical instruments, writing equipment and scientific instruments. It is housed in a former electro-plating factory and the modern Locomotive Hall (1972). *Tel.* Birmingham (021) 236 1022.

Sarehole Mill, Cole Bank Road, Hall Green, Moseley, Birmingham B13 0BD (139/SP 099 818). Last survivor of more than 50 watermills in the Birmingham area, in its present form it dates from the 1760s; one wheel was used to drive a cornmill, the other to grind edge tools. Milling ceased in 1919. Now re-opened, it has displays of milling and blade-grinding. *Tel.* Birmingham (021) 777 6612.

Dudley: Black Country Museum (139/SO 948 917)

Some museums, like Avoncroft or St Fagan's, are created on green field sites. Others, like Ironbridge and this museum, develop sites where industry was previously carried on.

The core of this museum is the Dudley Canal, on either side of which there are impressive banks of limekilns which were supplied with coal and limestone by barge. The first stage of the site is now being developed as a typical Black Country village and already a chapel, a row of houses with a general store from Old Hill and chemist's shop from Netherton, a bakehouse, a rolling mill and chain yard (where there are demonstrations) have been re-erected and a canal-bank dock has been constructed.

At an extra charge, trips can be taken by canal boat through the *Dudley Tunnel*, almost two miles long, which from a narrow width of 7 feet 2 inches opens out into huge caverns from which limestone has been excavated. A 3-feet 6-inches Dudley and Stourbridge electric tramcar takes the visitor from the entrance past the area on the 26-acre site where a typical headgear of a Black Country colliery has been erected, to the village. A local

Birmingham Museum of Science and Industry – Engineering Hall

transport collection includes trolleybuses, motor cars, bicycles and canal boats.

Address: Black Country Museum, Tipton Road, Dudley, West Midlands. *Tel.* Birmingham (021) 557 9643.

Also Worth Visiting in the West Midlands

Balsall, Berkswell Windmill, Windmill Lane (139/SP 249 757). A brick tower mill worked by wind from 1826 until 1933, now restored and working again. *Tel.* Berkswell (0676) 33403.

Brierley Hill, Delph Locks (139/SO 920 866). Eight locks built in 1858 to replace the original nine link the Dudley Canal with the Stourbridge Canal. The top and bottom locks were incorporated into the new structure and the remaining chambers, which can still be seen, were abandoned.

Coventry, Museum of British Road Transport, Cook Street (140/SP 335 794). A collection of some 400 cycles, motorcycles, commercial and private vehicles alongside petrol pumps, car manuals and other items. *Tel.* Coventry (0203) 25555 ext. 2315.

Walsall, The Lock Museum, Willenhall District Library, Walsall Street, Willenhall (139/SO 965 983). Exhibits illustrate the development and design of locks, a local industry. *Tel.* Walsall (0922) 21244 ext. 3115.

Black Country Museum – Canal Street bridge from Wolverhampton

Northern England

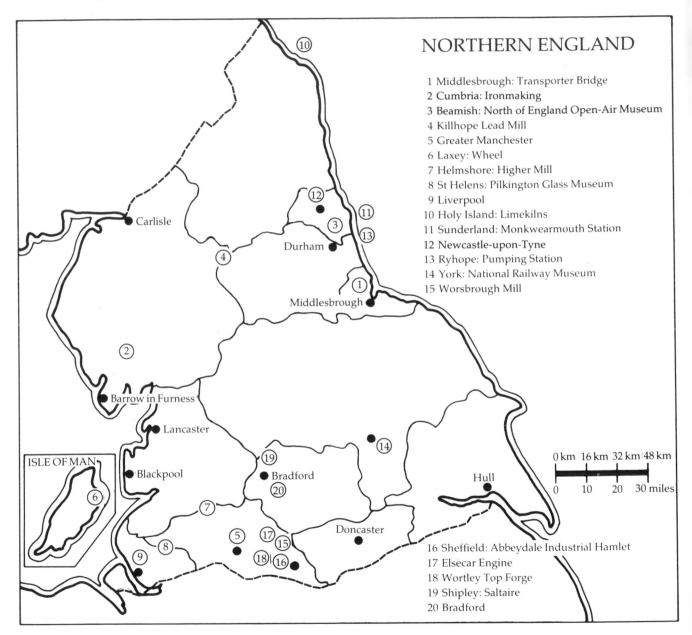

NORTHERN ENGLAND

1 Middlesbrough: Transporter Bridge
2 **Cumbria: Ironmaking**
3 **Beamish: North of England Open-Air Museum**
4 Killhope Lead Mill
5 Greater Manchester
6 Laxey: Wheel
7 Helmshore: Higher Mill
8 St Helens: Pilkington Glass Museum
9 Liverpool
10 Holy Island: Limekilns
11 Sunderland: Monkwearmouth Station
12 **Newcastle-upon-Tyne**
13 Ryhope: Pumping Station
14 York: National Railway Museum
15 Worsbrough Mill

16 Sheffield: Abbeydale Industrial Hamlet
17 Elsecar Engine
18 Wortley Top Forge
19 Shipley: Saltaire
20 Bradford

Carlisle

Durham

Middlesbrough

Barrow in Furness

Lancaster

ISLE OF MAN

Blackpool

Bradford

Hull

Doncaster

0 km 16 km 32 km 48 km

0   10   20   30 miles

CLEVELAND

The sites in this new county are mainly in the ports of the Tees estuary and the mines of the Cleveland Hills.

Middlesbrough Transporter Bridge (93/NZ 500 213)

One solution to the problem of providing a crossing for road traffic across a navigable waterway was provided by the transporter bridge. That at Middlesbrough, which has become a symbol of the area, was built by Sir William Arrol & Partners in 1911 to replace a vehicle ferry. With a total length of 850 feet and approach spans 225 feet high, the bridge provides a clear span of 570 feet for a height of 160 feet. The platform, suspended by 30 cables from a trolley, driven by an electric motor on the south side, can carry nine vehicles and 600 passengers between Middlesbrough and Port Clarence.

It can be crossed (in emergency) by pedestrians using the staircases in each tower and the high-level walkway.
Address: Ferry Road, Middlesbrough, Cleveland. *Tel.* Middlesbrough (0642) 247563.

Middlesbrough, Newport Bridge, (93/NZ 479 199), built in 1926, takes the A1130 across the Tees between Middlesbrough and Stockton. It is the largest remaining lift-span bridge in the world. The lifting span, 270 feet long and 66 feet wide, contains 1,530 tons of steel.

Also Worth Visiting in Cleveland

Boulby, alum works (94/NZ 761 191). The site of the last Cleveland alum works. The remains of the stone-built alum house, the storage cisterns, the culvert and several flues can be traced in the quarries.

Darlington Railway Museum, North Road Station, Station

Road (93/NZ 289 158). Housed in the original Stockton & Darlington Station opened in 1842, the museum has a number of locomotives, including *Locomotion* and *Derwent*, and other rolling stock and related railway exhibits on display. *Tel.* Darlington (0325) 60532.

Elwick Windmill (93/NZ 449 316). This semi-derelict brick tower mill is the second most complete in north-east England.

Greatham Viaduct (93/NZ 490 260). Built in 1840 by John Fowler, it originally had 92 arches but only 34 are now visible.

Hartlepool, HMS Warrior, Old Coal Dock (93/NZ 517 329). The first ironclad warship, launched in 1860, is now being restored. *Tel.* Hartlepool (0429) 33051.

North Yorkshire Moors Railway runs between Grosmont (94/NZ 828 052) and Pickering (100/SE 797 842). Built by George Stephenson, it is now operated by the North Yorkshire Moors Railway Company. *Tel.* Pickering (0751) 72508.

Redcar, old lifeboat station (94/NZ 607 252) on the Promenade. Built in 1877, it houses a small maritime museum, and contains one of the famous Redcar lifeboats. *Tel.* Redcar (0642) 485322 or 479500.

Saltburn, cliff railway (94/NZ 666 217). The present line, 270 feet long, was opened in 1884; it replaced an earlier vertical lift of 1869 which was one of the first cliff railways to be built. *Tel.* Guisborough (0287) 22013.

Skelton Park, iron mine (94/NZ 644 180). This mine was sunk in 1872 and finally ceased production in 1938. The buildings which remain represent the most complete minehead complex in the Cleveland iron field.

Stockton-on-Tees, Green Dragon Heritage Centre, Green Dragon Yard, off Finkle Street (93/NZ 446 190) has material from the Stockton & Darlington railway, as well as exhibits illustrating local industries, eg shipbuilding, trams and friction lights invented by John Walker of Stockton. *Tel.* Stockton-on-Tees (0642) 602474.

Stockton-on-Tees, Preston Hall Museum, Yarm Road (93/NZ 430 160) has collections of industrial material but is devoted more to crafts and features five working craftsmen. The museum plans to develop the heavy industrial side with emphasis on the metal trades. *Tel.* Stockton-on-Tees (0642) 602474.

CUMBRIA

Slate, metal mining, textiles (wool, cotton and flax) and the associated transport services predominated in what is largely the Lake District with coal and shipbuilding on the coast.

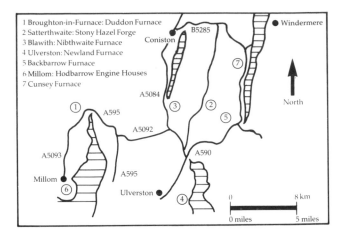

1 Broughton-in-Furnace: Duddon Furnace
2 Satterthwaite: Stony Hazel Forge
3 Blawith: Nibthwaite Furnace
4 Ulverston: Newland Furnace
5 Backbarrow Furnace
6 Millom: Hodbarrow Engine Houses
7 Cunsey Furnace

Ironmaking in Cumbria

Based on local ore, an iron industry was carried on in Cumbria from pre-Roman times although traces of the pre-18th-century industry are limited. However there are more substantial remains of later ironmaking.

Backbarrow Furnace (96/SD 356 846). Though in private ownership, the furnace on the River Leven can be seen from the road. Operated from 1712, the blast furnace was partially rebuilt in 1870. Charcoal was used until 1926 when coke was substituted. This is a striking but dilapidated 19th-century small furnace unit, with adaptations made between 1920 and 1963 when it closed.

Nearby is **Backbarrow Cotton Mills** (96/SD 356 849). The shell of the second cotton mill, originally built *c* 1785 and largely rebuilt in 1857, and the workers' housing *c* 1800 survive. The mill made dolly blue from the 1890s to 1981.

Cunsey Furnace (96/SD 383 937). The remains of this furnace, which was operated for a period by a company set up in 1710, adjoins a sawmill powered by a Gilkes water turbine on Cunsey Beck. A considerable slag heap nearby can be seen from the lakeshore path. About a mile inland, accessible by a footpath, is the site of a finery-forge (96/SD 377 936). Iron workings nearby are marked on the OS map.

Duddon Furnace (96/SD 196 884). This charcoal blast furnace operated from 1736 to 1867. Since overgrown, the site, which contains the furnace stack, charcoal stores, iron store, smithy and ironmakers' houses, is now being excavated. The most complete 18th-19th-century furnace site of the charcoal-using era, it lies to the west of the road not far from Duddon Bridge. Access is subject to permit. *Tel.* Kendal (0539) 24555.

Millom, Folk Museum, St George's Road (96/SD 174 800). Its display of ironmaking includes a full-scale model of a drift of the Hodbarrow mine, complete with an actual cage. *Tel.* Millom (0657) 2555.

Duddon Furnace

Millom, Hodbarrow engine houses (96/SD 180 784). Three engine houses, which worked from the 1870s to the 1960s, stand near the eastern end of the inner sea barrier, built to protect mining as the workings extended seawards.

Newland Furnace (96/SD 299 798). Iron was made here from about 1746 to 1903. The furnace structure, the casting floor, a charcoal barn and a row of workers' cottages built near the charging ramp of the furnace can be seen together with other housing along the Newland Beck.

Nibthwaite Furnace (96/SD 295 883). This furnace, with cast-iron lintel dated 1736, operated until *c* 1850 when a bobbin mill was built on top of the furnace and loading ramp. The charcoal barn has been converted into a house. On private land.

Satterthwaite, Stony Hazel Forge (96/SD 336 897). The remains of a site, which has been partially excavated, of one of the forges which re-worked the brittle cast iron produced in the furnaces at Backbarrow, Cunsey and Duddon into malleable wrought iron. It operated till about 1725 and is probably unique in Europe. Not easy to find, it lies north of an unclassified road about ¼ mile south-west of Rusland church.

Also Worth Visiting in Cumbria

Allonby, Crosscanonby Salt Pans (85/NY 066 402). Clearly visible on the west (seaward) side of the B3500 road are the earthworks of two settling tanks, almost the last traces of the Cumberland salt trade which closed down *c* 1790.

Beetham, Heron Watermill (97/SD 495 799). A mid-18th-century limestone three-storey mill with drying kiln and a 16-foot pitchback waterwheel. *Tel.* c/o Milnthorpe (044 82) 3363.

Boot, Eskdale Watermill (89, 90/NY 176 013). An early mill, it worked commercially until 1930 and has now been restored with a milling exhibition. *Tel.* (County Planning Officer) Kendal (0539) 21000.

Borrowdale, Honister slate quarry (89/NY 210 143). One of the earliest slate quarries in the Lake District – first mentioned in 1643 – this quarry, which is still active, produces green slate which was originally taken to Ravenglass by packhorse until the roads were improved in the later 19th century. The old tramroad from the head of Honister Pass is now a walkers' footpath.

Carlisle industrial trail (Map 85) provides a view of some local industries. Start from the *Canal Basin* (NY 391 560), the terminus of the Port Carlisle Canal, opened in 1821. Along Port Road you pass *Carr's Biscuit Factory* (NY 392 559) where Jonathan Carr, who invented a biscuit-cutting machine, carried on his business. On the left in Bridge Street is the *Old Brewery* (NY 394 561) with

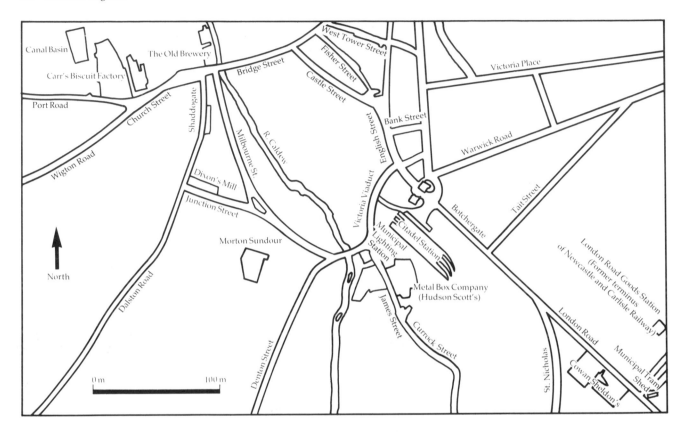

its high-pitched slate roof and kiln cowl (view from Caldew Bridge). Turn right into Shaddongate and at the corner of Junction Street is *Dixon's Mill* (NY 395 557), a seven-storey sandstone structure built in 1836 with framing designed by William Fairbairn. The adjacent engine house has a 350-foot chimney. Further along Junction Street on the left is the *Morton Sundour (Glendon Textile) Factory* (NY 395 554) with an enclosed yard and a double row of terraced cottages. Continue and at the junction of James Street and Rome Street is the former *Municipal Lighting Station* (NY 400 554) of 1889 which provided power for the tramway system. Turning into James Street, the *Metal Box (Hudson Scott) Works* (NY 402 553) where decorated tinplate boxes were made can be seen. Return to Victoria Viaduct and off

Botchergate is *Citadel Station* (NY 402 555), an exercise in cathedral Gothic by William Tite, opened in 1847. Continue down Botchergate to the London Road where *Cowan Sheldon's Works* (NY 407 552) can be seen on the right. The St Nicholas Works has an entrance lodge and gates and erecting shops behind for the dockyard cranes made there. On the opposite side of the road is the former *Municipal Tramshed* (NY 408 552) and behind London Road to the east is the *London Road Goods Depot* (NY 415 550), the former terminus of the Newcastle & Carlisle Railway. A single-storey row of sandstone offices, the large goods shed and the coaling house can be seen together with the station hotel opposite.

Carlisle, Guildhall Museum, Greenmarket (NY 401 560), an

example of medieval timber frame construction, has displays illustrating the history of the guilds and the city. *Tel.* Carlisle (0228) 34781.

Embleton, Wythop Watermill (89, 90/NY 179 295). Built as a cornmill, it was converted to a sawmill in 1860. *Tel.* Bassenthwaite Lake (059 681) 394 or 525.

Finsthwaite, Bobbin Mill, Stott Park (96/SD 373 882). Built in 1835 and closed in 1971, this is the most complete mill surviving in Cumbria, most of them being located in the south of the county. It contains much of its original machinery. Restored by the Department of the Environment, it is open to the public. *Tel.* Newby Bridge (0448) 31087. See also the ruined bobbin mill at *Caldbeck* (90/NY 318 398).

Kendal, Museum of Lakeland Life and Industry, Abbot Hall (97/SD 517 922) has displays of printing, clothmaking, engineering, mining, woodturning and other local industries. *Tel.* Kendal (0539) 21374.

Lakeland & Haverthwaite Railway, Haverthwaite Station (96/SD 349 843) operates a 3½-mile-long section of the former Furness Railway from Haverthwaite to Lake Windermere. *Tel.* Newby Bridge (0448) 31594.

Penrith, Little Salkeld Watermill (90/NY 566 360). An 18th-century cornmill with two overshot waterwheels. *Tel.* Penrith (0768) 81523.

Ravenglass, Muncaster Watermill (96/SD 096 977). The mill and drying kiln, last worked in 1961, have been restored and are operating. *Tel.* Ravenglass (065 77) 232.

Ravenglass & Eskdale Railway (96/SD 086 965). Opened in 1875 as a 3-foot-gauge iron ore line, it now carries passengers as a 15-inch-gauge line between Ravenglass and Dalegarth. *Tel.* Ravenglass (065 77) 226.

Shap Granite Quarries (90/NY 557 083). Pink granite, much valued for monumental buildings, was obtained from here from 1864 when railways made the area accessible. About 2 miles further north (NY 565 106) a second quarry produces blue granite for railway ballast. About 1900 the company also began producing pre-cast concrete near the blue quarry and the route of the mineral railway linking the three sites can be seen.

Whitehaven, Candlestick Chimney (89/NX 968 182). All that survives of an engine house, built in 1850 by Sydney Smirke, as part of a 'medievalization' of local pitheads.

Whitehaven, Duke Pit Fan Casing (89/NX 969 182). This vaulted 'medieval' casing, built in 1836, which housed a 36-foot wooden Guibel fan, is now preserved in an incongruously landscaped position.

Whitehaven, Harbour (89/NX 973 184) has dated bollards, a

Two displays at the Museum of Lakeland Life and Industry – farm bedroom c 1900, and wheelwright/joiner's shop

wooden capstan and an early lighthouse of 1730. The last coal-fired dredger in Britain can be seen working here.

Windermere Steamboat Museum, Rayrigg Road, Bowness, Windermere (96/SD 402 977) houses a collection of Victorian and Edwardian steam launches and other craft. *Tel.* Windermere (096 62) 5565.

Workington, Jane Pit Engine House (89/NX 995 277). Impressive pithead structures, built by Henry Curwen, with two battlemented chimneys and a crenellated engine house.

DURHAM

A shrunken county which still has important coal and lead mining sites.

Beamish North of England Open-Air Museum (88/NZ 212 549)

The Beamish Museum was established in 1958 on a 200-acre site to study, collect, preserve and exhibit buildings, machinery, objects and information, illustrating the development of industry and the northern way of life. Running through the site is a reconstructed tramline which takes the visitor past a huge 100-ton Bucyrus steam excavator built in 1931. Nearby are the Foulbridge cottages built originally for workers on the Beamish estate and now used to portray a typical pitman's cottage, a farm worker's cottage, a blacksmith's shop, a tinsmith's and general hardware store and a cooper's workshop. Opposite the cottages stands a gipsy caravan of about 1900 while at the end of the row of cottages is a garage housing some motor vehicles, including fire engines, motor buses, an electric trolley bus, cars and a steam roller. Close at hand is the vehicle store and tram depot.

Beyond the visitor centre is the home farm with its farmhouse and piggeries, a horse-powered threshing plant (or gin-gan), a steam threshing plant and a display of farm carts, implements and livestock.

In the colliery area a typical 19th-century engine house and head gear with 1885 winding engine, coal-sorting screens, coal wagons and locomotives and a drift mine can be seen with a row of pit cottages from Hetton-le-Hole, near Sunderland, and a coal drop from Seaham Harbour.

At the other end of the site, Rowley Station from the Stanhope & Tyne Railway, built in 1867, has been re-erected, together with a footbridge, a signal box and goods sheds. Some rolling stock is on display and visitors can ride in old passenger coaches pulled by an 1889 locomotive.

In Beamish Hall itself, the home of the Percys, there are a number of collections including a chemist's shop and a pottery display.

Address: Beamish North of England Open-Air Museum, Stanley, Co. Durham, DH4 0RG. *Tel.* Stanley (0207) 31811.

Weardale: Killhope Lead Mill (87/NY 827 429)

In previous centuries the northern dales were an important leadmining area; one of them was Weardale. Before the lead ore mined at Park Level was dispatched for treatment, it had to be dressed (broken into fragments so that the lead could be separated out). At Killhope are to be found the remains of one of these lead ore crushing mills, built *c* 1860. Because the ore was hard, it could not be crushed by hand and so rollers were used. The four sets were driven by a waterwheel 33 feet 6 inches in diameter, the most prominent feature now surviving on the site. After processing, the dressed ore was sent by the Carriers' Way north to Allenheads, west to Nenthead and east to Rookhope. As the diagram shows, on the site a stone building (1) provided leadminers' accommodation and smithy. Nearby is the entrance

to Park Level leadmine (2), out of which ran a narrow rail track (3), to cross the *bouse-steads* (4) where ore was stored until required. (5) Settling troughs for washed ore. (6) Earth ramp, continued originally by a wooden bridge at (7), to carry trucks of ore up to the crusher driven by the wheel (8). Mounted separately from the building, the wheel was powered by water brought in a trough supported on stone plinths (9). Inside the building (10) the crushed ore was washed and concentrated. Nearby is the earlier building (11), alongside which once was another water-wheel at (12).

Also Worth Visiting in County Durham

Barnard Castle, Thorngate Mill and weavers' cottages (92/NZ 049 160). Thorngate Street is lined with three-storey weavers' cottages with workshops on the top floor and at the end is the four-storey 19th-century weaving mill.

Gainford, Alwent Watermill (92/NZ 145 184). This late-18th century cornmill is one of the most complete in the area. See also *Demesne Mill*, Grey Lane, Barnard Castle (92/NZ 053 158), a three-storey rubble-built mill with a 15-foot diameter water-wheel.

Hamsterley, Derwentcote steel cementation furnace (88/NZ 131 565). A stumpy stone-built cone rising above a ruined building is a unique furnace used to convert wrought-iron to steel in the 18th century.

Shildon, Timothy Hackworth Museum, Hackworth Close (93/NZ 234 257). The home and workplace of a colleague of George Stephenson, it now contains a railway museum. *Tel.* Spennymoor (0388) 772036.

Tanfield, Causey Arch (88/NZ 201 559). Built in 1727 with a span of 105 feet to carry a horse-drawn tramway across the Tanfield Beck, it is the earliest railway bridge in the world.

There are a considerable number of *limekilns* still to be seen in the county as at: *Annfield Plain* (88/NZ 152 518), a bank of six kilns; *Ferryhill* (93/NZ 301 314 and 304 322); *Frosterley* (92/NZ 019 374 and 029 360); *Irehopeburn* (92/NY 849 385); *Muggleswick* (87/NZ 062 489); *Sherburn* (88/NZ 332 404); and *Stanhope* (87/NY 989 401).

HUMBERSIDE

Now united by the Humber Bridge, it is largely agricultural with ports (Hull, Grimsby and Immingham) and some iron manufacture. Sites to see include:

Flamborough Head, Clough Tower old lighthouse (101/TA 250 708). Built in 1674, an octagonal four-storey tower, it is the only intact coal light in England.

    Goole, Company town (105/SE 748 234). Terraces of small brick-built houses with pubs, shops and a hotel built at its terminus by the Aire & Calder Navigation from 1825.

    Horkstow, suspension bridge (112/SE 973 190), one of the oldest in Britain, built in 1834, still has a simple plank deck.

    Kingston-upon-Hull, Town Docks Museum, Queen Victoria Square (107/TA 097 288). The museum is housed in one of the city's most distinctive and imposing buildings, the former offices of the Hull Dock Company, erected 1868–71. It contains collections which reflect Hull's maritime past, including one devoted to whaling. *Tel.* Hull (0482) 223111.

    Skidby Windmill (107/TA 021 334). A six-storey tower mill of 1821 with granary, stables and modern roller plant; it is being developed as a milling museum. *Tel.* (Beverley Borough Council) Hull (0482) 882255.

    Wrawby Windmill (112/TA 025 088). A late-18th-century post mill with roundhouse restored to working order. *Tel.* Brigg (0652) 53699.

ISLE OF MAN

Agriculture and tourism now predominate but mining was formerly important.

Laxey Wheel (95/SC 432 851)

In the past a main industrial activity on the Isle of Man was metalliferrous mining, particularly of lead and zinc. It has left behind one of the single most impressive monuments of industrial archaeology in the British Isles; this great waterwheel, 6 feet in width and 72 feet 6 inches in diameter with 168 buckets, is the largest extant waterwheel in the country. It was designed by a Manxman, Robert Casement, to operate the pumps to drain the local copper, lead and zinc mine; for much of its history the mine produced more zinc blende than the total production of all other British mines as well as lead with a high silver content. Known as

the 'Lady Isabella', after the wife of the Governor who started it turning on 27 September 1854, the wheel, powered by water brought in pipes from a reservoir above in the Laxey valley, pumped water from a depth of over 200 fathoms and had a horsepower rating of 200. It is mounted separately from the building. It ceased working when the mine closed in 1919 but has now been restored.

    In the neighbourhood in the Laxey valley there are a number of other sites of interest. The 'Laxey Mines Trail' starts at the Manx Electric Railway station at Laxey, the junction between the MER and the Snaefell Mountain Railway, which still retains its original booking office. Nearby, what is now the Mines Tavern was formerly the Station Hotel and earlier still the mine captain's house. At the southern entrance to the station is the White House Café which once housed the Laxey Village Co-operative Stores set up by the miners. Follow the signs to the Laxey Wheel. Below the main road the Laxey River passes the washing floors, remains of which can be seen in the ornamental gardens which now occupy the site. Above the main road, on the left, is Dumbell's Terrace, a row of miners' cottages. The footpath to the Wheel runs through the mine's yard and crosses the river by the adit; the works of Manx Engineers, visible on the access road, were once a flour mill. Above the wheel the trail leads to the engine shaft, the turbine house and the Welsh shaft. There is also a woollen mill, St George's mill, in the lower valley.
Tel. Douglas (0624) 26262.

Also Worth Visiting in the Isle of Man (Map 95)
Calf of Man lighthouses are one of the finest series in the British Isles. There may be the remains of a medieval beacon tower. The twin lights built by Robert Stevenson in 1818 survive in a dilapidated state (SC 148 657); they operated until they were replaced by the Chicken Rock Lighthouse in 1875 and this was in turn replaced by a new light on the islet itself (SC 143 639) in 1968. Access to the Calf is by boat from Port Erin or Port St Mary.

Castletown. The *Harbour* (SC 266 675) is protected by a breakwater erected in 1844 with a lighthouse at its seaward end; the lifeboat house, in use from 1856 till 1922 and now a private house, has a slipway into the outer harbour. The wheelpit and the position of the sack hoist of a mill, probably a tidemill, can be seen in *Castle Rushen* (SC 265 674). *Tel.* Castletown (0624) 823326. The *Nautical Museum*, Bridge Street (SC 266 675) is based on the yacht *Peggy* of 1790 in her original boathouse with the owner's room above while other exhibits include a sail loft, ship models and a ship's biscuit making machine. *Tel.* (c/o Manx Museum) Douglas (0624) 5522. There is the shell of a stone tower *windmill* (SC 264 677) built in 1828; the mill buildings are now a private dwelling.

Cregneash, Folk Museum (SC 189 672). An open-air museum which illustrates 19th-century Manx crofting life. *Tel.* (c/o Manx Museum) Douglas (0624) 5522.

Dhoon National Glen, Dhoon Mine wheel case (SC 455 864) is the remains of one of over 50 mine wheels on the island.

Douglas has *harbourworks* of considerable interest and a wide range of dates including a *swing bridge* (SC 384 753). Note the memorial to Sir William Hillary, founder of the RNLI, below the site of his former residence. The *Camera Obscura* (SC 388 748) is one of the few to survive in the British Isles in working order and is still privately owned. *Clinch's Brewery*, North Quay (SC 381 754), built in 1779 and altered *c* 1868, is typically tall to facilitate movement through the processes by gravity.

Foxdale is another leadmining area with some remains. At Glen Rushen, *Cross's Mine* (SC 263 780) has an engine house of *c* 1840. *Beckwith's Mine* (SC 253 778), worked from *c* 1831 to *c* 1870, is marked by the ruins of an engine house and stack, a washing floor and a crusher house.

LANCASHIRE

Now a much smaller county where textiles were the major industry.

Helmshore: Higher Mill (103/SD 777 217)
Though Lancashire is thought of as a cotton-manufacturing area, woollen cloth was also made there. One of the final processes of manufacture is fulling which is used to produce heavy dense fabric such as blankets. Higher Mill, one of the first fulling mills to be built in Rossendale some time after 1789, operated until 1967.

The most impressive feature of the mill is the fulling stocks which were driven by an overshot waterwheel 18 feet in diameter, fed by a leat from a reservoir upstream of the mill. Also on display are a wetting-out machine, rotary milling machines, a flock maker, a scouring machine, a mangle, a tenter frame, a teazle raising gig and a cloth folding machine. There is also a small beam engine brought from a file manufactory at Stockport and a small fire engine.

Address: Higher Mill Museum, Holcombe Road, Helmshore, Rossendale, Lancashire. *Tel.* Rossendale (0706) 226459.

Other museums related to the textile industry
The Lewis Textile Museum, 3 Exchange Street, Blackburn (103/SD 682 283) has a display of textile machinery. *Tel.* Blackburn (0254) 667130 or 55201 ext. 66.

Tonge Moor Textile Museum, Tonge Moor Road, Bolton, Greater Manchester (109/SD 728 106) has a collection of early textile machinery, including Crompton's mule, Hargreaves's jenny and Arkwright's water frame. *Tel.* Bolton (0204) 21394.

Hall i'the Wood Museum, Green Way, off Crompton Way, Bolton, Greater Manchester (109/SD 728 111). This late-15th-century manor house was the home of Samuel Crompton in 1779 when he invented the spinning mule. Some Crompton relics are on display. *Tel.* Bolton (0204) 51159.

Also Worth Visiting in Lancashire
Blackpool, North Pier (102/SD 305 364). The earliest of the three Blackpool piers, it is 1,070 feet long and was opened in 1863.

Carnforth, Steamtown Railway Museum, Warton Road (97/SD 496 707). Over 30 main-line industrial and continental locomotives are housed in an ex-British Rail depot with vintage carriages and a working coaling plant. *Tel.* Carnforth (0524) 734220.

Clitheroe, Low Moor (103/SD 730 418). A fine example of an industrial community: several streets of stone cottages, two chapels, village school and co-operative store; but the mill has now gone.

Colne, Museum of Mines, Old Grammar School, School Lane, Earby (103/SD 890 398). A collection of leadminers' tools, mine tub, lead crusher and other items. *Tel.* c/o Earby (0283) 843210.

Fleetwood lighthouses (102/SD 339 484, 337 486). The upper light in Pharos Place is a tall circular tower and the lower Beach Lighthouse is an elaborate three-stage structure. Both were built in 1836–41 by Decimus Burton as part of the planned development of the port.

Lancaster, Lune Aqueduct (97/SD 484 639). Built by John Rennie in 1797, it carries the Lancaster Canal by five arches across the Lune. See also the *Wyre Aqueduct, Garstang* (102/SD 491 448) which carries the same canal across the Wyre by a single arch.

Lytham St Annes Windmill, East Beach (102/SD 371 270). A white-washed brick tower mill, built about 1804 as a cornmill, in use until *c* 1926 and recently restored.

Quernmore, Castle Watermill (97/SD 520 609). Built in 1818, it has an unusual stone wall and roof cladding protecting a later 36-foot-diameter overshot waterwheel with a rim gear.

Thornton Cleveleys, Marsh Windmill (102/SD 335 426). An 18th-century tower mill, recently restored. *Tel.* Cleveleys (0253) 826295.

Whalley Viaduct (103/SD 728 363). Built in 1848, this 48-arch brick viaduct carries the railway over the Calder.

Many *textile mills* have been demolished but see: *Preston, Centenary Mill*, New Hall Lane (102/SD 551 297), built by

Horrocks in 1895; and *Rawtenstall, Whitehead's Mill*, New Hall Hey (103/SD 810 225), built in 1862.

GREATER MANCHESTER

This county includes the major surrounding textile centres as well as coal and a wide range of other industries.

Manchester (Map 109)
In recent years much of the centre of Manchester has been rebuilt. Of what remains, see:

Barton Arcade, Deansgate (SJ 837 985). An elegant three-storey glass and iron shopping arcade built by Corbett, Rabey and Sawey in 1871.

Central Station, Lower Mosley Street (SJ 837 977). Built in 1880 and closed in 1969, the station has a fine iron arch roof 90 feet high and its span of 210 feet is exceeded only by St Pancras Station, London. The forecourt and yard are now used as a car park.

Great Northern Railway Warehouse, Deansgate (SJ 836 978), a fine example of 1895–8 with goods stations at two levels connected by inclines, an internal steel structure and road, rail and canal interchange. It is under conversion to a multi-storey car park.

Greater Manchester Museum of Science and Industry, Liverpool Road Station, Liverpool Road, Castleford (SJ 830 979) occupies the original terminus of the Liverpool & Manchester Railway (1830). Displays include textile machinery, steam power, internal combustion and electric engines, machine tools, papermaking and printing, and other industries of the north-west with some working exhibits. *Tel.* Manchester (061) 832 2244.

Water Street Warehouses (SJ 827 978). A range of Victorian warehouses along the River Irwell between New Bailey Bridge and Regent Street including New Botany, Marshall's Side and the Victoria and Albert Warehouses. The *Ducie Street railway warehouses* (SJ 848 981) were built by the different railway companies and *Castlefield* (SJ 831 975) was the terminus of the Bridgwater Canal with two surviving warehouses.

Also Worth Visiting in Greater Manchester
Salford Museum of Mining, Buile Hill Park, Eccles Old Road (109/SJ 799 994), deals with the history of coalmining. *Tel.* Manchester (061) 736 1832.

Manchester – Liverpool Road Station before redevelopment

Pilkington Glass Museum – model 16th-century glass kiln

There are a number of impressive canal and railway works: see, for example, *Marple, Peak Forest canal aqueduct* (109/SJ 955 901) across the River Goyt; *Eccles, Barton swing aqueduct* (109/SJ 767 976) which carries the Bridgwater Canal across the Manchester Ship canal; *Worsley, Bridgwater canal basin* (109/SD 749 006), two entrances to the underground tunnel system connecting with the collieries of this, the first successful canal in the north of England, built to carry coal to Manchester. At *Stockport*, the *Mersey railway viaduct* (109/SJ 890 906–893 901) which dominates the town – 110 feet high and 1,780 feet long – carries the main line to Manchester.

Though many have been destroyed, a number of substantial textile mills can still be seen, for example: *Bolton* (Map 109), *Swan Lane Mills* (SD 708 079), a late-19th-century spinning mill, and *Atlas Mills* (SD 701 101), 1862, where the Northern Mill Engine Society is establishing a museum, *Tel.* Rochdale (0706) 58528 or Halifax (0422) 60874; *Bury, Burrs Mill* (109/SD 799 127), a water-powered cotton mill and community from the 1780s and later; *Milnrow, Ellenroad Ring Mill* (109/SD 931 116), 1892 and still working; *Oldham* (Map 109), a group of mills in the Hathershaw area, *Belgrave Mills* (SD 932 035), 1881 and 1908–14, *Earl Mill* (SD 929 032), 1890, and *Maple Mills* (SD 931 033), 1904 and 1915; and *Stockport, Reddish Mills* (109/SJ 891 933), a large group of mills built in the 1860s with its associated community.

MERSEYSIDE

This county is dominated by Liverpool but also includes Birkenhead and St Helens.

St Helens: Pilkington Glass Museum (108/SJ 502 945)
For long St Helens has been a major glass-making centre. Little remains now in the town, though on the Pilkington's site the old manager's house, stables and some cottages survive. Attached to the head office of Pilkington's, the major British glass manufacturer, is this museum which has a series of displays concerned with glass-making. Two dioramas are of particular interest. The first shows what a 16th-century Wealden kiln was like; the second a team or 'chair' consisting of the master glassblower (gaffer), the chief assistant (footman) and a boy in action. Other displays illustrate the various applications of glass: in building, in lamps, as windowglass and as decorated glassware.
Address: Pilkington Glass Museum, Prescot Road, St Helens, Merseyside. *Tel.* St Helens (0744) 28882.

Within the adjacent *United Glass Ravenhead Glass-bottle Works* (SJ 504 944) there still survives a 'tank' furnace of 1886, a rare example of the Siemens regenerative principle, once the basis of the industry.

Remains of the glass industry can also be seen elsewhere. In *Bristol*, Avon, a truncated glass cone forms part of the Dragonara Hotel, Prewett Street (172/ST 593 723). The oldest of the surviving cones, built *c* 1740 and 60 feet high, is at *Catcliffe*, South Yorkshire (111/SK 425 886). An 87-foot high cone built *c* 1780 has been preserved by Stuart Crystal at their works in Stuart Street, Wordsley, *Stourbridge*, West Midlands (139/SO 894 856).

Liverpool (Map 108)

The major port in the north-west and an early centre of railways, Liverpool has suffered much from demolition but still retains many important sites.

The Dock area has a number of points of interest including: at the Pier Head, the *Cunard Building* (SJ 339 904) and the *Royal Liver Building* (SJ 339 903), the first multi-storeyed reinforced concrete frame building, 1908–11, both familiar features of the Liverpool skyline. *Merseyside Maritime Museum* (SJ 339 900), immediately to the south, is situated round the Canning Docks, two 18th-century graving docks rebuilt in the 1840s. The visitors' centre is the old pilotage building. The collection concentrates on local maritime matters: a number of boats are afloat, there is a boat hall, a maritime park with heavy cargo-handling equipment and a temporary exhibition gallery. *Tel.* Liverpool (051) 236 1492. In 1984 an extension is planned into the *Albert Dock*, Canning Place (SJ 341 898). The most important of the Liverpool docks to survive, this dock was built to the designs of Jesse Hartley, 1843–6. Five-storey warehouses surround the 8-acre dock on all sides. The Dock Traffic Office (1847) in the north-east corner, by Philip Hardwick, incorporates an enormous classical portico. Other docks and warehouses can be seen along the dock road which is bordered by the *dock estate wall*, begun *c* 1830, which contains an imposing series of gate openings which range from the stern classical to gothic whimsy. *Stanley Dock* (SJ 337 921) has a pair of fireproof warehouses, one hidden behind a 13-storey brick tobacco warehouse of 1900 by G. F. Lyster. At *Wapping* (SJ 345 894) there is another fireproof warehouse and a castellated hydraulic station of 1856. An enormous German steam-powered *floating crane* of *c* 1910, *Goliath*, is still used occasionally in the Northern Docks.

Edge Hill railway station and cutting (SJ 373 899). The station is now refurbished and still partly in use and its external appearance remains very much as George Stephenson would have known it in 1836. Nearby is the cutting through which the Liverpool & Manchester Railway ran, where the remains of the Moorish Arch, the boiler houses, the stables and staircases cut out of the rock can be seen. Plans are in hand for restoration. Until 1870 Edge Hill was the point at which the steam locomotives took over from the ropes which hauled the carriages up from **Lime Street Station** (SJ 352 905) which has twin train sheds with iron roof trusses.

Higson's Brewery, Stanhope Street (SJ 350 889) is a fine example of a Victorian tower brewery, built in the style of a Bavarian castle by Robert Cain in 1896–1902.

Among other buildings of note are **Oriel Chambers** (SJ 341 905), the first cantilevered clad construction, of 1864 and the **Royal Insurance Building**, North John Street (SJ 344 904), an early steel frame building, 1897–1903. Two 'cast iron' churches by Rickman & Cragg, 1812–15, can be seen at **St George's, Everton** (SJ 355 925) and **St Michael in the Hamlet** (SJ 369 870). At the entrance to the Mersey is a **fort** (SJ 309 947) built in 1826–9 to defend the river. Of the several lighthouses, the earliest (1763) is at **Leasowe** (SJ 253 914).

Liverpool – north side of Edge Hill railway cutting before recent excavation

Also Worth Visiting in Merseyside (Map 108)

Birkenhead, Bidston Windmill (SJ 287 894). A late-18th-century tower mill replacing an earlier post mill, it ceased working about 1875. In the care of Wirral Borough Council, it is the best surviving example in the area.

Birkenhead Docks date essentially from the late 1850s, though Morpeth and Egerton Docks (SJ 325 895) were completed in the late 1840s. Of special interest are the *Central Hydraulic Generating Station* (SJ 322 899) of 1863 by Hartley, still operating; the *Alfred Basin river entrance* (SJ 327 902) whose gates are still operated by hydraulic power; and the *Impounding Station* (SJ 327 899) at Wallasey Dock, where Gwynnes pumps are still driven by steam turbines. At Birkenhead Woodside the ferry from Liverpool moors at the only remaining early *floating landing stage* (SJ 331 893) which dates from 1861 and has a wood and cast-iron booking hall.

Birkenhead, Mersey Railway Pumphouse, Shore Road (SJ 328 893) still contains one of two 'grasshopper' compound beam engines supplied by Andrew Barclay in 1886 to drain the railway tunnel under the river. The only large engine of this type surviving in the world, it worked until 1959.

Liverpool & Manchester Railway passed to the south of St Helens, through *Rainhill* (SJ 491 914) where the site of the famous 1829 locomotive trials is recorded by a commemorative board and there is a fine *skew bridge*, the crossing of a 1753 turnpike road over the railway. The railway crosses the Sankey Valley by a *viaduct* (SJ 568 947) of nine semi-circular arches, constructed in 1827–30 by George Stephenson. To the south of *Earlestown*, a railway town created by the railway works, is the *Vulcan Foundry* (SJ 585 940), now part of Rustons, which was established in 1834 expressly for the construction of railway locomotives. Though nothing earlier than 1907 now remains in the works, immediately to the south (SJ 586 938) is *Vulcan Village*, an industrial village dating from the 1840s.

Port Sunlight (SJ 348 845) is an industrial village built by Lever Brothers from 1898 to the 1930s. The spacious model settlement of gabled houses with generous bedroom and bathroom provision compared favourably with the regimented terraces of Saltaire and New Lanark.

Prescot Museum, High Street (SJ 465 928) has some machinery and other relics of the local watch-making industry of which some disused *workshops* can be seen in St Helens Road (SJ 468 928) and the factory of the *Lancashire Watch Company* (SJ 472 928), in Albany Road, which operated 1889–1910.

St Helens, Old Double Locks, Sankey Canal (SJ 536 961) are the first pair of staircase locks built on an English canal. Dating from 1758 and much altered, they have the typical barrel shape of early locks. Compare the *New Double Locks* (SJ 519 962), 1 mile west, which date from *c* 1772.

Southport pier (SD 335 176). Opened in 1860 and subsequently extended, it has since been shortened to 3,650 feet. It was one of the earliest true pleasure – as distinct from landing – piers. Nearby are some typical cast-iron seaside shelters.

Coalmining was important in the St Helens area. At *Haydock* (SJ 573 976) can be seen the workshops of Richard Evans & Co. while the *Sutton Manor Colliery* (SJ 518 908) has an array of two-cylinder cross-compound steam winding and compressing engines and a stand-by ventilating fan engine (Fraser & Chalmers, 1906; Yates & Thom, 1914; and three by Walkers of various dates).

NORTHUMBERLAND

The industries mainly consist of coal and leadmining and lime burning.

Holy Island Limekilns (75/NU 138 417)

In many parts of the country, often close to rivers or coasts, limekilns were built from the 16th century onwards to produce burnt lime which was placed on the soil to reduce its acidity, and used for making mortar for building purposes. The kilns or furnaces were top-loaded and the burnt lime was raked out from the hearth at the bottom.

Lime had been quarried on Holy Island for centuries but about 1860 a Dundee company began operations on a commercial scale, building a large new kiln immediately east of Beblowe Crag. Limestone was brought to the kilns by a railway (the line of which can still be seen) from quarries north of Lindisfarne Castle. In the second half of the 19th century crushed lime replaced burnt lime and limekilns ceased to be used. The Holy Island kilns were banked for the last time at the turn of this century. Recently restored by the National Trust, they are a particularly impressive set.

Tel. (Administrator, Lindisfarne Castle) Berwick-upon-Tweed (0289) 89244.

Other limekilns can be seen along the Northumbrian coast, notably at *Beadnell* (75/NU 238 285); at *Bamburgh Castle* (75/NU 185 351); and at *Rennington*, Little Mill (81/NU 228 173).

Holy Island Limekilns

Also Worth Visiting in Northumberland

Allendale smelt mill and flues (87/NY 832 567–814 538). Flues several miles long lead from the smelt mills to two chimneys on the moorland above. Lead from Killhope was processed here.

   Berwick-upon-Tweed, icehouse (75/NT 997 529), a commercial icehouse built into Bankhill to store ice for use in the salmon-netting industry.

   Berwick-upon-Tweed, Royal Border Bridge (75/NT 992 532) was built by Robert Stephenson and T. E. Harrison in 1847–50 to carry the main east coast railway line by 28 arches at a height of 126 feet across the Tweed. The construction involved up to 2,700 men and 180 horses at a cost of £200,000.

   Blyth, staithes (81/NZ 306 830), two sets of wooden coal staithes, the North Side Staithes (1896) and the West Side Staithes (1928).

   Corbridge, Walker's Pottery Works, Milkwell Lane (87/NY 992 652). A rural pottery which went out of use in 1906, it has substantial remains of kilns, drying floors, manufacturing sheds and a water-powered pug mill.

   Ford, Heatherslaw Watermill (74/NT 933 384). The building housed two mills with undershot wheels which worked until 1949; it is now being restored. *Tel.* Crookham (089 082) 338.

   Stocksfield, Hunday National Tractor and Farm Museum, Newton (87/NZ 037 653). Housed in a typical stone-built early-19th-century Northumbrian farm, it includes over 200 tractors and engines, blacksmith's and joiner's shops, a watermill and a horse-whim house, farming equipment and animals. *Tel.* Stocksfield (0661) 842553.

   Wylam-on-Tyne, George Stephenson's Cottage (88/NZ 126 650). Approached by a footpath along the river; a small stone cottage built about 1750 where George Stephenson was born in 1781. *Tel.* Wylam (066 14) 3457.

TYNE AND WEAR

The main industry here was coalmining served by the ports of the two rivers.

Sunderland: Monkwearmouth Station (88/NZ 396 577)

Opened in 1848 as the Sunderland terminus of the York, Newcastle and Berwick Railway, the present station with its impressive classical façade designed by Thomas Moore replaced an earlier station. At the rear there was an ironframed train shed over the platform and track; but the track section was removed in 1928. When the line was extended over the Wear to a new station at Sunderland Central by the North-East Railway in 1879, Monkwearmouth Station lost much of its importance but it continued to have some traffic until after 1945. In the following 20 years the number of passengers using the station declined considerably and it was closed in 1967, to be reopened as a museum of land transport in 1973. It contains a restored booking office, displays relating to the station itself, land transport in north-east England and a survey of public street transport to Newcastle, South Shields and Sunderland from the 1900s to the 1970s.

In 1977 the footbridge was refurbished and the former siding area was reopened to provide accommodation for a display of rolling stock including a 1915 NER goods train van and an LNER covered carriage truck.

Life is given to the museum since trains on the busy Newcastle–Middlesbrough line pass through the station though they no longer stop there.

Tyne bridges

Address: Monkwearmouth Station Museum, North Bridge Street, Sunderland, Tyne and Wear SR5 1AD. *Tel.* Sunderland (0783) 77075.

Newcastle-on-Tyne (Map 88)

Newcastle-on-Tyne is famous for its bridges:

Dean Street Bridge (NZ 251 640) was built to carry the York, Newcastle and Berwick Railway over Dean Street in 1848. It was widened in 1894.

High Level Bridge (NZ 252 637), the most notable engineering work in Newcastle, carries both the road and the main-line railway across the Tyne. Designed by Robert Stephenson and Thomas Harrison and opened in 1849, it consists of six main spans with cast-iron ribs.

King Edward Railway Bridge (NZ 247 633) was built in 1906 to enable through-running on the east coast main line.

Newcastle Swing Bridge (NZ 253 637) was built in 1876 to replace an earlier fixed bridge which interrupted navigation up the river. When built, it was the largest of its type in Britain. It consists of a 281-foot main section, weighing 1,200 tons, which was originally turned by steam pumps driving a hydraulic engine. It is now electrically powered and opens two or three times a day.

Tyne Bridge (NZ 254 638) was opened in 1928 to deal with the expansion of road traffic. A two-pin arch bridge, it was at the time of its construction the longest of its type in Britain.

Also of interest in Newcastle-on-Tyne

Newcastle Central Station (NZ 246 638), designed by John Dobson in 1850 with an arcaded portico by Thomas Prosser. It has an all-over iron and glass roof on a curve.

Victoria Tunnel (NZ 237 657). Almost 2 miles long, this tunnel was built in 1839–42 to enable coal to be brought from the outskirts of the city to the Tyne. Closed in 1860, it was used as an air raid shelter during World War II. Part has recently been converted into a sewer but access is possible at the western end.

Museum of Science and Technology, Blandford House, West Blandford Street (NZ 241 639). Apart from Sir Charles Parson's SY *Turbinia*, the world's first turbine-driven ship which is still in Exhibition Park on the outskirts of the city (NZ 247 658), the collections relating to engineering, shipbuilding, mining and transport are now housed in a former warehouse. *Tel.* Newcastle-upon-Tyne (0632) 326789.

Ryhope Pumping Station (88/NZ 404 525)

One of the problems which had to be tackled with the growth of towns in the 19th century was the supply of water. The Sunderland and South Shields Water Company was formed in 1852. A water supply from Ryhope was first proposed in 1858 but it was not until 1865 that firm plans were drawn up to extract water for public supply from the permeable magnesium limestone lying below the surface in this part of County Durham. Two 100-hp double-acting rotative beam engines and pumps were installed at Ryhope to deliver 3 million gallons of water a day from a depth of about 250 feet to a service reservoir in the station grounds from which it was supplied to Sunderland. The steam engines were in use from 1869 until 1 July 1967. The steam came from six Cornish boilers, replaced in 1908 by three larger Lancashire boilers. As was typical of the time, the engines are a visual delight with ornamentation on the parallel linkages, valve chests, valve gears and elsewhere. They are housed in a structure which looks more like a chapel than a powerhouse. The other buildings – boiler house, coal store and workshops – are also elaborate while the chimney is impressive. And considerable effort was made to provide an attractive setting for the engine house with lawns, trees and flower beds. Solidly-built houses were also provided on site for the workmen.

The trust which runs the pumping station has set up displays in the coal store, illustrating the history of water supply, and also a 'clean and decent' display of domestic sanitary equipment.

Address: Ryhope Pumping Station, Ryhope, Tyne and Wear. *Tel.* Sunderland (0783) 210235.

Also Worth Visiting in Tyne and Wear (Map 88)
Fulwell Windmill (NZ 392 595). The most complete windmill in north-east England, it is a limestone tower mill of 1821. The exterior was restored in the 1950s and the machinery recently.

Newburn, Lemington glass cone (NZ 184 646), built in 1787, has been reduced in height from 130 feet to 110 feet.

Springwell, Bowes Railway (NZ 285 587). Remains of a mineral line which include a gravity incline, stationary engines and locomotives as motive power. About 1¼ miles of this 15-mile system is being restored.

Washington, F. Pit colliery winder (NZ 303 575). The engine house and headgear of this pit have been preserved as a mining museum.

NORTH YORKSHIRE

Its industrial past includes brewing, leadmining and textiles.

York: National Railway Museum (105/SE 595 515)
One of the vital communication developments of the modern age was the steam railway. The first trains in operation were in the north of England: the Stockton to Darlington Railway began running in 1825 and the Liverpool and Manchester in 1830. Moreover, York was an important railway centre and it was George Hudson's town. It is therefore appropriate that the National Railway Museum should be in York. Housed in the Round House of the old York North Steam Motive Power Depot,

the Museum has a wide ranging collection. It has normally some 25 locomotives, an exhibition including the earliest 0–4–0 *Agenorica* (1829), the record-breaking 4–6–2 *Mallard* (1938) and *Evening Star* (1960), an example of the last BR steam locomotives. There are also electric and diesel locomotives, a wide range of rolling stock (freight and passenger), signalling equipment and other material associated with the past 150 years of railways in the United Kingdom. In addition, there is a considerable collection of models. The museum also has an impressive collection of illustrative material, photographs, posters and technical drawings.
Address: National Railway Museum, Leeman Road, York. *Tel.* York (0904) 21261.

Also Worth Visiting in North Yorkshire

Bedale, Crakehall Watermill (99/SE 272 882). A 17th-century building with a top floor of about 1800 on an ancient site which milled until the 1930s. It has been restored. *Tel.* Bedale (0677) 23240.

Grassington, Linton Cotton Mill (98/SE 002 633). Built to take advantage of the water power available from the River Wharfe, when it closed in the 1930s it had five turbines and an auxiliary steam engine. It then became an electricity generating station for a period and four diesel engines were added. See also the former hemp mill at *Pateley Bridge* (99/SE 148 664), built *c* 1887 with a 35-foot-high breastshot waterwheel and now converted to a country inn.

Masham, Theakston's Brewery (99/SE 224 816). A small family brewery founded in 1827 in a stone-built complex with fine maltings.

Skipton, Canal Warehouse, Coach Street (103/SD 983 511), on the Leeds and Liverpool Canal, is now used as the Dales Outdoor Centre.

Skipton, High Corn Mill (103/SD 993 520). This mill is now the George Leatt Industrial and Folk Museum with machinery driven by one of the two waterwheels. *Tel.* Skipton (0756) 2883.

York, Castle Museum, Tower Street (105/SE 605 514), contains a series of period rooms, reconstructed streets, a restored watermill from near Pickering, other types of mill and collections relating to Yorkshire history. *Tel.* York (0904) 53611.

There are a number of ruined mining and metal working sites: see, in particular, mine engine house, *Cononley* (103/SD 980 462); a small powder house 1 mile east of *Glaisdale* (94/NZ 787 055); the ruined cupola smelter, flue and chimney on *Grassington Moor* (98/SE 030 667); the *Grinton smelt mill* with its flue, near Reeth (98/SE 050 964) and the *Surrender smelt mill* (92/NY 988 003).

SOUTH YORKSHIRE

This county is dominated by Sheffield with coal, iron and steel, glass and pottery.

Worsbrough Mill (110/SE 349 034)

Worsbrough Mill was probably constructed on the site of Domesday mills about 1625. It is a two-storey stone-built cornmill with three pairs of stones powered by an overshot waterwheel driven by water from a millpond supplied by the River Dove. Because of increased demand, a three-storey steam mill was erected to the north of the watermill in 1843. The steam engine drove two pairs of stones and ancillary machinery. While Worsbrough Mill made only stone-ground flour for brown bread, by 1900 white bread made from flour produced by roller mills was more popular. Demand for Worsbrough flour fell and in 1922 the steam engine was scrapped while the watermill continued to produce animal feed until the 1960s.

The mill has now been restored as a working museum and a 1911 oil engine has replaced the steam engine. An adjacent Interpretative Centre contains a display on the history and development of the mill.

Behind the mill is the dam forming the Worsbrough Reservoir and Basin of the Derne & Dove Canal, opened in 1804 to connect the collieries of the Barnsley area to the Don Navigation. The footpath from the mill follows the mill leat which was diverted around the reservoir and crosses its outfall by an attractive masonry bridge.
Address: Worsbrough Mill Museum, Worsbrough, Barnsley, South Yorkshire S70 5LJ. *Tel.* Barnsley (0226) 203961.

Sheffield: Abbeydale Industrial Hamlet (Maps 110, 111/SK 326 820)

While many steelworks today are huge concerns, two centuries ago the scale of manufacture was much smaller. At the small industrial complex at Abbeydale a whole range of processes was carried out around a small courtyard until 1933. From the later 18th century steel was refined here in small clay crucibles, which were themselves made on the site in the pot room. Charged with 56 lbs of broken blister steel and a little lime as flux, the crucibles were placed in the furnace where the charge was melted at a temperature of about 1,550° centigrade for three to four hours. The pots were then taken out of the furnace by the puller-out and the molten metal was poured into an ingot mould. After the ingots had cooled they were tested and then sent off site to a rolling mill further up the river and reduced to a 1-inch-square

Worsbrough – old mill, c 1625, left, *and new mill, c 1843,* right

section. Brought back, the ingots were reheated, the air supply being provided by a water-driven blowing machine. Under water-driven tilt-hammers dating from 1785 or in the rolling mill the metal was forge-welded to produce the forged or 'crown' scythe. The roughly forged scythes were straightened and hardened in small hand-forges and sharpened by water-driven grindstones. In times of drought these were powered by an 1855 Davy Brothers horizontal single-cylinder steam engine. To complete the set-up were the offices, the warehouse and stabling for six horses. Accommodation was also provided for three key workmen in cottages, one of which has been furnished in late-18th-century style, and for the manager, whose house has been

Abbeydale – the tilt forge

furnished as it would have been in the 19th century. In its rural setting, Abbeydale provides a very good example of a restored 18th-century small-scale scythe works.

Address: Abbeydale Industrial Hamlet, Abbeydale Road, Sheffield, South Yorkshire S7 2QW. *Tel.* Sheffield (0742) 367731.

Sheffield Museums have also restored the late-16th-century water-powered cutlery grinding establishment, **Shepherd Wheel**, Whiteley Wood, Sheffield 11 (110, 111/SK 317 854), which provides a strong contrast and complement to Abbeydale. And they have established the **Sheffield Industrial Museum** on Kelham Island (110, 111/SK 352 882) in a former electriciy generating station to illustrate a range of local industries. *Tel.* Sheffield (0742) 22106.

Elsecar Engine (110, 111/SK 387 999)

A key invention that enabled Britain to become the first industrial nation was the stationary steam engine which allowed coal and metals to be won from deeper pits. The last Newcomen engine on its original site has been preserved by the National Coal Board at Elsecar. Built in 1787, though probably not in use until 1795, it was modified in 1836 with a cast-iron beam with parallel motion replacing the original wooden beam. The cylinder, with a top open to the atmosphere, installed in 1801 is 4 feet in diameter with a 5-foot stroke and the engine has an indicated horsepower of 13·16. It could raise 50 gallons per stroke at a rate of six strokes per minute from a depth of 130 feet. It worked continuously until 1923 when it was replaced by electric pumps. When these were flooded in June 1928 the Newcomen engine was put to work again until the electric pumps were able to restart. It last ran for demonstration purposes in 1954. Nearby is the industrial village of Elsecar (SE 386 003) which was enlarged on a planned basis in the middle of the 19th century by Earl Fitzwilliam, including terraced housing (Reform Row alongside the colliery was built in 1830), a model lodging house, an estate market house, a steam cornmill, a school, a church, mineral offices and a private railway station. Very little survives of the ironworks which provided employment for those who lived at Elsecar.

Address: National Coal Board, Elsecar, Barnsley, South Yorkshire. *Tel.* Barnsley (0226) 742531.

Wortley Top Forge (110/SK 294 998)

Sheffield is synonymous with iron and steel. The visitor to Top Forge who stands near the older helve can justifiably say that he is on the spot where wrought iron was made from 1620 to 1912. Founded by Sir Francis Wortley, the forge moved into the

ownership of the Spencer partnership after the Civil War. The forge appears to have been extended by a second waterwheel and hammer added in the early 18th century when the works produced rod and bar iron. Most of the plant now visible at Wortley – the massive spring-assisted belly helve hammer worked by a 13-feet 6-inches breastshot waterwheel and the three jib cranes – dates from the middle of the 19th century when Wortley produced railway iron, particularly wrought-iron axles.

Wortley Top Forge – helve hammer

In 1850 Top Forge came into the possession of the Andrews family and shortly after 1907 into the ownership of the Wortley Iron Company which closed Top Forge in 1912.

Other displays include a 19th-century machine shop, joiner's and blacksmith's shops and a range of early steam and oil engines.

Tel. c/o Darley Dale (062 983) 4374.

WEST YORKSHIRE

West Yorkshire has the heart of the Yorkshire textile industry.

Shipley: Saltaire (104/SE 140 381)

The village of Saltaire owes its existence to Sir Titus Salt, a Victorian textile magnate who had made a fortune pioneering the

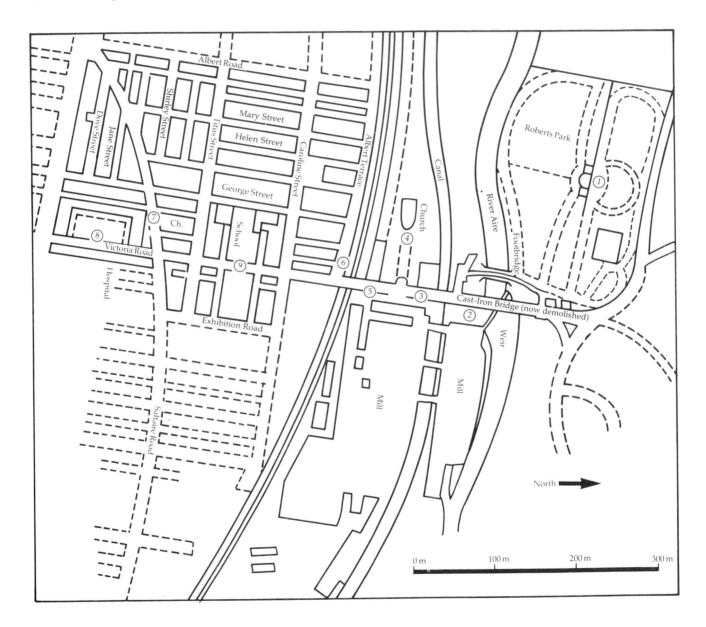

Albert Road

Mary Street

Helen Street

George Street

Shirley Street

Titus Street

Caroline Street

Jane Street

Dove Street

Albert Terrace

Church

Canal

River Aire

Roberts Park

①

Footbridge

⑦

Ch.

⑧

Victoria Road

School

⑨

⑥

Hospital

Exhibition Road

Saltaire Road

④

⑤

③

②

Cast-Iron Bridge (now demolished)

Weir

Mill

Mill

North ➤

0 m   100 m   200 m   300 m

use of the alpaca fleece. Dissatisfied with employment and housing conditions in nearby Bradford, he used his fortune to establish a model industrial village on the banks of the River Aire from 1851.

Dominated by the mill, the village provided shops, alms-houses, a hospital and other public buildings to cater for the workers' physical and spiritual welfare. The Congregational church is regarded as one of the most distinguished examples of Italian-style architecture in Britain. There are no pubs as Sir Titus Salt preached against the evils of alcohol.

A walk gives a good impression of the village. Starting at (1) the statue of Sir Titus Salt in Roberts Park, (2) the view from the bridge shows the location of (3) the works between the River Aire and Midland Railway; the Leeds–Liverpool Canal runs through the site. Nearby can be seen (4) the Congregational church and on Victoria Road itself (5) the works dining-room, with mono-gram and family crest over the door. The housing (6) consists of single two-storey cottages. A view of the streets can be obtained by walking along Albert Terrace and then along Albert Road which contains the houses intended for overlookers and execu-tives. Then turn left along Saltaire Road passing (7) the Wesleyan Methodist chapel. Victoria Road is reached again and (8) the almshouses built between 1868 and 1871 can be seen to the right. To the left in Victoria Road are Victoria Square, the school and the Institute.

Bradford and its Industrial Museum (Map 104)

Bradford was once the major centre of the woollen textile industry. The **Wool Exchange** in Market Street (SE 164 332), opened in 1867, was the hub of the wool trade. The carved heads high on the outside walls range from Christopher Columbus to Sir Titus Salt. Built in 1887, the **General Post Office** in Foster Square (SE 166 333) provided a focal point for the Victorian town planning of Bradford. A little distance north-west of the city centre, the **Conditioning House** (SE 154 339), built in 1902 to provide an impartial assessment of the quality of local textiles, is the only such structure in Britain. East of the city centre the hill slope, between Leeds Road and Church Bank, once the centre of wool merchanting, became known as **Little Germany**. Most of the *warehouses* here (SE 168 330) were built between *c* 1850 and *c* 1874. Given up largely to the reception and bulk disposal of piece goods, yarns and to a lesser extent wool, the area remains pretty much as it was before World War I.

On the outskirts of the city there are three mill buildings worth noting:

Illingworth's Mill, Buttershaw (SE 137 293). The mid-19th-century buildings include a plain five-storey spinning mill, an engine house and a preparation shed with workers' housing adjacent.

Manningham Mills (SE 146 348) were built in 1873. With their two six-storey blocks, they provide an example of the grand scale of mill architecture. Owned by Samuel Lister, their main pro-ducts were velvet and plush.

Bradford Industrial Museum, Moorside Mills, Moorside Road, Eccleshill (SE 186 357), is a typical worsted spinning mill complex dating from 1875. It now houses displays of textile machinery, motive power and transport. *Moorside House*, in the grounds, was originally the home of the first owner of the mill and has been furnished to show the domestic life of a middle-class family in the late Victorian and early Edwardian era. *Tel.* Bradford (0274) 631756.

Also Worth Visiting in West Yorkshire

Bingley Five-Rise Locks (104/SE 108 399). Opened in 1774, this staircase of five locks on the Leeds and Liverpool Canal is extremely steep, rising about 60 feet, and is the most impressive flight in the country.

Golcar, Colne Valley Museum, Cliffe Ash (110/SE 102 153). Housed in a terrace of weavers' cottages of 1845 on a steep hillside, this most attractive little museum has a clogger's room, a weaving workshop and an example of a 19th-century living-room. Craft demonstrations are given. *Tel.* Huddersfield (0484) 659762.

Halifax Piece Hall, Horton Street (104/SE 095 250). Built in 1779, this most impressive building, three storeys high enclosing an open square, was formerly occupied by cloth merchants. It has recently been restored with shops, galleries and a textile museum. *Tel.* Halifax (0422) 68725.

Keighley and Worth Valley Light Railway, Haworth Station (104/SE 035 373). The line opened in 1867 and was closed in 1962 but it now operates as a steam railway over 5 miles and there is an exhibition of locomotives etc. *Tel.* Haworth (0535) 43629.

Leeds, Middleton Colliery Railway, Hunslett Moor (104/SE 303 322). The site of a horsedrawn waggon way of 1758 and the first commercial railway to be worked by steam locomotives in 1812. Three miles of standard-gauge track is now run as a steam railway. *Tel.* c/o Leeds (0532) 645424.

Leeds, Museum of Industry and Science, Armley Mills, Canal Road (104/SE 276 341). Housed in a largely 1805 iron-framed fireproof construction building, once the largest woollen mill in

Bradford Industrial Museum – Moorside Mills

the world, the collections include material relating to local industries; water, steam and petrol power; and a wide range of technological models. *Tel.* Leeds (0532) 637861.

Leeds, Temple Works, Marshall Street (104/SE 295 326). An Egyptian-style flax mill built in 1840 for John Marshall, the stone walls are 6 feet thick at the base; it was lit from above and a uniform temperature all year was achieved by hypocaust-like air chambers in the basement.

Leeds, Thwaite Putty Mills, Thwaite Lane (104/SE 328 312). A water-powered milling complex dating from 1823–5 with two large late-19th-century iron breastshot waterwheels which successively crushed oil seed and ground corn, crushed flint, and ground chalk for the manufacture of putty. *Tel.* c/o Wakefield (0924) 367111 ext. 4769.

Marsden, Standedge Canal Tunnel north portal (110/SE 040 120). Completed in 1811, it is the longest canal tunnel in Britain at 3 miles 125 yards. It formed part of the summit level of the Huddersfield Canal but is now closed.

Stanley, Stanley Ferry aqueduct (104/SE 355 230) carries the Aire and Calder Navigation in a cast-iron trough across the Calder. A single bow-string arched structure, it was opened in 1839.

Wakefield, Aire and Calder Navigation Offices (104/SE 338 202). This neo-classical building was built in 1800 and extended in 1820. Joseph Priestley, the canal historian, worked in it as a clerk. The building stands on land once occupied by the yard of the navigation basin.

Wales

WALES

1 Pontcysyllte Aqueduct
2 **Bersham Industrial Trail**
3 Carew: French Mill
4 Dre-Fach Felindre: Museum of The Woollen Industry
5 Pumpsaint: Dolaucothi Gold Mines
6 Merthyr Tydfil: Iron Trail
7 St Fagan's: Welsh Folk Museum
8 Swansea
9 Cefn Coed Coal and Steam Centre
10 **Blaenavon: Ironworks and Big Pit**
11 Newport: Transporter Bridge
12 Tywyn: Talyllyn Railway
13 Llanberis: The Welsh Slate Museum
14 Penryn Castle and Industrial Railway Museum
15 Beaumaris: Gaol
16 Llanidloes: Bryntail Leadmine
17 Elan Valley Dams

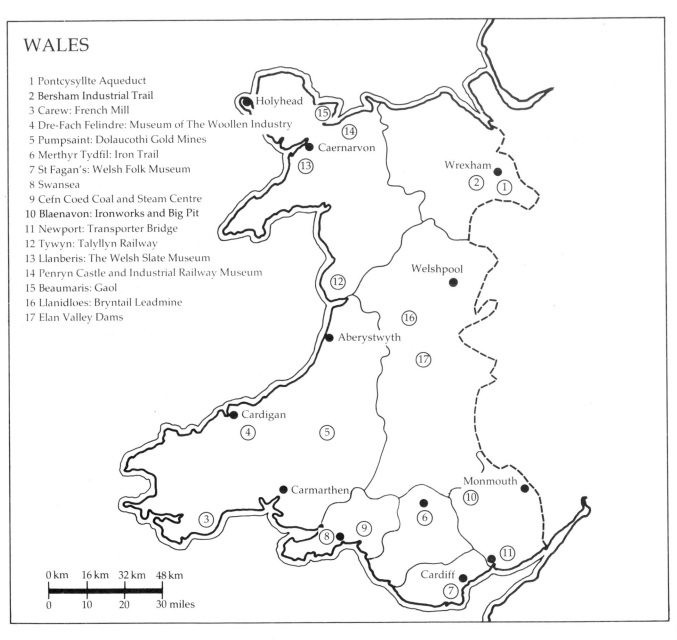

Holyhead

Wrexham

Caernarvon

Welshpool

Aberystwyth

Cardigan

Carmarthen

Monmouth

Cardiff

0 km   16 km   32 km   48 km

0   10   20   30 miles

CLWYD

Clwyd (formerly Denbigh and Flint) had metal mining and working and textiles as its principal activities.

Pontcysyllte Aqueduct (117/SJ 271 420)

One of the most spectacular stretches of canal in Britain is the branch of the Shropshire Union Canal designed by William Jessop and Thomas Telford to link the border towns of Shrewsbury and Chester via the ironworks of Wrexham and Ruabon. On this branch is one of Telford's great achievements, the Pontcysyllte aqueduct, built between 1794 and 1805, which carries the canal on stone pillars across the Dee valley at a height of 127 feet above the river. The aqueduct has 19 iron arches, each with a span of 53 feet, making a total width of 1,007 feet. The canal is contained in a cast-iron trough with a towpath on one side.

There is a *Canal Exhibition Centre* at the canal wharf on the edge of Llangollen (117/SJ 209 428), housed in an early-19th-century warehouse. *Tel.* Llangollen (0978) 860702.

Not far away is the *Chirk aqueduct* (126/SJ 287 372), built in 1801, 600 feet long with 10 arches, to carry the Shropshire Union Canal at a height of 70 feet over the River Ceirwig. The original cast-iron plates were replaced by a cast-iron trough in the 1870s.

Close by is the *Chirk viaduct* of 16 bays built in 1848 to carry the Shrewsbury and Chester Railway across the valley.

Bersham Industrial Trail (117/SJ 272 518–315 492)

Ironmaking began at Bersham about 1670 and developed under

the Wilkinson family, particularly John Wilkinson, about a century later. It ceased at the end of the Napoleonic War. In this area there is evidence also of other economic activity such as leadmining and cornmilling.

The trail begins beside the village green in the leadmining village of Minera. Nearby is the site of Minera mill. On the right of the mountain road to Llangollen the remains of two reservoirs which provided water for the operations of the New Minera Mining Company are visible. Near Roy's turning are the mortuary and blacksmith's building with dated boundary stones marked 'OWEN JONES 1859'. Follow the B5426 and a ruined Cornish beam engine house can be seen on the right opposite the City Arms.

Turning off the B5426 to the left to follow the River Clywedog the road passes some mid-18th-century cottages, a ford, coalpit sites, the day level exit from some leadmines, the ruins of the new cornmills and Nant Mill. Approaching Bersham the Caeau Dam can be seen. Built in the 18th century, it provided water to the leat for what is now the cornmill (possibly John Wilkinson's boring mill). Here too is the millrace which conveyed the water to the mill and the sluice which controlled its flow. The road then crosses the Clywedog and passes mid-18th-century cottages which are separated from the cornmill by a track to the coking bank. Opposite is the accounts house. The safe is still incorporated in the extended part of the building on the south-east wall. If the left fork of the road is taken the octagonal building (now a

Bersham – Bridge Cottages

barn) which may have been the cannon foundry can be seen. Further on are the remains of the blast furnaces (117/ST 308 492). And on the right is the furnace field which was the main centre of operations for John Wilkinson's New Bersham Company. Further to the east is the weir which provided water for the East Works. The race runs under the road, where it can be seen, and then set back from the road are Bunker's Hill Cottages, built between 1775 and 1785 by John Wilkinson and thought to be the earliest surviving examples of industrial workers' dwellings in Wales. The road continues to the site of Turkey Paper Mill, Felin Puleston Corn Mill and Erddig.

Also Worth Visiting in Clwyd

Dyserth, Cwm (116/SJ 072 777). There are substantial remains here of extensive ironworkings with deep shafts and of buildings dating from the mid 19th century. At *Pennant* (116/SJ 087 754) are remains of a Cornish engine house and stack and at *Talargoch* (116/SJ 057 802) another ruined engine house, both connected with leadmining.

Erddig (117/SJ 325 480). Built 1684–7 and extended in the 1720s and 1770s, the Servants' Hall contains a series of portraits of the staff begun in the early 18th century while the outbuildings include a sawmill and smithy and a display of veteran cars. Adjacent is the *Felin Puleston Agricultural Museum* built round a 17th-century barn. *Tel.* Wrexham (0978) 55314.

Holywell Textile Mills (116/SJ 185 764). A large mill, more like textile mills in Lancashire and Yorkshire than rural Wales, the present building dates from 1884 when it replaced the earlier mill of 1777, destroyed by fire in the previous year. The mill is still operating. *Tel.* Holywell (0352) 712022.

Mold, Afonwen papermills (116/SJ 131 714). A sizeable complex of buildings on the River Wheeler, with chimney stack and boiler house, part now used for textile manufacture.

Pentrefoelas Watermill (116/SH 873 516). Dating from about 1750, this mill is still worked commercially. *Tel.* Pentrefoelas (069 05) 603 or 610.

Whitford, Mostyn Quay (116/SJ 158 810) was developed by an iron company as a tidal port.

DYFED

Dyfed (formerly Cardiganshire, Carmarthenshire and Pembrokeshire) was the scene of coal and metal mining, iron and steel manufacture and quarrying.

Carew: French Mill (158/SS 042 038)

As in England, tides as well as the wind and the streams and rivers were harnessed to provide power. The fenestrated ruins of Carew Castle look down on the 23-acre pool of the French Mill which lies on the south side of the Carew estuary. It is not known how early a mill was built here but the first recorded reference dates from 1558. The present mill building which replaced an earlier dates from the late 18th or early 19th century. One of the few tidemills still operational in Britain and the only one in Wales, the Carew mill was worked in the 19th century in conjunction with a similar mill which stood in the shadow of Pembroke Castle (the remains can still be seen). The source of power was provided by the tidal waters of the Carew River. On the flowing tide, the waters filled the millpool upstream of the mill. Then, as the tide ebbed, the gates of the pool were pushed shut and the ebbing waters then flowed through sluices to drive the two undershot wheels which each powered three pairs of stones. A century ago one set was used for grinding barley and the other for bonemeal fertilizer.

The stone-built slate-roofed mill has four floors with a two-storey granary at the north end. From the third floor (the garner floor) the grain flowed by gravity to the bin floor, to be milled on the first floor and bagged on the ground floor. In layout a tidemill is therefore a conventional watermill.

The French Mill ceased operating early in this century and was restored and opened to the public in 1973.

Address: Carew Castle Estate Office, Eastgate House, Pembroke, Dyfed. *Tel*. (Carew Castle Estate Office) Carew (064 67) 2706.

There are also a number of ordinary water-powered cornmills in Dyfed:

Narberth, Blackpool Watermill, Canaston Bridge (158/SN 061 144). Built in 1813, this mill was powered first by a waterwheel, then by a turbine and now by electricity. There is also a museum of 19th-century steam engines at the site. *Tel*. Llawhaden (099 14) 233 (summer only).

Newcastle Emlyn, Felin Geri Mill, Cwm Cou (145/SN 301 423). Corn has been ground here since at least 1604. Alongside is a water-powered sawmill which was added in the late 19th century. *Tel*. Newcastle Emlyn (0239) 710810.

Dre-fach Felindre: Museum of the Woollen Industry (145/SN 355 388)

Woollen manufacture has long been carried on widely in Wales but from 1860 to 1930 the villages of the middle Teifi valley and in particular Dre-fach Felindre were the most important manufacturing centre in Wales. After 1930 the Welsh rural textile industry declined and although there has been a slight recent resurgence, largely to meet the needs of the tourist industry, the making of woollen cloth in the Welsh countryside on a strictly commercial basis has virtually come to an end.

Recognizing that the essentials of the industry ought to be

caught before the final demise, the National Museum of Wales opened this museum in part of a working mill in 1976. The museum itself has a collection of textile machinery from the 18th century while the first floor is equipped with spinning jennies. Next door to the museum display on the ground floor, which illustrates the history of the textile industry from the Middle Ages, the looms of the Cambrian mill continue to produce woollen textiles.

Linked with the museum is a trail about a mile long which illustrates the various stages in the development of cloth-making in rural Wales, including several woollen mills (built to harness the power of the swiftly flowing Bargod and Esger streams) and a terrace of weavers' cottages.

Address: Museum of the Woollen Industry, Dre-fach Felindre, Dyfed SA44 5UP. *Tel.* Velindre (0559) 370453.

There are other working woollen mills in the neighbourhood:

Ambleston, Wallis Woollen Mill (157/SN 014 256). Founded about 1800, the mill specialized in knitting yarns in the 19th century. It now produces Welsh weaves. *Tel.* Clarbeston (043 782) 297.

Llandyssul, Maesllyn Mill (145/SN 368 447). Built in 1886, this

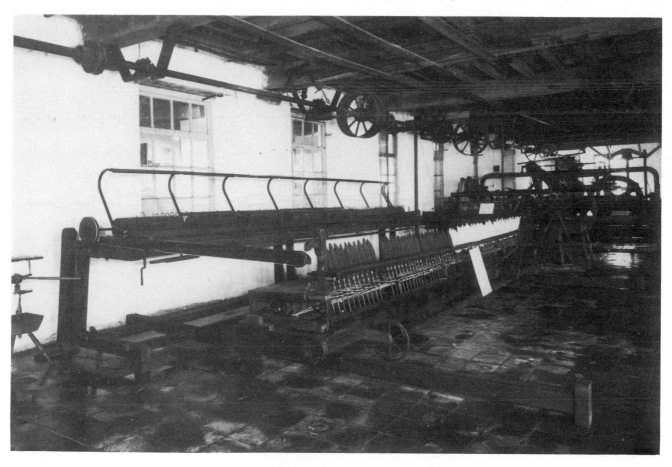

large factory-type woollen mill operated until 1964 and was restored in 1976 as a working museum. *Tel.* Rhydlewis (023 975) 251.

Llandyssui, Rock Mills, Capel Dewi (146/SN 452 423). Some of the original machinery remains in this woollen mill, founded in 1890, which is still water-driven. *Tel.* Llandyssul (055 932) 2356.

Pumpsaint: Dolaucothi Gold Mines (146/SN 664 405)

Here, far into Wales, where the Celts had previously worked on a small scale, the Romans had workings for gold about AD 70. To obtain the precious metal, their workings consisted of open quarries, large caves and a number of adits driven into the rock, using only hand tools. Associated with these workings are two watercourses. One of them runs 7 miles from the Afon Cothi below Pwll Uffern, the other runs from the Afon Annell to the south-east. The water appears to have been used for flushing away the soil to expose ore-bearing rock and for other purposes. Fragments of a drainage wheel used to raise water found on the site are now in the National Museum of Wales in Cardiff which also has a conjectural model of the wheel. The washed-out auriferous quartz, collected at the bottom of the hill, was run through grinding wheels (probably water-driven) to be crushed before proceeding to stepped washing tables (cut out of the hillside and connected to an aqueduct) which finally separated gold from quartz. The gold dust so obtained was then taken down to an industrial area below the mine for processing into bullion to be shipped (probably through the Roman port of Carmarthen) to the imperial mints, either in London, Lyons or perhaps Rome.

More than fifteen hundred years later, there were renewed attempts to mine gold between 1845 and 1938. Concrete capping of the modern shaft can be seen in the centre of the mine yard.

Signposted walks constructed by the National Trust enable the visitor to explore the site of these early attempts to win gold from wild Wales and to see the remains of Roman adits, open-cast workings and aqueduct systems as well as of more recent activity. During the summer guided tours of three of the adits can be taken.

A gold pendant and chain found at Dolaucothi can be seen in Carmarthen Museum. *Tel.* Pumpsaint (055 85) 556.

Also Worth Visiting in Dyfed

Aberaeron forge (146/SN 459 627) produced sickles and shovels from 1850 to 1940; it had a tilt-hammer driven by a waterwheel.

Dyfi Furnace (135/SN 685 952). Built in 1755 and in production until 1810, this water-driven blast furnace is being restored by the Welsh Office. It has a 31-foot waterwheel.

Frongoch Leadmine (135/SN 723 745) was worked from 1759 until 1910. Though its three Cornish engine houses and other buildings are in a sorry state, this site has probably the best collection of 19th-century mine buildings in Wales.

Kilgetty, Stepaside Ironworks complex (158/SN 142 073). Established in 1846, the ruins of this important ironworks site include the engine house and some walls of the cast house. Nearby is the site of Grove Colliery, opened in 1853 to supply fuel to the ironworks. The route of the tramroad which linked the pits to Saundersfoot Harbour is a waymarked walk.

Llandybie Limekilns (159/SN 613 165). Unusual limekilns designed in the 1850s by R. K. Penson (a Welshpool architect better known for his churches and schools) alongside the Panty-llyn limestone quarries. At first glance the remains, with their pointed arches and corbelled parapets, look like the ruins of a medieval castle.

Ponterwyd, Llywernog Silver-Lead Mine (135/SN 735 808). A restored mining site which was worked from 1740 until 1914, it also has additional displays including buddles and waterwheels. *Tel.* Ponterwyd (097 085) 620.

Porthgain Harbour (157/SM 815 327). Quarries (SM 812 325, 806 327), broken foundations of crushing and grading plant, large brick-built hoppers and other buildings can be seen above the harbour quay from which the stone was exported.

MID-GLAMORGAN

Mid-Glamorgan stretches from the iron and steel capital of South Wales, Merthyr Tydfil, through the Rhondda to the coast in the region of Porthcawl.

Merthyr Tydfil Iron Trail (160/SO 03 09 and 05 09)

Based on local coal and iron ore, Merthyr was the cradle of the Industrial Revolution in South Wales and, in terms of real effect, in Great Britain. But as the iron industry waxed so it has later waned. The centre of Welsh ironmaking has now moved to the coast and determined efforts have been made to eradicate the signs of Merthyr's industrial greatness. Little now survives of the mighty Plymouth Works started by Anthony Bacon *c* 1780 (to be taken over by Richard Hill soon after), whose site is now occupied by the Hoover factory, but there are some scattered remains. If Merthyr is entered by the A4102 from the roundabout on the A465 Heads of Valleys road at Caeharris the road runs down past the site of the Dowlais Works established in 1759 and to be developed to world fame by Sir John Guest. The red-and-yellow-brick *engine house* of *Dowlais Works* (erected in the later 19th century) can be seen to the south. On the other side of the road is the Grecian bulk of the *Guest Memorial Library*, designed by Sir Charles Barry and built in 1863 for the workers at a cost of £7,000, now used as a recreational centre. Just behind, regrettably in ruinous condition, are the *Dowlais Stables* (160/SO 067 079) built in 1820 for the 200 horses used in the Dowlais Works. The upper storey later housed the first school in Dowlais. Continuing down past the site of Homfray's *Penydarren Works* we enter Merthyr Tydfil. Near the parish church, the elaborate cast-iron fountain canopy erected in 1907 to commemorate Robert and Lucy Thomas (160/SO 051 057), the pioneer coal exporters of the 1820s, can be seen. Behind the Merthyr Technical College can be seen the four-storey sandstone engine house and the remains of four blast furnace stacks of the *Ynysfach Works* (160/SO 045 060), built as a subsidiary to the Cyfarthfa Works in 1801. Nearby is some terrace housing built for the workers.

As the road proceeds north towards Cefn Coed and the Brecon Beacons it passes on the left the site of *Cyfarthfa Works* (160/SO 038 070) started in 1765 by Anthony Bacon and sold to Richard Crawshay in 1786. Under the Crawshay family the works, like Dowlais, developed into one of the largest in the world. Remains

Cyfarthfa Castle

of six massive furnaces can be viewed; whilst in desperate need of repair, they are excellent examples of the 'Welsh method' of iron manufacture. Slightly to the left standing in its park is *Cyfarthfa Castle* (160/SO 041 073), built in castellated Gothic style by Robert Lugar for William Crawshay II, the 'Iron King', in 1825. It now houses a museum and art gallery.

Also Worth Visiting in Mid-Glamorgan
Aberdare, cast-iron bridge, Robertstown (170/SN 997 037). A cast-iron bridge built in 1811 to carry the Hirwaun–Abercynon tramroad across Afon Cynon. The centre walkway is specially ridged to prevent the horses which hauled the trams from slipping.

Aberdare, industry trail (170/SN 999 026). This trail, which runs from St John's church, follows the line of the old Dare Valley Railway for most of its length from the site of the old Gadlys colliery to Bwllfa Dare colliery, passing the piers of the Brunel viaduct built in 1857 which carried the Vale of Neath Railway across the Dare. There are no visible remains of the Cwmdare and Merthyr Dare collieries.

Blaencanaid iron furnace (170/SO 035 042). The remains of a small stone 16th-century furnace.

Glamorganshire Canal was opened in 1794 from Cardiff to Abercynon and extended to Merthyr Tydfil in 1798. The canal, which had 52 locks, can be traced in sections during its 25-mile length. Ironworkers' cottages and other buildings survive on the length which runs from *Merthyr* (160/SO 047 062) to *Abercanaid* (170/SO 060 038) where there are substantial remains of the canal. A further length runs from Nightingale's Bush, ¼ mile east of *Pontypridd* off the A470. The walk, which starts behind the 'Bunch of Grapes' (170/ST 076 903), includes disused locks, a bridge and canalside cottages.

Hengoed, Maesycwmmer Viaduct (171/ST 155 949). An impressive 15-arch stone viaduct by Charles Liddell built in 1857 to carry the Newport, Abergavenny & Hereford Railway across the valley.

Penydarren Tramroad was built by the ironmasters in 1802 to bypass the many locks on the Glamorganshire Canal between Abercynon and Merthyr. Originally 10 miles long, several sections can still be traced: from Abercynon (170/ST 085 950) to Quakers Yard (171/ST 097 965) and for a mile between there and Pontygwaithe Bridge (170/ST 083 966). Large masonry bridges carrying the tramroad over the River Taff can be seen at Quakers Yard (171/ST 090 965 and 094 962) and a small overbridge at Pontygwaithe (170/ST 081 977). Near Merthyr is the tunnel which carried the tramroad under the charging bank at Plymouth Ironworks (170/SO 055 049).

Pontypridd Bridge (170/ST 074 904). This single-arched pack-horse bridge, constructed by William Edwards in 1755 to span the Taff, was the largest single-span arch bridge in the world when built.

Rhymney, Butetown (161/SO 104 092). This model village, with three parallel terraces of stone houses, reputedly designed by R. Johnson, the manager of the ironworks *c* 1825, was restored in 1975.

Rhymney iron furnace (161/SO 109 093). The remains of Rhymney's first iron furnace, originally more than 20 feet high, can be seen. The *Lawn Shop* (161/SO 112 075), opposite the railway station in Rhymney town, was the last company shop to survive in Wales, being in use until 1885; it is now much altered from its original state.

SOUTH GLAMORGAN

South Glamorgan, dominated by Cardiff, has remains of coal, iron and steel and earlier transport systems.

St Fagan's, Cardiff: Welsh Folk Museum (171/ST 115 774)
Following the pattern of the Scandinavian Skansen, a Welsh Folk Museum was established in the grounds of St Fagan's Castle on the edge of Cardiff in the late 1940s. Since that date buildings from various parts of Wales have been re-erected there. Of the 16 buildings, see in particular:

Melin Bompren. This three-storey cornmill built in 1852 formerly stood on the banks of the River Soden between New Quay and Cross Inn in Cardigan (now Dyfed). With its adjacent corn-drying kiln, it is typical of the small rural cornmill of the early 19th century. It was re-erected at St Fagan's in 1977. It now has a cast-iron wheel and two pairs of stones.

Esgair Moel Woollen Mill. This mill, built about 1780 at Llanwrytyd Wells (Powys), was re-erected at St Fagan's in 1953. Woollen cloth is still made here in a traditional way with water-driven equipment.

Rhayader Tannery represents an activity of which surviving examples are rare. Originally built about 1860, the Rhayader tannery was the last oak bark tannery to operate in Wales. It was re-erected at St Fagan's in 1968. In the yard are the leaching pits and suspender pits, the lime pits, the offal pit and the water pit while in the buildings around the yard are the layer pits, the handler or floating pits and the beam house. On one side is the bark store and the bark mill which is water-driven. On the other side are the office, the weighing room and the cellar, used mainly for the storage of horn.

Other structures include the Penparcau tollhouse, the smithy from Llawr-y-glyn and the replica of the Chepstow boathouse and net house. Among the additional twelve buildings still to be erected at St Fagan's are a water-driven mill from Clwyd, a pottery kiln from Ewenni, a terrace of six iron-workers' dwellings from Rhyd-y-Car, Merthyr and a communal baking oven also from Merthyr.

It is obviously preferable that these rural industries should be pursued in their original locations; but a folk museum such as St Fagan's enables the scale and nature of such operations to be appreciated, albeit divorced from their environment.

Address: Welsh Folk Museum, St Fagan's, Cardiff CF5 6XB. *Tel.* Cardiff (0222) 569441.

Two other parts of the National Museum of Wales are worth a visit:

The *National Museum of Wales* (171/ST 183 769) has a Department of Industry with five main galleries including a mining gallery, an iron and steel gallery, a shipping gallery and a modern industries gallery.

Address: National Museum of Wales, Cathays Park, Cardiff CF1 3NP. *Tel.* Cardiff (0222) 397951.

The *Welsh Industrial and Maritime Museum* (171/ST 191 744), which occupies a new building adjacent to Bute West Dock Basin, has exhibits relating to coal, iron and steel and other Welsh industries, but its display consists mainly of a wide range of power units from a waterwheel to a jet engine. Among its outdoor exhibits are a pilot cutter, a canal barge, a saddle-tank loco, cranes and a railway footbridge.

Address: Welsh Industrial and Maritime Museum, Bute Street, Cardiff CF1 6AN. *Tel.* Cardiff (0222) 371805/6.

From here, Cardiff docks and the dockland area can be explored. The *West Dock*, built by the Bute Dock Company in 1839, has been filled except for the walls of the dock basin, the catch pit to the north and the sea walls in front of the Pierhead Building and Industrial and Maritime Museum. When first constructed, it was the largest purpose-built dock in the world. The *Bute East Dock* (171/ST 192 757), constructed in 1853–5 and extended in 1857–9, has been partly filled at its southern end. At its northern end is situated a fine *warehouse* (ST 191 759) erected in 1861 as a bonded warehouse; it has a cast-iron frame supported by cast-iron Doric columns. The most notable section of

Welsh Folk Museum – Rhayader Tannery: in the foreground can be seen the tan pits in which the hides were soaked

the dockland area is the fine former commercial centre of the
South Wales coal industry in Mount Stuart Square.

Also Worth Visiting in South Glamorgan

Barry Docks (171/ST 11 67, 12 67, 13 68, 13 67) opened in 1889 for
the coal trade and are now largely disused. The headquarters and
office of the Barry Railway are now the headquarters of the
British Transport Board (Barry).

Glamorganshire Canal was opened in 1794 from Cardiff to
Abercynon and extended to Merthyr Tydfil in 1798. Portions of
the canal can be traced northwards from *Maendy* (171/ST 178 780)
and *Galbalfa* (ST 163 785) following the line of the Galbalfa
cycleway. From *Whitchurch* (ST 143 803) to near *Tongwynlais* (ST
135 817) a section is in water. Note particularly a cast-iron
towpath bridge dated 1851 with stone abutments over the
overflow channel to the former Melingriffith Tinplate Works (ST
142 799).

Porthkerry Viaduct (170/ST 083 668). An impressive structure
in rock-faced stone with twenty semi-circular headed arches,
imposts and parapets, it spans Porthkerry Country Park. It was
built to connect Barry with the collieries of the Glamorgan valleys
and the agricultural Vale of Glamorgan.

Treforest Tinplate Works (170/ST 087 880) was built in 1833 by
William Crawshay II. Five long, narrow white-washed stone
buildings, which can be seen from the outside, remain; they are
at present unused. The parapet of the feeder is inscribed 'WC
1831'.

Whitchurch, Melingriffith Tinplate Works water pump (171/ST
142 799). On the site of the tinplate works is this water-powered
beam engine erected in 1807 to lift water from the works feeder
up to the canal alongside.

WEST GLAMORGAN

West Glamorgan, with Neath, Port Talbot and Swansea, has
been largely engaged in mining and metal working.

The Lower Swansea Valley: a trail (Map 159)

As the iron industry was centred on the hill works in the Merthyr
area, so copper smelting in the 18th and 19th centuries was
concentrated in the lower Swansea valley. Although much of the
evidence of past industrial activity has been removed since 1961,
there is still something to be seen. *Swansea Maritime and
Industrial Museum* (159/SS 657 925), now housed in a converted

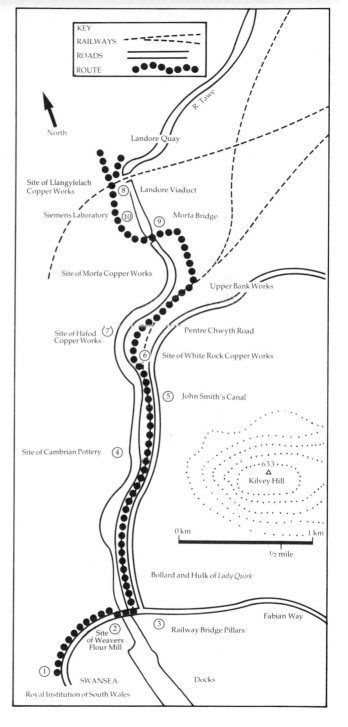

White Rock copper works from Wood, *Rivers and valleys of Wales* (1811)

warehouse on the north side of the South Dock, has a working woollen mill and a Swansea Canal exhibition.

A convenient starting place for the trail is (1) the **Swansea Museum** (Royal Institution of South Wales) (159/SS 659 927) founded in 1835. The present building, erected in 1841, has a small exhibition on the lower Swansea Valley. From the Museum, walk eastwards. Beyond the roundabout, Fabian Way crosses the old entrance to the **North Dock** and then the River Tawe, on the west side of which is (2) the site of **Weaver's flour mill** (159/SS 662 932), claimed to have been the first multi-storey reinforced concrete frame building in Europe, demolished in early 1984. The present bridge across the New Cut replaced an iron swing bridge of 1897 which opened to allow vessels to sail up the river. (3) To the south of the road bridge can be seen the pillars of the railway bridge which carried the Swansea & Neath Railway across the river. The **New Cut** itself was made in the 1840s to straighten the Tawe and so enable the original course of the river to be used as the North Dock. Take the footpath which runs northwards along the east side of the New Cut. Immediately above on the right is the site of the former **St Thomas Station** (1860–1950). Along the river bed as you proceed can be seen the remains of a number of vessels. Looking west across the river, (4) the site between High Street Station and the river was occupied by the copper works founded in 1720 by the Quaker, James Griffiths. Later the Cambrian Pottery was also carried on here from 1764 to 1860. Examples of its products are on display in

Swansea Museum. Follow the railway line north and pass through a small wood planted in 1961 on a derelict railway siding. (5) At the northern end it is possible to make out the basin of **Smith's Canal** (159/SS 664 946) built in 1784. The canal ran three miles from Llansamlet to bring coal to the smelters at Foxhole and for export. Make your way through what remains of the (6) **White Rock Works** and its tips. Across the river can be seen (7) the sign 'V & S Ltd No. 1 Shed', the initials of Vivian & Sons, copper smelters, who formerly occupied **Hafod Works** (1810–1924). Swansea Canal (1798) ran on the far side of the Morfa and Hafod Works. Continue north towards the Addis factory, in which is incorporated the refinery building of the old **Upper Bank Works**, and round the right of the factory to reach Morfa Bridge. Prominent in front is (8) **Landore viaduct**, which replaced Brunel's 1850 timber viaduct. On the skyline are the remains of **Morris Castle** (159/SS 662 968) (1768–75), an early example of industrial housing. Cross the Tawe by (9) **Morfa Bridge** (SS 665 955). Nearby can be seen (10) **Siemens' Laboratory** (SS 662 957) where he perfected in 1867 the open-hearth method of steel production. Turn away from the river towards the spire of St Paul's Church, Landore, crossing the former low-level railway line and the filled-in **Swansea Canal** (159/SS 664 964), 1798–1931, passing the site of the 18th-century Llangyfelach Copper Works. A bus will provide transport back to Swansea.

As a considerable amount of reclamation is being carried out, some of the features described may alter in the years to come. The walk can also be taken in the reverse direction from Landore (159/SS 663 960).

Crynant: Cefn Coed Coal and Steam Centre (170/SN 784 033)

South Wales was a major coal-producing area in the 19th century, but the decline of coal consumption and the concentration of working in a few large pits have been accompanied by the removal of pithead gear and the flattening or grassing over of spoil heaps, as local people have tried to put the past behind them. The construction of the Neath & Brecon Railway in 1864 enabled the coal resources of the Dulais valley to be exploited from the 1870s. After several earlier attempts had failed, Cefn Coed Colliery was eventually sunk in 1926 by the Amalgamated Anthracite Company. Coal was raised in 1930 from a depth of nearly half a mile, the deepest anthracite working in the world. Modernized after nationalization, it subsequently became uneconomic and was closed in 1968. The men were transferred to the adjacent Blaenant Colliery where a new drift was opened in 1975.

The centre tells the story of coal and steam power with

particular reference to the Dulais valley. Some of the surface plant of the Cefn Coed Colliery can be visited, including the boiler house which houses the engine which wound the cages up and down the shaft and the compressors which provided power for the machinery. There are a number of items of machinery displayed outside and changing exhibitions are on display in the compressor room. In the underground mining gallery, displays trace the development of mining techniques.

It is also, for comparison, possible to see operations currently at work on the surface at the adjoining Blaenant Colliery.

Unlike earlier pits, no village grew up around Cefn Coed and it was a colliery of commuters with miners coming from as far away as Swansea, Aberdare and Merthyr.

Address: Cefn Coed Coal and Steam Centre, Blaenant Colliery, Crynant, West Glamorgan. *Tel.* Crynant (063 979) 556.

Of related interest is the **Welsh Miners' Museum** in the Afan Argoed Country Park just north of Port Talbot which has some displays relating to the history of coalmining.

Also Worth Visiting in West Glamorgan
Aberdulais, Dulais Ironworks (170/SS 772 994). Used for industrial purposes from the 16th century, the site has a fine weir, sluices, watercourses and a wheelpit. On the east side of the A465 the aqueduct built in 1823–4 which carried the Neath Canal across the River Neath, the slipway and the canal basin can be seen. Also nearby is the skew bridge which carried the Neath Canal

Blaenavon Ironworks

Blaenavon Big Pit

towpath over the junction with the Tennant Canal, the tollhouse, lock-keeper's cottage, remains of two barges and disused lock gates. The Neath Canal has been restored in parts between Neath and Abergarwed. The buildings of the Aberdulais tinplate works (1830–1939), now occupied by Calor Gas, can be seen nearby.

Neath Abbey Ironworks (170/SS 738 977). These two enormous furnaces, 60–70 feet high, in the grounds of Matt Price & Sons Ltd, were established in 1792.

Llansamlet, Scott's Pitt (170/SS 698 984). The engine house of this colliery which operated from 1835 to 1838 was one of the first of its type in South Wales.

GWENT

Gwent has the collieries and ironworks of the eastern valleys, with Newport as outlet.

Blaenavon Ironworks (161/SO 248 093) **and Big Pit** (SO 238 088) With Merthyr as its centre, in the late 18th century the iron industry stretched across the north-eastern rim of the South Wales ironfield at places at the heads of the valleys where iron ore, coal and limestone were readily available. Now the best preserved of these ironworks is that at Blaenavon, founded in 1789. The works reached a peak of production in the 1820s and then encountered a number of difficult years with falling demand before production ceased in the 1860s.

The remains on the site consist of five furnaces (three of which were built in 1789), cast houses, coke ovens and a water-balance tower which was used to raise raw materials to the upper level of the furnaces. Like limekilns, the blast furnaces were built into the hillside so that their charging platforms were level with the ground area behind where the raw materials were prepared for charging. There are also on the site the remains of an early-19th-century open-ended square of cottages, known as Stack Square, built to house the ironworkers.

After it finished commercial production the Blaenavon Ironworks was associated with the experiments of Sidney Gilchrist Thomas towards finding a suitable lining for the Bessemer converter so that it could be used with phosphoric iron ore.

Although conservation is some way from completion, a viewing platform has been erected so that visitors can get a good view of the site.

Address: Blaenavon Ironworks, North Street, Blaenavon. *Tel.* (Welsh Office) Cardiff (0222) 824249.

The need of the ironworks for coal was satisfied by local pits. Of these, **Blaenavon Big Pit**, sunk in 1860, was until its closure in 1980 the oldest working mine in South Wales. The pit, 293 feet deep, has now been reopened as a colliery museum. Visitors can go underground and also visit the mine workshops, the pithead showers and changing rooms and a typical miner's cottage of the 1940s on the surface. There are plans to link the colliery railway lines with the track of the Pontypool & Blaenavon Railway Society.

Address: Big Pit Museum Trust, Blaenavon, Gwent NP4 9XP. *Tel.* Blaenavon (0495) 790311.

Newport Transporter Bridge (171/ST 318 863)

One of the ways of crossing a river used by ocean-going ships was the vehicle ferry, but in a relatively few cases transporter bridges, a form of suspension bridge, were constructed. The arrangement was for a platform suspended from a high-level bridge between tall towers to be propelled from one shore to the other carrying vehicles and passengers. The finest surviving example is at Newport, Gwent. Here, where it was proposed to build a tunnel in 1888, a transporter bridge was constructed in 1906 at a cost of £98,000 to replace a ferry and provide a crossing of the River Usk. The towers are 242 feet high and the bridge has a span of 645 feet. The platform is 33 feet long and 40 feet wide, with covered accommodation for the foot passengers each side of the roadway, and is powered by an electric motor in a motor-house on the east bank. It is suspended from the trolley by 16 suspension cables. The upper catwalk can be crossed by those able to climb up the towers and down again. The bridge was designed by F. Arnodin (the builder of the Rochfort bridge) and R. H. Haynes (then Borough Engineer of Newport).

Also Worth Visiting in Gwent

Abersychan, Cwnbyrgwm water balance wheel (171/SO 251 033). The last winding gear of its type in its original position in South Wales. To find it an OS map is essential.

Clydach Gorge has extensive industrial remains of early iron-works, industrial housing, quarries, limekilns and tramways. See in particular the Llanelly charcoal furnace (161/SO 232 138), a late 17th-century furnace with the furnace keeper's house of 1693

nearby; and the Clydach coke blast furnace (161/SO 229 132). The Clydach Ironworks operated from 1795 to 1860; remains of two furnaces with a charge house behind can be seen together with a small cast-iron bridge (1824) over the River Clydach.

Cwmavon, Forge Row (161/SO 270 064). With its high standard of construction and, for its time, relatively generous floor area, this row is one of the best examples of early industrial housing. Across the main road is the site of Varteg Forge where the men would have worked.

Rogerstone, Monmouthshire Canal: Fourteen Locks (171/ST 279 885). This, the Crumlin arm of the canal – 11 miles in length – was built in 1798 rising 358 feet through 32 locks from Newport to Crumlin. From the Information Centre there are waymarked walks which follow the towpath, past this impressive flight of locks with side-ponds. *Tel*. Newport (0633) 894802.

Tredegar, Clock Tower (161/SO 142 088). Erected in 1858, this 68-foot clock tower is constructed of cast iron.

Tredegar, Sirhowy Ironworks, Dukestown (161/SO 143 102). The ruins of this works which operated from the late 18th century to the late 19th century have now been excavated. *Tel*. Ebbw Vale (0495) 303401, or Cwmbran (063 33) 67711.

Tredegar, Trefil Viaduct (161/SO 130 107–134 107). This disused railway viaduct in rock-faced masonry with nine arches can be seen from the A465 near the junction with the A4048 road to Tredegar.

GWYNEDD

Gwynedd (Anglesey, Caernarvonshire and Merioneth) has had slate and metalworking as its main industries.

Tywyn: Talyllyn Railway (135–124/SH 585 005–671 063)
To enable the mineral resources of Wales to be developed, a

number of small lines, most of them narrow gauge, were constructed in the 19th century. Mining for slate began at Bryn Eglwys in the hills of Merioneth in the late 1840s. In the 1860s the owners sold out to a group of Manchester businessmen who planned to develop the quarry by building a railway from Bryn Eglwys quarry to Aberdovey. The arrival of the main line at Tywyn however rendered the latter part of the construction unnecessary and so, following an Act of 1865, the Talyllyn Railway, a 2-feet 3-inches line, was built from Tywyn to Abergynolwyn, a distance of 6¾ miles. From Abergynolwyn there was to be a further line for mineral traffic only to quarries at Bryn Eglwys. The railway began business in December 1866 and from the start carried passengers as well as the slate traffic for which it was built.

The quarry did good business before 1914 but after that sales declined. After World War II, when only half a dozen men were still at work in the quarry, the end came quickly. In 1946 the underground chamber in which they worked collapsed and from then on the Talyllyn Railway was virtually a passenger line. On the death of the owner of the quarry and railway, Sir Henry Haydn Jones, a preservation society was founded which still operates the railway. In 1976 an extension of the line from Abergynolwyn to Nant Gwernol was opened. In addition to two steam locomotives – *Talyllyn* and *Dolgoch* – built for the line, the railway has three other steam locomotives and three diesel locos. Some of the passenger coaches belonged to the original line, while some have been built since.

Address: Talyllyn Railway, Wharf Station, Tywyn, Gwynedd LL36 9EY. *Tel.* Tywyn (0654) 710 472.

A number of other narrow-gauge railways now cater for

Welsh Slate Museum

holiday traffic in Wales: the *Bala Lake Railway* (Llanuechllyn and Bala); the *Ffestiniog Railway* (Porthmadog to Tanygrisiau) which has a museum at Harbour Station, Porthmadog; the *Llanberis Lake Railway*; the *Snowdon Mountain Railway* (Llanberis to the summit); the *Vale of Rheidol Railway* (Aberystwyth and Devil's Bridge); and the *Welshpool and Llanfair Light Railway* (Llanfair Caerinion and Sylfaen). The *Brecon Mountain Railway* (Pant to Pontsticill) and the *Welsh Highland Railway* (Porthmadog) are standard-gauge lines. See also the miniature *Fairbourne Railway* (Fairbourne to Barmouth).

There is a cable tram service at Llandudno up Great Orme and a cliff railway at Aberystwyth.

Llanberis: Welsh Slate Museum (115/SH 586 603)
The major industry in North Wales in the past 200 years was slate quarrying, and the hills bear the scars of this and other evidence of it in mounds of discarded slate. From the late 18th century there were several small quarries on the mountain slopes of Llanberis and Llanddeiniolen parishes. Begun in 1788, a 'great new quarry' above Llyn Peris was to incorporate many of these quarries: in time it became known as Dinorwic quarry. Close at hand are the workshops, built in 1870 to house the engineering trades necessary to keep the Dinorwic slate quarry, by the end of the 19th century one of the largest slate quarries in the world, in operation.

These workshops, in the form of a quadrangle with an impressive archway flanked by twin towers, housed stand drills, lathes and other machinery powered initially by line shafting from an 1870 waterwheel 50 feet 5 inches in diameter – almost as large as the Laxey wheel – which developed 80 horsepower, and later (from 1925) by a Pelton wheel. The water supply is obtained by pipe from across the valley to an overhead tank. A woodworking department, a pattern shop, a foundry, smithies, fitting shops and locomotive sheds enabled the quarry company to make and maintain the tools and machinery required for the quarrying, dressing and transport of the slate. There are now also cutting and dressing machines on display here brought from other parts of the quarry or, in some cases, from elsewhere.

The workshop ceased to function when the quarry closed in 1969. Since then the site has been taken into the guardianship of the Secretary of State for Wales and is operated jointly with the National Museum of Wales. It now forms part of the Padarn Country Park which also has a marked footpath into sections of the *Vivian Quarry* and the *Llanberis Lake Railway*, a narrow-gauge railway, which runs 2 miles along the shores of Lake Padarn. Just to the north is the Hafod Owen, an example of a table incline used for lifting slate from the quarry floor. It has been moved from the site of the Dinorwic Pumped Storage Scheme. The quarry area can be explored by climbing the zigzag path, which crosses the Dinorwic incline. Above can be seen Y Tre Newydd, the quarrymen's barracks, where the men used to live during the week. The Country Park Warden's House used to be the Quarry Office: the men queued for their wages along the north wall. Along the lake can be seen factory cottages, originally a woollen mill but later converted to a slate factory manufacturing articles such as school slates. Now privately owned, Glan y Bala was the quarry manager's house. To the south-west of the museum can be seen the 24-inch pipe which carries water from the waterfall beside the Snowdon Railway to operate the machinery in the museum.

Address: North Wales Quarrying Museum, Gilfach Ddu, Llanberis, Gwynedd. *Tel.* Llanberis (028 682) 630.

Penrhyn slate quarries, Bethesda (115/SH 62 65) are no longer worked but extensive galleries and terraces, inclines and ruins of incline houses remain.

There are three places where the visitor can go underground in former slate quarries:

Blaenau Ffestiniog, Gloddfa Ganol (115/SH 698 470). Surface displays include quarrymen's cottages. There is direct entry to chambers and tunnels of old workings. *Tel.* Blaenau Ffestiniog (076 681) 664.

Blaenau Ffestiniog, Llechwedd Slate Caverns (115/SH 708 471). Surface displays include a slate museum. Two inclines give access to some of the 16 levels of the Llechwedd Deep Mine. *Tel.* Blaenau Ffestiniog (076 681) 306.

Llanfair Quarry Slate Caverns (124/SH 596 298). Entry to caverns and tunnels of the old workings. *Tel.* Harlech (0766) 780 247.

Penrhyn Castle and Industrial Railway Museum (115/SH 603 719)
In South Wales, Cyfarthfa Castle is an example of a house built by a wealthy ironmaster; Penrhyn Castle is a more splendid residence built by a rich quarry owner, George Hay Dawkins, in a more beautiful setting overlooking the Menai Strait. Intended to impress, Penrhyn Castle was designed by Thomas Hopper. The neo-Norman castle was built around the great hall of an earlier castle designed by Samuel Wyatt (*c* 1782) which incorporated in its turn the remains of a medieval mansion built by the Tudors of Penmynydd in the early 14th century and enlarged by Gwilym ap Gruffyff in the 15th century on the site of the palace of Rhodri

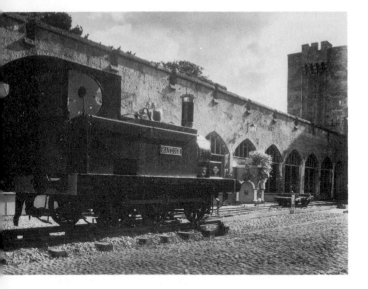

was built in 1829 as a result of the Gaol Act of 1823 which aimed to rectify the existing scandalous state of the prisons. Even so, the new prison was grim enough. Beaumaris Gaol was a prison for a comparatively short period. Under an Act of 1877 prisons were transferred from the control of the local authorities to the Home Office. Among the 38 small prisons which were closed as a result was the Beaumaris Gaol which then became a police station and lock-up for the town. For eight years before its closure the prison only had a daily population of about 10. From 1878 prisoners were sent into custody at Caernarvon. The gaol is now open to the public. The visitor is able to visit much of the prison including the cells, the workrooms, the kitchen, the laundry, the nursery, the infirmary and the governor's room and offices. The route from the condemned cell to the scaffold can be followed.

In the courtyard is a treadwheel, the only one of its kind in Britain and in its original position, to which prisoners sentenced to hard labour were committed. It could accommodate six prisoners at a time and operated a pump which supplied the watertanks in the roof of the gaol and so provided the building with running water.

Address: Beamaris Gaol, Bunkers Hill, Beaumaris, Anglesey, Gwynedd. *Tel.* Beaumaris (0248) 810921.

Molwynog, the 8th-century prince of Gwynedd, so there is a long tradition of habitation on this site. But it is the enormous 19th-century castle with its massive keep, which took 13 years to complete (1827–40), which impresses today. For all its splendour, it must have been an uninviting place in which to live. The *nouveaux riches* of the 19th century clearly placed conspicuous display ahead of comfort.

A bonus at Penrhyn is the industrial railway museum, housed in the stables of the castle. There are locomotives, rolling stock and trackwork from the Penrhyn Slate Quarries (115/SH 62 65) which operated between the quarries near Bethesda and Port Penrhyn (115/SH 593 730), locomotives and rolling stock from the Dinorwic Quarry Railway and a number of industrial locomotives. Signs, models and other material complete the display which documents particularly well the nature of the slate quarry narrow-gauge railways.

Address: Penryn Castle, Bangor, Gwynedd. *Tel.* Bangor (0248) 5308.

Beaumaris Gaol (115/SH 604 761)

While lock-ups still exist in some towns and villages, an obsolete prison is a rarity. An abandoned medieval prison still stands at Lydford (Devon) but at Beaumaris is an improved prison which

Also Worth Visiting in Gwynedd

Amlwch port, Anglesey (114/SH 449 934). From here copper ore mined on Parys mountain – a major mining area, dominated by a ruined windmill, but no longer accessible to the public – was exported in the late 18th century. Storage bins, quays, dock gates and a dry dock can be seen.

Bangor pier (115/SH 585 733). A charming little pier with pagoda-like shelters.

Bangor, Menai Suspension Bridge (114, 115/SH 556 714). A road bridge (which now carries the A5) built by Telford in 1819 with a span of 579 feet, 100 feet above the Manai Strait.

Bangor, Britannia Railway Bridge (114, 115/SH 542 710). Originally a tubular bridge like that at Conway also built by Robert Stephenson, it was constructed between 1846 and 1850. Following a fire in 1970 the dual tubes were replaced by open tracks.

Conway bridges (115/SH 787 777). The suspension bridge, designed and built by Thomas Telford in 1826 as a crossing of the River Conway, was bypassed in 1959. The old tollhouse is used for exhibitions. Alongside is the tubular bridge, 410 feet long, built to carry the railway by Robert Stephenson in 1846–8.

Dolbenmaen, Cwm Ystradllyn Slate Mill (124/SH 550 434). Built

Beuumuris Gaol – treadwheel

in 1855, this massive three-storey building (now roofless) was supplied by a railway running on a curved embankment. Here slates were sawn and dressed with water-powered machinery.

Garn Dolbenmaen, Brykir Woollen Mill, Golan (124/SH 527 424). Established in 1830, this mill was originally powered by an overshot waterwheel, which is now preserved, and now uses a water turbine and mains electricity. *Tel.* Garn Dolbenmaen (076 675) 236.

Llandudno, Great Orme tramway (115/SH 783 829). This cable tramway, operated in two sections from the town to the top of Great Orme, was opened in 1902.

Llansantffraid, Felin Isaf Watermill, Glan Conwy (116/SH 804 747). This mid-18th-century mill was disused early this century but has been restored and now grinds regularly. *Tel.* Glan Conwy (049 268) 646.

Porthmadog, Gwynedd Maritime Museum, Oakley's No. 3, The Harbour (124/SH 570 384) has an exhibition in a former slate shed depicting the maritime history of the locality. Also here is the wooden ketch *Garlandstone*, built on the River Tamar by James Goss in 1905–9. *Tel.* Porthmadog (0766) 3736.

Snowdon, The miners' track (115/SH 648 556) was built from Pen-y-pas on the A4086 (Llanberis–Beddgelert) road in the 19th century to the Britannia mine at Glaslyn to serve the miners. The mine was abandoned in 1917. The ruins of the miners' barracks can be seen on the shores of Llyn Llydaw. The causeway across the lake was originally built by the miners in 1853. The derelict

sorting and crushing mills are by the lakeside. Above, near Llyn Glaslyn, are the old barracks where the miners lived during the week.

POWYS

Powys (formerly Breconshire, Montgomeryshire and Radnorshire) has had mining and textiles but is more rural than other Welsh counties.

Llanidloes: Bryntail Leadmine (136/SN 913 869)
There was much mining in mid-Wales in the 19th century. Nestling under the massive 287-foot dam of the Clwyedog reservoir, the tallest mass of concrete in Britain, are the remains of a small mine which was opened in 1770. In its first phase it was worked for lead. Its most profitable period was from 1845 to 1867 when over 2,000 tons of lead were mined. From 1872 until the 1930s the upper workings of the mine produced barytes.

The clearance of the site has revealed the two phases of the mine's activity. There are two waterwheel pits, ore bins, drying ovens and settling tanks. With the care previously lavished on ruins of medieval castles or churches, these industrial remains have been conserved by the Welsh Office in whose care the site is now placed.

Not far to the east of Bryntail, north of Fan Pool, are the remains of the *Van Leadmine* (136/SN 941 878), said to have been the most profitable mine in mid-Wales. As well as ruins of the mine, including two yellow-brick chimneys high on the hillside, there are terraced houses, chapels, ruined buildings and reservoirs, the survivals of a prosperous mining community.

The Elan Valley Dams (147/SN 920 630)
As cities grew in the mid-19th century the need for pure drinking water became increasingly imperative. With local supplies exhausted, water could only be obtained by building reservoirs and conveying the water by underground pipes with the assistance of steam pumping engines.

With no convenient high ground with valleys that could be flooded (as was the case with Sheffield and Manchester) Birmingham was forced to seek supplies from central Wales. Following an Act of 1892 three reservoirs with impressive high masonry dams, *Caban Coch*, *Pen-y-garreg* and *Craig Goch*, were completed in 1904. To assist the construction a railway was built for 8 miles from the former main Cambrian line just south of the Rhayader tunnel. And to house the labour force of over 1,000 workers and their families a village was constructed of timber huts at the foot of the Caban Coch. Access to it was by a small suspension bridge, built by David Rowell & Company, which is still there. Elan village, with pairs of cottages to house the maintenance staff, was built in two stages, from 1906. Eleven houses, including one for the schoolteacher, a house/shop, and a house/office for the superintendent, were completed on the south side of the river. Between the wars four houses were constructed on the north side of the river at Glan-yr-Afon and, in connection with the construction of Claerwen Dam, which began in 1946, six bungalows were erected behind the Elan Valley Hotel. The *Claerwen*, a further larger reservoir, has a mass concrete dam 184 feet high, faced with gritstone with a capacity of 10,620 million gallons (compared with Caban Coch's 7,800 million gallons, Pen-y-garreg's 1,330 million gallons and Craig Goch's 2,030 million gallons) and was completed in 1952. An aqueduct with gravity flow carries the water from the Elan reservoirs to terminal storage reservoirs near the south-west boundary of Birmingham.

Elan Valley -- Craig Goch Dam

Also Worth Visiting in Powys

Church Stoke, Bacheldre Watermill (137/SO 243 929). Probably built in the 17th century and last worked in 1963, this mill has been restored. *Tel.* Church Stoke (058 85) 489.

Montgomeryshire Canal, built 1796–1821, a branch of the Ellesmere Canal, ran from Newtown (136/SO 139 930) through Welshpool (126/SJ 226 075). A section 8 miles long north of Welshpool to Llanymynech (126/SJ 279 227) has been restored. Much of the towpath can be walked. Notable features include the *Vyrnwy aqueduct* (126/SJ 253 196) and the *Newbridge salt warehouse* nearby; the *Carreghofa locks* (126/SJ 253 202); and Belan locks and limekilns, the Powis estate sawmills and canal monuments accessible along the towing path both ways from the *Canal Yard, Welshpool* (126/SJ 226 073).

Newtown Textile Museum, 5–7 Commercial Street (136/SO 107 919). Built *c* 1830 as six tiny back-to-back houses, their upper two floors, open from end to end, housed looms between the casement windows. They now contain displays illustrating the history of the woollen industry. *Tel.* Newtown (0686) 25815. Many examples of former three- and four-storey red-brick woollen factories and warehouses can be seen in Newtown.

Welshpool and Llanfair Light Railway, a 2-feet 6-inches line, built with steep gradients and sharp curves, was opened in 1903 and operated until 1956; 5½ miles have been restored and the railway has been operated as a passenger line from Llanfair Caereinion (125/SJ 106 068) to Sylfaen (125/SJ 175 064) since 1963. It has rolling stock from Austria, France, West Africa and the West Indies. *Tel.* Llanfair Caereinion (0938) 810 441.

There are remains of the *iron industry* at *Abercrave*, a blast furnace of the Hen Noyadd ironworks (160/SN 811 125); *Hirwaun*, remains of four blast furnaces (160/SN 957 057); *Llanelly*, remains of a blast furnace (161/SO 236 140); and *Ystradgynlais*, remains of the Ynyscedwyn ironworks (160/SN 782 094).

Scotland

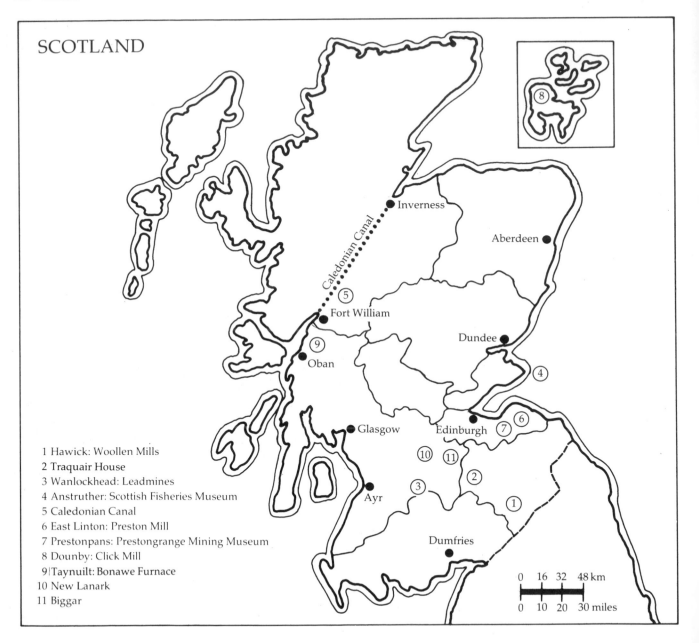

SCOTLAND

Caledonian Canal

⑧

● Inverness

Aberdeen ●

⑤

● Fort William

Dundee ●

⑨

Oban ●

④

● Glasgow

Edinburgh ● ⑦ ⑥

⑩ ⑪

③

② ①

Ayr ●

Dumfries ●

1 Hawick: Woollen Mills
2 Traquair House
3 Wanlockhead: Leadmines
4 Anstruther: Scottish Fisheries Museum
5 Caledonian Canal
6 East Linton: Preston Mill
7 Prestonpans: Prestongrange Mining Museum
8 Dounby: Click Mill
9 Taynuilt: Bonawe Furnace
10 New Lanark
11 Biggar

0   16   32   48 km

0   10   20   30 miles

BORDERS

Textiles have been the most important industry in the Borders region.

Hawick Woollen Mills (Map 79)

Of the hosiery branch of the Scottish textile industry, the largest concentration of the old-type works is in Hawick where a number of buildings, some of them dating from the early 19th century, are to be found. Three- or four-storey blocks often have single-storey workshops attached. The **Wilton Mills** in Commercial Road (NT 502 152) were built in the early 19th century over an external lock system and consist of a large complex with a three-storey and attic three-by-eight bay block with a clock tower and a three-storey fifteen-by-nine bay block with a castellated stair tower in the front. Offices are housed in a two-storey seven-by-two bay French Renaissance block and the front range was completed by an older, plainer two-storey three-by-nine bay building, now demolished. At the rear were three- and four-storey eight-bay blocks, a five-storey six-by-six bay building on an L plan and the monumental pedimented structure of a large chimney. These have gone to make way for a vehicle depot and paper salvage yard and the collection of textile machinery formerly housed here has been transferred to the museum at Wilton Lodge.

In Hawick there are a number of other mills of interest: the **Pringle of Scotland Company's works**, **Victoria Mills**, Victoria Road (NT 498 147), the **Dangerfield Mills**, Commercial Road (NT

502 150), the *Eastfield Mills*, Mansfield Road (NT 507 153), the *Glebe Mills* off Duke Street (NT 509 152), *Hoggs Hosiery Works*, Millbank Factory (NT 504 153), *Mansfield Mills*, Mansfield Road (NT 506 153), *Tower Mill*, Bridge Street (NT 502 144), partly situated on a bridge over the Slitrig Water, and *Weensland Mills*, Weensland Road (NT 514 154). There is an old stocking shop, formerly operated by William Beck and said to date from the 18th century, behind 21 High Street (NT 502 145).

Wilton Lodge, a mansion remodelled in 1859 set in Wilton Park, has displays of local industries including the woollen industry as well as a new art gallery. *Tel.* Hawick (0450) 3457.

There are also mill buildings of interest in neighbouring towns:

In *Denholm*, the late-18th-century *Westside Mill* (80/NT 567 183), a three-storey rubble building with small windows for individual stocking frames in the upper floors, represents the intermediate stage between the cottage industry and the large mills. It is being converted to a house.

In *Galashiels* (Map 73) see *Nether Mill* (NT 506 353), built in 1805 and extended in 1866; *Netherdale Mill* (NT 494 360), a four-storey mid-19th-century mill; *Valley Mill* (NT 494 359), founded in 1793, the main four-storey fifteen-bay block of which

was built in the mid-19th century; and *Tweed Mill* (NT 483 369), built in 1852 and the first steam mill in Galashiels. Most of these mills have a beam engine house.

In *Jedburgh* (Map 74) see *Allars Mill* (Laidlaw's) (NT 651 203), an early-19th-century mill now used as a fertilizer depot; and *Bongate Mill* (NT 656 213), a late-19th-century mill.

In *Selkirk* (Map 73) see especially *Ettrick Mill* (NT 473 293), of which the main block was built in 1836–50; *Philiphaugh Mill* (NT 457 282), a late-19th-century mill; and *Yarrow Mill* (NT 470 292), a massive four-storey late-19th-century mill with separate engine and boiler house.

Traquair House and Brewery (73/NT 331 354)

Houses of landowners as well as the houses of workers and industrialists fall within the scope of industrial archaeology. Traquair House claims to be the oldest inhabited house in Scotland. It is approached by an impressive quarter-mile avenue lined with sycamores. The oldest part dates from about 1107 but the main building is of later date; the 'modern' wings were completed between 1660 and 1680 and nothing has been added since that date. Typical of a Lowlands landowner's house,

Traquair has a number of noteworthy features including an 18th-century library.

Country gentlemen often had their own brewhouses. The brewhouse at Traquair, typical of such, consists of two rooms, one containing a boiler (which when it was installed in 1739 cost £8), mash tub and two cooling trays, while the other has three fermenting tuns. Used until *c* 1790, the brewhouse was restored to production in 1965 and brewing takes place regularly (except in July and August).

In the old stables a number of crafts, including pottery, candlemaking, screen printing and weaving, are carried on. *Address:* Traquair House, Innerleithen, Borders. *Tel.* Innerleithen (0896) 830323.

Also Worth Visiting in Borders

Eyemouth Harbour (67/NT 947 642) was originally built by John Smeaton in 1768 but altered since. Facing the harbour are some warehouses which probably date from the late 18th century. Built *c* 1849, *Eyemouth Mill* still has two large overshot waterwheels. There is a kiln with a pyramidal asbestos roof attached.

Hutton, Union suspension bridge and tollhouse (74, 75/NT 934 511). Built in 1820 and strengthened in 1902–3, this bridge, the greatest work of the engineer Captain Samuel Brown, was the first large suspension bridge built in Britain. The three sets of chains each side are composed of Brown's patented wrought links. The single-storey tollhouse survives at one end of the bridge. See also the similar but smaller suspension bridges at *Kalemouth* (74/NT 709 274) and *Melrose* (73/NT 545 346). North British Railway Company. Features include the wooden platform awning and cast-iron columns with lotus capitals.

Peebles, Neidpath Viaduct (73/NT 233 402). A seven-arched curved skew viaduct opened in 1864 by the Symington, Biggar & Broughton Railway.

Roxburgh Viaduct (74/NT 702 304). A fine curved viaduct with six main arches and four smaller ones, built in 1850 to carry the North British Railway. There is a small footbridge on the down-stream side. See also *Leaderfoot Viaduct* (73/NT 573 347), built in 1865 with 19 spans.

Walkerburn, Tweedvale Mill (73/NT 365 372). A complex of buildings founded in 1855 is now the Scottish Museum of Woollen Textiles. *Tel.* Walkerburn (089 687) 208.

Yarrow, Ashiestiel Bridge (73/NT 439 351). When built in 1847 it was reputedly the longest (132 feet) single-span rubble bridge in the world. Other bridges of note in Borders include Smeaton's *Coldstream Bridge* (74/NT 848 401) of 1767, Rennie's *Kelso Bridge* (74/NT 728 336) and the *Ladykirk-Norham Bridge* (74/NT 890 473); all three have tollhouses.

CENTRAL

Central has had a wide range of industries including textiles, iron and steel, brewing and glass.

Alloa (Map 58): The *Kilncraige Mills* (NS 888 927) are an extensive group of multi-storey buildings dating from the 1860s and later; originally powered by steam engines, they now have three steam turbines and a now-rare wooden cooling tower. The tannery at *Tullibody* (NS 863 951), the largest surviving in Scotland, dating from *c* 1860, has louvred upper floors for ventilation and a tall brick water tower. The late-19th-century *Thistle Brewery* (NS 888 927) is one of the two surviving active small Scottish breweries. In the middle of the modern glassworks (NS 881 923) can be glimpsed the one remaining glass cone in Scotland (*c* 1825).

Alva (Map 58) contains a number of interesting woollen mills. The finest is *Strude Mill* (NS 887 975), *c* 1820 or later, a 25-bay rubble building of six storeys and attic. Others include *Braehead Mill* (NS 884 974), a three-storey rubble building, now a store; *Coblecrook Mill* (NS 878 969) which has a projecting semi-circular stair tower; *Glentana Mills* (NS 878 972), brick single-storey buildings dating from the late 19th and early 20th century; the long red and white brick *Ochilvale Mills* (NS 888 969); early to mid 19th-century mills in *Brook Street* (NS 884 970); and the L-shaped mill in *Henry Street* (NS 884 969), now a hosiery works.

The *Edinburgh & Glasgow Union Canal* runs through the Central Region from west of Linlithgow (65/NS 967 758) to its terminus west of Falkirk (NS 865 794). Built in 1818–22 by Hugh Baird, interesting features include the 12-arched masonry and cast-iron *Avon Aqueduct* at the eastern boundary; a small *dry dock* (NS 965 758) and the *Slamannan Railway basin* (NS 962 762) nearby; and Scotland's only surviving canal tunnel south of *Falkirk* (NS 881 790–884 784). The locks which linked this with the *Forth & Clyde Canal* were filled in in 1923 but the *Union Inn* can be seen beside lock 16 on the Forth & Clyde where they joined (NS 868 801) and further locks remain east of this point. Built by John Smeaton in 1768–73, the Forth & Clyde runs from west of Grangemouth (65/NS 905 816) to the Clyde north-west of Glasgow (64/NS 450 736).

Falkirk (Map 65) is the most important industrial centre in the

Central Region. There are a number of ironworks, some now used for other purposes: **Camelon Ironworks** (NS 881 805) has an attractive entrance with a belfry and two disused cupolas at the rear; **Castlelaurie Ironworks** (NS 890 813) has two cupolas and a tall red-and-white-brick fitting shop and a similar building can be seen at **Falkirk Ironworks** (NS 889 811); **Grahamston Ironworks** (NS 885 805) has an ornamental cast-iron gateway made for an exhibition. At Bonnybridge, to the west, the **Caledonian Stove and Iron Works** (NS 822 798) is a typical late-19th-century light foundry; the **Columbian Foundry** (NS 824 800) is a large complex on the canal; the *firebrick works* (NS 839 796), one of the last such small works in the country, has a two-vent firebrick kiln and a red-brick moulding shop.

Grangemouth Docks (Map 65) were built by the Forth & Clyde Canal and the Caledonian Railway: the **Old Dock** (NS 925 825), 1838–43, entered from the River Carron and linked with the canal by a short cut which was widened in 1859 to form the Junction Dock; *Carron Dock* (NS 927 825) was added in 1883 and *Grange Dock*, with its associated Western and Eastern Channels and new entrance lock (NS 940 827), opened in 1906.

Larbert, the Carron Ironworks (65/NS 880 824) was founded in 1759. Most of the older buildings have gone but the 1876 main office block remains and opposite it can be seen the canal which linked the works to the Carron. There is a long leat from the river at NS 856 820 to reservoirs just west of the works to supply water for the processes.

Stirling (Map 57): the *Station* (NS 798 936) was rebuilt in 1912 by the Caledonian Railway; it has 9 platforms and the main offices, in a single-storey ashlar building on the principal down platform, include a circular booking office. *Hayford Mills* (NS 776 928) is a striking complex in red and white brick, now used as warehouses.

DUMFRIES AND GALLOWAY

Dumfries and Galloway are predominantly agricultural but with mining in the uplands.

Wanlockhead Leadmines (78/NS 860 130–890 155)

In Scotland non-ferrous metal mining was rarely a large-scale operation. The most extensive remains are to be found in the Wanlockhead–Leadhills area which now straddles the Dumfries and Galloway–Strathclyde border. Here silver and gold and

particularly lead have been mined for many centuries and there are many remains of the 18th- and 19th-century lead mines while much of the landscape has been formed by the surface workings and spoil tips. Wanlockhead itself is largely a leadmining settlement with single-storey houses, a school, a library and now a museum. A trail runs from the museum, which has displays of mineral specimens and mining relics, past the more significant remains; the adit of the Loch Nell mine can be entered at times. Unique are the surface remains of a water-bucket pumping engine (78/NS 873 125), constructed of wood with iron fittings, which drained the Straitsteps mine; it is now in the keeping of the Secretary of State for Scotland. Three ruined but-and-ben cottages nearby housed miners. A little beyond are the remains of the Pates Knowes smelt mill where the annealing oven and other remains have recently been consolidated under a job creation programme; a sign at the site explains the process and the surviving structures. On the other side of the valley at this point is an indicator plinth pointing out features of the village. At the Bay Mine lead was mined to a depth of 600 feet during the past two centuries; there is a stone column for a water engine similar to the one surviving at Straitsteps mine and the foundations of engine and boiler houses, including the stone base for an engine built by William Symington. Nearby is a large waterwheel pit which provided auxiliary pumping for the mine. Leadhills is also a former leadmining settlement, larger than Wanlockhead, with single-storey miners' houses. On the road from Wanlockhead through Leadhills down to Elvanfoot further signs of leadmining can be seen by the side of the road.

Address: Museum of the Scottish Lead Mining Industry, Goldscaur Row, Wanlockhead, Dumfries and Galloway. *Tel.* Leadhills (065 94) 387.

Also Worth Visiting in Dumfries and Galloway

Annandale Distillery (85/NY 194 683). A pleasant little complex, founded in 1830, rebuilt in 1883 but now disused, which includes maltings, kiln, bonded stores and proprietor's house, now a farm.

Dumfries has a number of impressive mills: *Dumfries Mill*, a cornmill built *c* 1780 (84/NX 970 758), *Tweed Mill, Kingholm Quay c* 1840 (84/NX 975 753), now a potato store, *Nithsdale Mill*, built 1857, a tweed mill, now a potato store (84/NX 976 754), *Rosefield Mill*, built 1886–94 (84/NX 974 753) and *Troqueer Mill*, built 1866, now split into a number of units (84/NX 973 754). *Dumfries Museum* (84/NX 968 758) incorporates a fine tower windmill (without sails) of 1797. In *Bank Street* (84/NX 973 760) there are several impressive neo-classical bank buildings: two Royal Bank premises, the Clydesdale Bank and the former National Bank.

Gatehouse-of-Fleet has a number of buildings worth seeing: a large three-storey *brewery* (83/NX 599 563), Thomas Scott's six-bay *cotton mill* (now a dwelling), built *c* 1790 (83/NX 603 564), and a *tollhouse* of about the same date on the road to Laurieston (83/NX 602 566).

Hoddam, windmill and horse-gin house, Shortrigg (85/NY 162 744). A tapering rubble tower with a conical slate cap but without sails and a roundhouse which contained the horse gear adjacent.

Kirkmaiden, Port Logan harbour (82/NX 094 405). The pier, now decayed, was built in 1818. There is an attractive light tower.

Langholm gasworks (79/NY 364 844). A small town gasworks which operated 1836–1971, housed in white-washed rubble buildings; the purifiers are under an open-sided shelter.

FIFE

Fife has industry in the west and agriculture in the east.

Anstruther: Scottish Fisheries Museum (59/NT 565 037)

Fishing is an activity which has been carried on in many places around the coasts of Great Britain. Anstruther is a small fishing village on the Fife coast which has three harbours to provide refuge: Cellardyke Harbour (NO 577 038) was built in the 16th–18th centuries and improved in the early 19th; Anstruther Easter Harbour (NO 568 034) was rebuilt 1866-77 and again in the 1930s – on the breakwater is an octagonal concrete light tower and on the pier a cast-iron light tower; Pittenweem Harbour (NO 550 023) was built in the late 19th century. Overlooking Anstruther Easter Harbour is the collection of 16th–20th-century buildings which house the museum, opened in 1969. In the seven galleries there are various displays concerned with maritime crafts, with whaling, with model vessels and with navigation instruments. In the courtyard two fishing boats together with fishing gear are on display. In the harbour itself a 70-foot 'Fifie', a fishing vessel of *c* 1900, has been restored.

The North Carr lightship, built in 1933 and taken out of commission in 1975, is also open to visitors.

Address: Scottish Fisheries Museum, St Ayles, Anstruther, Fife KY10 3AB. *Tel.* Anstruther (0333) 310628.

Also Worth Visiting in Fife

Along the coast of Fife there are a number of harbours which have lost their former importance: see, in particular, *Aberdour harbour* (65/NT 194 851) with an 18th-century pier; *Burntisland* (66/NT 233 854) built 1876–1902 for the export of coal; *Crail harbour* (59/NO 612 073) whose east pier dates from the 16th century while the west pier was built in the early 19th by Robert Stevenson & Sons; *Charlestown harbour* (65/NT 064 833) built for coal and limestone export, serving as the port of Dunfermline – the limekilns, a long range of 14 built into the cliff, the largest group in Scotland (65/NT 065 835), were linked to the harbour by a horse tramway and later by rail; *Dysart harbour*, Kirkcaldy (59/NT 302 928) enclosed in the 17th century with an inner basin built in 1831 for coal shipment; *St Andrews harbour* (59/NO 517 166) with an inner harbour on a stretch of the river bank; and *Methil Harbour, Wemyss* (59/NT 375 995) built in 1887 for coal export and later extended.

The two main towns have a number of notable buildings. In *Dunfermline* these include: a number of linen works, for example, the *Baldridge factory*, built *c* 1845 (65/NT 083 880), the Renaissance-style *St Leonard's Works* (65/NT 097 867), the *St Margaret's Works* (65/NT 090 878) and the *Victoria Works* (65/NT 092 879) which has an Italianate office block.

In *Kirkcaldy* see the two flint mills, both converted from cornmills, *Balwearie* and *Hole Mill* (59/NT 265 902), the *West Bridge Mills* (flax) built 1856 (59/NT 276 902), *the linoleum works*, founded in 1847 (59/NT 287 927) and *St Mary's Canvas Works* (59/NT 285 921) built in 1869 and rebuilt 1914.

Scottish Fisheries Museum – part of the harbour frontage

At *Markinch*, see the *Thornton beam engine house* (59/NT 292 973), a three-storey engine house, which operated *c* 1800–50, with associated buildings, including a dwelling house. It is now a farmstead.

There are a number of attractive railway stations: see in particular *Ladybank Station* (59/NO 307 097), built in 1847 for the Edinburgh & Northern Railway, and *Cupar Station* (59/NO 377 143) built in the same year for the same company.

GRAMPIAN

Agriculture, fishing and whisky distilling have provided most of the jobs.

Aberdeen (Map 38) is the major town in the region. The oldest part of the *harbour* (NJ 95 06) is the north pier (1775–81) by John Smeaton; this was extended in the 19th century and a southern breakwater and various docks were established. See on *Mullhew's Quay* the two-storey harbour workshops; on *Regent's Quay* the two-storey rubble warehouse (*c* 1900), the *Harbour Offices* (1883–5) and the seven-storey sugar refinery, now a warehouse (late 18th–early 19th century); on *Waterloo Quay* a mid-19th-century ashlar flour mill, now offices. There are a number of 19th-century warehouses in the area north of the harbour. The handsome *Girdleness Lighthouse* (NJ 972 053) was built by Robert Stevenson in 1833 with lanterns at two levels, the lower now disused. North of the harbour, on the site of the Aberdeen Gas-works (NJ 950 164), founded in 1840, two old gasholders and an exhauster house with two horizontal steam engines have been preserved. *Broadford Linen Mills*, Maberley Street (NJ 936 068) are an interesting group of 19th-century buildings including a four-storey, 15-bay windowless flax store with castellated details.

Aboyne, Station (37/NO 530 986), rebuilt *c* 1900 and now closed, has an impressive granite building on the up platform and glazed awnings on cast-iron frames on both platforms.

Banff (Map 29). The *harbour* (NJ 689 648) is divided into three basins; the inner harbour dates from 1775 and it was extended in 1816 by Thomas Telford. Nearby are two ranges of late-18th- or early-19th-century warehouses (NJ 691 642 and 689 644) and the *Gordon Granaries* (NJ 691 641). See also the *brewery* (NJ 688 646), now an aerated water factory.

Craigellachie Bridge (28/NJ 285 452), built 1812–15 by Thomas

Craigellachie Bridge

Telford, is one of the finest cast-iron bridges in Britain. The single-arched span has ashlar abutments.

Cruden Bay, Port Errol Harbour (30/NK 094 356) was created in the late 19th century by two concrete L-plan piers enclosing a basin; there are net-drying poles and an upturned boat used as a store. Nearby the *Port Errol Salmon Fishery* is a low single-storey rubble building with tall chimney stacks, a wood store and a net-boiling tub with tripod.

Dufftown is the heart of the whisky-producing area. Among the distilleries open to the public are: *The Glenfiddich Distillery* of William Grant & Sons (28/NJ 324 410). *Tel*. Dufftown (0340) 20375; and G. & J. G. Smith's *Glenlivet Distillery* (36/NJ 196 290). *Tel*. Glenlivet (080 73) 202. Other distilleries in the Grampians are open to visitors but some require advance notice.

Elgin, Oldmills Watermill (28/NJ 206 630). A late 18th- or early 19th-century working meal mill with two low breastshot wheels which worked commercially until 1967, it has recently been restored. *Tel*. c/o Elgin (0343) 45121.

Elgin, woollen mill (28/NJ 216 634) was founded in 1875 and has two-storey buildings on the west side of the road and one- and two-storey rubble buildings with a brick chimney on the east.

Fraserburgh (Map 30) is an important fishing port. The construction of the modern *harbour* (NK 000 670) began in 1807; it is a complex of eight piers and a breakwater forming a series of basins. North of the harbour is the *Kinnaird Head Fish Canning Works* (NK 000 674), a group of one- and two-storey buildings of various dates from its foundation in 1883, and a brick chimney. Just north again is *Kinnaird Head lighthouse* (NJ 999 677), a square tower of 1570 with a short circular tower on top which was leased by the Northern Lighthouse Company in 1787; nearby are the flat-roofed keepers' houses. Returning towards the town, there are fish-smoking houses at NJ 993 670 and NJ 997 672 which have tall slate-roofed smoking houses with marine-type ventilators.

Inverurie, Paper Mills (38/NJ 782 192). Founded in 1858, the complex is dominated by a five-storey brick tower. A 10-foot-diameter, high-breast waterwheel survives in the repair shop and the site of two other wheels can still be seen. Today it gets some of its power from two water turbines.

Kemnay was the source of much of the stone for building the 'granite city'. Disused quarries, as at *Paradise Hill* (38/NJ 737 170), can be seen in the area.

Lossiemouth, Branderburgh Harbour (28/NJ 239 712) is an unusual harbour on an L-plan built in 1837–8 and extended south in 1852 and west in 1860. Note the three-storey block of gear stores and warehouses parallel to the south basin and the small steel-framed post crane with a wooden jib.

Portsoy Harbour (29/NJ 589 665) consists of the smaller old harbour of 1692–1830 to the south and the massive rubble piers creating the more recent and larger basin to the north. Lining the quays of the old basin are four rubble warehouses.

HIGHLANDS

Fishing, forestry and quarrying predominate in the Highlands.

Caledonian Canal (Maps 26, 34, 41: NN 096 767–NH 644 467)
The major canal in Scotland is the Caledonian Canal, built between 1804 and 1822 across the Great Glen from Fort William

Caledonian Canal – Mount Alexander aqueduct

to Inverness. It was financed by the government largely to provide a link between the North Sea and the Atlantic for the fleet. Built by Telford with William Jessop as consulting engineer, there are 29 locks in its 60-mile length and it can accommodate boats up to 160 feet by 36 feet; in the 1840s it was deepened to 17 feet. It has never been commercially viable but it includes some notable engineering features and passes through spectacular country. The canal begins just north of Fort William at *Corpach* where the entrance locks can be seen (NN 096 767). Nearby at *Banavie* a massive hand-operated steel bow truss swing bridge of 1901 carries the West Highland Extension Railway over the canal (NN 112 768) and there is a splendid flight of eight locks known as *'Neptune's Staircase'* (NN 114 770) which can be seen from the A830 which crosses the canal at the bottom of the flight or can be approached from the top where there is parking nearby. Proceeding along the canal there are three strange aqueducts, which seem more like tunnels under the canal embankment and are only visible from below, at *Mount Alexander* (NN 122 777) – with three arches, *Torcastle* (NN 132 792) and *Glen Loy* (NN 149 818). Then at *Moy* there is the only original swing bridge remaining (NN 162 826). Not far beyond there the canal enters Loch Lochy at *Gairlochy* and there are locks and a lighthouse. There is a short length of canal joining Loch Lochy and Loch Oich and then a section between Loch Oich and Loch Ness with a flight of five locks where it joins Loch Ness at *Fort Augustus* (NH 373 092). Nearby is the stump of an engine house (NH 378 091) used for draining the lock chambers during construction; this now forms part of a Museum of Life in the Great Glen. The last of the original lighthouses, a building with an octagonal end, can be seen at *Lochend* (NH 602 377) at the northern end of Loch Ness. Mooring rings and bollards can be seen along the A82 to the north of Lochend. At *Muirtown*, on the west side of Inverness (NH 653 456), there is a flight of four locks leading down to Muirtown Basin, beyond which are the entrance locks at *Clachnaharry* (NH 644 467). The Highland Railway crosses the canal at a 65-degree skew on a hand-operated steel bowed plate girder swing bridge, 126 feet long. Alongside the basin are the workshops of the canal and Clachnaharry village contains a group of mainly single-storey small cottages built for canal employees.

The Canal is accessible for much of its length from the A82. It can, of course, be followed in the opposite direction from Clachnaharry to Fort William. The A82 is part of General Wade's military road, built in 1726, which linked Fort George and Fort William.

Also Worth Visiting in the Highlands

Dornoch, The Mound (21/NH 769 978–774 982), an embankment with a bridge at the north end spanning the end of Loch Fleet and carrying the A9, was built in 1814–16 by Thomas Telford. The bridge arches are fitted with non-return valves to prevent sea water flowing up the River Fleet.

Foyers, Aluminium Works (26/NH 497 211). Founded in 1896, this is no longer operating but the surviving buildings are impressive. Nearby is a quay for shipment through the Caledonian Canal and to the south (NH 497 209, 499 202) are the white-painted houses built for the workers.

Inverness (Map 26) has four interesting suspension footbridges: those linking Ness Island from either side of the river are cantilever bridges of 1853–4: *General Well's Bridge* (NH 661 436) is 97 feet long and *Island Bank Road Bridge* (NH 664 439) is 83 feet long. The others – *Infirmary Bridge* (NH 664 446) with a total length of about 273 feet and *Greig Street Bridge* (NH 665 454) – are true suspension bridges, built by local foundries in 1881.

Iona, marble quarry (48/NM 275 223) worked from the Middle Ages until 1907–14. The actual workings and a small quay can be seen and some machinery from the 1907 reconstruction.

Kingussie, Highland Folk Museum (35/NH 760 007). The major folk museum in the Highlands, its displays include agricultural material, textile crafts and a click mill from the township of Back in the Isle of Lewis. *Tel.* Kingussie (054 02) 3070.

Lybster, Harbour (11/ND 245 349) was built in 1849 as a fishing harbour and rebuilt in 1882. It has four basins; at the entrance is a small octagonal lighthouse; there are two storehouses and the ruins of another store and a mill.

Raasay, Suisnish Pier (24/NG 554 341) was built about 1914 for the shipment of iron ore; it is now used by the ferry from Skye. On the coast adjacent to the pier are the bases of four ore-calcining kilns and a large concrete ore bin which discharged into a conveyor carrying ore to the pier, dating from the same time.

Skye, Glendale Watermill (23/NG 168 498). A small stone-built mill with a thatched roof and a metal overshot wheel installed in 1902. It last worked commercially in 1914 and was restored to working order in 1972. *Tel.* Glendale (047 081) 223.

Thurso, Forss Mill (12/ND 037 687) is an early 19th-century three-storey rubble building with a 16-foot-diameter overshot wheel. See also *Achingale Mill*, Watten (12/ND 241 544), an L-plan building with a double kiln and two external wheels.

Ullapool (19/NH 12 94) is a planned village developed from the late 18th century for the fishing industry. It has a short rubble pier extended in wood and concrete and four fine storehouses, the best of which have been converted into shops and a bar. ✓ *Wick, Pultneytown Harbour* (12/ND 368 505) was built in 1824 by Thomas Telford with later additions; it has two large irregularly shaped basins and a massive breakwater with an octagonal lighthouse. In the street facing and leading away from the harbour are a number of early- to mid-19th-century warehouses (ND 364 509), mainly associated with the salt-herring industry but including two coal stores. There is a local heritage museum.

Railway viaducts are a characteristic feature of the Highland landscape and some of the most notable are the following. Highland Railway: *Culloden Moor* (27/NH 763 450), west of Inverness (1898), has 28 masonry spans, the longest such in Scotland; *Aultnaslanash*, Moy (27/NH 759 349), 1897, a five-span wooden trestle retained because of the difficulty of securing foundations for a steel or masonry bridge; *Tomatin* (35/NH 803 290), 1897, a nine-span masonry structure; *Findhorn* (35/NH 806 288), nine spans of steel trusses on masonry piers; *Slochd Mhuic* (35/NH 847 237), eight masonry spans built in 1897. Inverness & Aberdeen Junction Railway: *Nairn* (27/NH 886 563), four masonry spans of 1857 over the A96. Inverness & Ross-shire Railway: *Alness* (21/NH 655 695), over the river, two ashlar segmental-arched main spans and a small arch of 1863; *Conon Bridge* (26/NH 540 557), 1862, four arches on a skew. Sutherland Railway: *Shin* (21/NH 579 953), over the Kyle of Sutherland, a 230-foot iron truss with arched approaches of 1867.

On *Skye* there are three museums established in old crofters' thatched cottages to show what life was like there until fairly recently:

Colbost, Skye Black House (23/NG 215 485) depicts life there about 100 years ago. It also has a stable and a replica illicit whisky still.

Kilmuir, Skye Cottage Museum (23/NG 395 718) which has a loom and an old smithy. *Tel.* c/o Duntulm (047 052) 213.

Luib, Old Skye Crofter's House (32/NG 565 279). *Tel.* Broadford (047 12) 427.

LOTHIAN

Mining – coal, fireclay, iron and oil shale – was the major industry.

East Linton: Preston Mill (67/NT 595 779)

In Scotland, as in England, natural sources of power were essential before the 19th century. Preston Mill is a 17th-century water-driven mill. The low-breastshot wheel, whose cast-iron

frame was made at Carron in 1760, drives two pairs of stones housed in a rubble-construction, pantile-roofed building. Attached to the mill is a circular kiln with a cast-iron floor which was used for drying the barley before it was milled. This arrangement is typical of many sites on the east coast of Scotland.

Nearby on the estate is a dovecote, typical of many to be found in Scotland, capable of nesting 400 birds.

Address: Preston Mill, East Linton, near Dunbar, Lothian. *Tel.* East Linton (0620) 860426.

Prestongrange Mining Museum (66/NT 374 737)

Coal was to provide an improved source of heat and power. One of the key coal areas was in the neighbourhood of Prestongrange. Here the coal was mined as early as 1210. Nearby the first Scottish railway was constructed between Tranent and Cockenzie in 1722.

An important site in Scottish industrial development, its centrepiece is the colliery engine built by Harveys of Hayle, Cornwall in 1874, the last surviving beam engine in Scotland. With a cylinder 70 inches in diameter and a stroke of 10 feet, it was capable of raising 600 gallons a minute from a shaft 800 feet deep. It was enlarged in 1895 when a greater pumping capacity was required. After mishaps in 1916 and 1938, the engine ceased operation in 1954.

The power station of the colliery, a single-storey brick building with rounded windows, has been restored to house a collection of machinery and other artefacts associated with the history of coalmining. The Grant Ritchie steam winding engine of 1909 from Newcraighall colliery is being reassembled here; there is also a 100-year-old steam navvy and a 1914 0-4-2 steam locomotive. Nearby are the remains of a brick and fireclay works.

Address: (for information): Director of Physical Planning, East Lothian District Council, Council Buildings, Haddington. *Tel.* Haddington (062 082) 4161.

Also Worth Visiting in Lothian

Bo'ness, The Bo'ness and Kinneil Railway (65/NT 003 817). A steam railway centre established by the Scottish Railway Preservation Society. *Tel.* Bo'ness (0506) 822298.

Currie, Balerno Paper Mills (65, 66/NT 164 663), west of Currie, founded in 1810, are a large group of steel-framed brick buildings. See also the papermills in Currie itself (NT 188 680), founded in the 18th century; the 18th-century mills at *Polton*: Polton Paper Mill (66/NT 291 650) and Springfield Paper Mill (66/NT 287 647).

Dunbar, Belhaven Brewery (67/NT 665 784), rebuilt *c* 1814 and 1978, is an attractive range of rubble buildings with two pyramidal-roofed malting kilns. There are also three blocks of *maltings* by the harbour (67/NT 681 791), now all disused and one converted to flats, and one west of the town at West Barns (67/NT 654 781). On the coastal footpath east of the town at Catcraig (67/NT 715 772) there is a pair of restored mid-19th-century *limekilns* (less well-preserved limekilns can be seen in many parts of the Lothians).

Edinburgh, Royal Scottish Museum, Chambers Street (66/NT 258 734). Exhibits include an 1813 locomotive – *Wylam Dilly*, a Boulton & Watt steam engine of 1786 and a 25-foot-diameter waterwheel of 1826. *Tel.* Edinburgh (031) 225 7534. The Museum has a *Museum of Flight* at the wartime RAF East Fortune Airfield (66/NT 550 783). Exhibits include about 30 aircraft, rockets and relics of the R34 airship. *Tel.* Athelstaneford (062 088) 308.

Edinburgh, Leith Harbour (66/NT 26 77) was developed through the 19th century to serve Edinburgh. The area has a fine collection of warehouses, the three main groups being in the Timber Bush–Tower Street area, the Constitution Street–Mitchell Street area and the Water Street–Broad Wynd–Maritime Street area.

Edinburgh, at *Portobello* (66/NT 304 742) two bottle kilns of 1906 and 1909 have been preserved although the rest of the pottery has been demolished.

Edinburgh & Glasgow Union Canal, built in 1818–22 by Hugh Baird, runs from Lochrin Basin in central Edinburgh (66/NT 246 728) through to the border of the region west of Linlithgow (65/NS 967 758) although a short section of it has been filled in on the outskirts of Edinburgh at Wester Hailes. At *Linlithgow* a museum illustrating the history of the 31-mile canal has been set up in a former barge-horse stable at the Manse Road Basin (65/NT 004 770). Another range of stables can be seen just west of Linlithgow at *Woodcockdale* (65/NS 975 759). There are two large aqueducts on this section of the canal at *Slateford* (66/NT 220 707), on the outskirts of Edinburgh, and over the Almond west of *Ratho* (65/NT 105 706), both with cast-iron troughs. About 2 miles west of the latter is the maintenance depot at *Powflats* (65/NT 083 712). Close to the Edinburgh end of the canal is an unusual early-20th-century lifting bridge in *Gilmore Park* (66/NT 244 727). Stone milestones can be seen along the towpath and winding holes – widened parts of the canal used to turn boats and barges around – can be seen at regular intervals. The canal bridges are numbered from Edinburgh.

Haddington, Gimmers' Mills (66/NT 518 740) consist of a four-storey rubble building with a pyramidal-roofed kiln and an early-20th-century maltings block; they produce malt flour for baking. See also *Simpson's Maltings*, Distillery Park (66/NT 514 733), a large group with a four-storey main range with two kilns, and *Poldrate Mill* (66/NT 518 734) which has a steel waterwheel and is now restored as a community centre.

Queensferry, Forth Railway Bridge (65/NT 138 782–131 809), built in 1882–90, has a total length of 8,296 feet and the two main spans are each 1,700 feet long. In contrast, see the 36-span masonry Almond Viaduct of 1842 south of *Kirkliston* (65/NT 113 722).

Unique to Lothian was the *oil shale industry*. Pioneered by James Young in 1851, the industry continued until 1962. Its most conspicuous memorial are the usually flat-topped pinkish heaps of spent shale which can be seen at *Addiewell* (65/NT 005 628), *Broxburn* (65/NT 08 73), *Pumpherston* (65/NT 07 69) and *Winchburgh* (65/NT 097 747). At Five Sisters Bing at *West Calder* (65/NT 010 640) the heaps are conical. An interpretation point, 'The story of bing', can be seen on the B7015 to Livingston (65/NT 004 641), one of the points on a *Paraffin Young Heritage Trail* which starts at the BP Oil Grangemouth Refinery, Bo'ness Road, Grangemouth (65/NS 942 814). *Tel.* Grangemouth (0324) 483422. As well as the bings, many rows of shale-workers' cottages can be seen.

ORKNEY AND SHETLAND

Orkney and Shetland are two different groups of islands and are mainly concerned with grainmilling and fishing.

ORKNEY

Dounby, Orkney: Click Mill (6/HY 325 228)

The most primitive type of watermill used in the British Isles was the horizontal mill (Norse mill or click mill). In the past such mills were numerous in Shetland though some are to be found in the

Western Isles and in mainland Scotland (one has been preserved at the Kingussie Highland Folk Museum). The mill at Dounby, the last of its kind in Orkney, is such a mill. Probably built in the early 19th century, it follows the pattern of earlier mills. It is operated by a flow of water from a millpond which is controlled by a sluice and directed down a trough on to the fins of the horizontal waterwheel (or turl) which turns a vertical spindle and so drives the millstone above directly. The millhouse has two compartments: the lower houses the millwheel while the upper contains the millstones. At one end of this floor the entrance door is faced by a wind-door which allows the chaff to be separated from the grain.

Enquiries to Scottish Development Department (Ancient Monuments), 17 Atholl Crescent, Edinburgh. *Tel.* Edinburgh (031) 229 9321.

Also Worth Visiting in Orkney and Shetland

ORKNEY

Kirkwall (Map 6) is the main town. The *Harbour* (HY 449 113) was first built in 1811 and rebuilt in 1867 and 1880–5; the two piers form a basin with a cast-iron light tower at the seaward end of the main one; the pier office dates from 1871. *Ayre Mill* (HY 443 113), now a hotel, is a late-19th-century tidal cornmill. *Highland Park Distillery* (HY 452 095), south of the town, includes a range of maltings with a pair of kilns; see also *Scapa Distillery* (HY 434 089), about 2 miles south-west.

Boardhouse Mills, Birsay (HY 253 274) is a complex of three mills, the largest of which (1873) is still in use.

Hellicliff Mill, Woodwick (HY 388 241) is an L-plan 19th-century mill with two stones driven by an overshot wheel with rim gear.

Stenness, Tormiston Watermill (HY 319 125). This late 19th-century three-storey mill is now a craft shop and restaurant with the wheel and machinery preserved; note the fine stone aqueduct carrying the leat. *Tel.* Finstown (085 676) 372.

SHETLAND

Norse mills abound in Shetland; among the best examples are a group of seven at *Troswick* (4/HU 406 172–407 171), one of which was restored in 1929 and is still occasionally used; and three at *Southvoe* (4/HU 401 145), one of which has been restored by the nearby folk museum.

Lerwick Harbour (4/HU 47 41) was built *c* 1883. The main steamer and fish harbour has recently been reconstructed but to the north is the drystone rubble *Hay's Dock* with associated buildings; there are also a number of disused privately built piers and jetties. See also the masonry fish jetty with three winches for hauling boats at *Sand Lodge* (4/HU 437 249); and the massive 19th-century rubble pier at *Ollaberry* (3/HU 365 804).

STRATHCLYDE

This is a very large region with a wide range of occupations including mining, textiles, engineering and shipbuilding.

Taynuilt: Bonawe Furnace (50/NN 012 318)

Because of the availability of timber, a number of charcoal ironworks were set up in the Highlands in the 18th century. The most complete of these is Bonawe, Taynuilt which was estab-lished by a group of Lake District ironmasters in 1753. They made agreements with several local landowners for the supply of wood with which they made charcoal to smelt haematite iron ore brought by sea from Lancashire and Cumberland. The furnace could make up to 700 tons of iron a year for which it required the charcoal from 3,500 tons of wood, derived from cutting approx-imately 75 acres of woodland. Good quality iron was produced at a competitive price and the concern flourished, operating until 1874 when the buildings were abandoned or put to other uses. The whole site covers about an acre and the focal point is the furnace, constructed of local rubble masonry, chiefly granite, and with cast-iron or timber lintels, some of which bear the inscrip-tion 'BUNAW . F . 1753'. The brick furnace lining and chimney date from the second quarter of the 19th century when the furnace was raised in height. The furnace is about 86 feet 6 inches square at the base, reducing to 76 feet 6 inches at the top, and is 128 feet high. The bridgehouse, from which the furnace was loaded, survives and other ancillary buildings around the furnace – including a waterwheel house, the blowing-engine house, the casting-floor, a smithy and a store – can be seen in ruins. Close by are an ore shed and two charcoal sheds, each divided into sections. Since the firm was established on a rural site on the southern edge of Loch Etive, it was necessary to create a settlement for the workers and several blocks of workers' houses were erected together with a school for the children and a house for the manager. The latter survives along with two groups of

Glasgow – Museum of Transport

workers' dwellings, the larger a two-storey L-shaped block which was constructed in three stages through the lifetime of the furnace and the smaller – probably the original – a row of single-storey cottages. On the lakeside there is a rubble-built pier which served the furnace. Although local labour was used in the manufacture and transport of charcoal, the style of the buildings suggests that craftsmen and materials were brought from the Lake District for the construction work.

For early ironmaking, see also the Creleckan Ironworks at *Furnace* (55/NN 027 001). The square stone furnace with casting-house and blowing-house was built in 1755 by the Argyll Company.

Glasgow

Glasgow (Map 64) is Scotland's largest city and major industrial centre, the appearance of which has been radically altered in recent years. It was first of all an important trading centre, so see:

Argyll Arcade (NS 590 651), a good example of a glass-roofed shopping arcade with cast-iron supports.

Gardner's Warehouse, Jamaica Street (NS 588 650). Built by John Baird, 1855–6, it is an example of a cast-iron-framed building. See also in Union Street (NS 588 653) the cast-iron-framed warehouse of 1855 at nos 54–76, and the Ca d'Oro Building of cast-iron and glass designed by V. G. Gillespie in 1872.

Among noteworthy transport items are:

Harbour Tunnel terminals, Tunnel Street to Plantation Place (NS 571 650). Built 1890–6, these circular buildings with their domed roofs contained the hydraulic lifts which lowered vehicles to tunnel level.

Museum of Transport, 25 Albert Drive, G41 2PE (NS 581 633), near Eglinton Toll. Housed in a former tram depot, the museum has a collection of Glasgow trams, a reconstruction of the old Merkland Street subway, horse-drawn vehicles, locomotives, cars, cycles and models of Clyde ships. *Tel.* Glasgow (041) 423 8000.

New Lanark (71/NS 880 425)

'A magnificent and probably the most famous monument to the Industrial Revolution in Scotland', this settlement, which consists of mills and industrial housing, was established by David Dale and Richard Arkwright in 1784 in the splendid narrow wooded gorge of the Clyde. By 1799 the water-powered New Lanark works had become the largest cotton mill in Scotland. Marrying Dale's daughter, Robert Owen became managing partner of the concern and used the opportunity to put into practice

some of his ideas about the establishment of industrial communities. He built a new house for the poor-law apprentice children who worked in the mills, a store where provisions could be bought at low prices and a New Institution for the Formation of Character which was finally opened in 1816 and used as a school for children up to 10, a lecture room for adults, a dance hall and a church. He also established a separate school (1817) with a public kitchen, where workers could take food for cooking for the midday meal, thus helping to free married women for factory work. The settlement remained in the ownership of Owen's successors until the early 1960s when it was acquired by the Gourock Ropework Company which closed in 1968. Since then the Mill has been occupied by Metal Extractions and a New Lanark Conservation and Civic Trust has been set up to revivify the village.

Inevitably during the last 200 years or so there have been a number of changes. The eleven waterwheels have gone as has the early-19th-century boilerhouse and chimney, and the mills have been substantially altered inside. No. 1 mill (1787) has been reduced from five storeys to three, No. 2 mill was extended in brick about 1905.

Address: New Lanark Conservation, New Lanark, Strathclyde ML11 9DG. *Tel.* Lanark (0555) 61345.

Biggar: Gasworks and Gladstone Court Museum (Map 72)

Biggar Gasworks (NT 040 378). There was a Gas Company here from 1839 which supplied gas from the same site until 1973. Over the years alterations and replacements were made. The gas-holders date from 1858 (extensively rebuilt) and 1880. The horizontal hand-fired retorts, rectangular line purifiers and cast-iron condensers are typical of 19th-century simple gas-making technology. The old retort house was replaced by a new one in 1914 and became a coal store and new purification equipment was installed. The works remains very much as it was following the major reconstruction in 1914.

For further information contact: J. Wood, Royal Scottish Museum, Chambers Street, Edinburgh. *Tel.* Edinburgh (031) 225 7534.

The *Gladstone Court Museum* (NT 042 378), a folk museum,

Biggar – Gasworks

has a range of exhibits displayed in reconstructed premises – a joiner's workshop, a chemist's shop, a dressmaker's a photographer's, a printer's and stationer's, a cobbler's, a grocer's shop, a bank, a small telephone exchange, a watchmaker, an ironmonger and a schoolroom – arranged along streets with a Victorian postbox, handcarts and agricultural implements. This fine collection of bygones is thus realistically displayed. *Tel.* Biggar (0899) 20005.

Also Worth Visiting in Strathclyde

Ardrossan (70/NS 23 42) was laid out by Peter Nicholson for the Earl of Eglinton in 1806 in connection with the dock development with villas along the South Bay to create a resort. The harbour was created by improving a natural harbour and in 1886–91 an outer basin and new breakwater were added. There are some remains of the shipyard (NS 224 419) and an early-19th-century custom house (NS 228 420).

Beith, Giffen Limeworks (63/NS 364 507) functioned from the mid-19th century to 1972 and was probably the last traditional limeworks to operate in Scotland. There is a bank of two single-draw rubble kilns linked by conveyors to the crushing and bagging mill.

Bonhill, Argyll Motor Company factory, Alexandria (63/NS 390 807), was built in 1906 and only operated until 1913, but in its time was one of the largest car factories in Europe. It has a large range of single-storey workshops and a fine two-storey office block with central towers.

Crinan Canal (Map 55), connecting Loch Crinan and the Sound of Jura with Loch Gilp and Loch Fyne, was built in 1794–1809 by John Rennie. There are basins within the entrance locks at *Crinan* (NR 788 943) and *Ardrishaig* (NR 853 853) and two other groups of locks at *Dunardry* (NR 82 91) and *Cairnbaan* (NR 83 91). Note also lock-keepers' cottages and bridges along the canal, particularly the rolling bridge at *Dunardry* (NR 829 912).

Dalmellington, Ironworks, Waterside (70/NS 442 083), opened in 1848, is the remains of a typical mid-19th-century iron-smelting works. Most impressive is the Italianate blowing-engine house (1847), now part of a brickworks; note also the locomotive repair workshops and the slag heap.

Islay, Laphroaig Distillery (60/NR 387 452) was founded in 1815 and rebuilt in 1885 and 1954; it still makes malt whisky in the traditional manner. There are also a number of other distilleries on Islay, for example: *Ardbeg* (NR 414 462), *Bruichladdich* (NR 264 612), *Bowmore* (NR 309 599), *Caol Ila, Port Askaig* (NR 429 700), *Langavulin* (NR 404 457) and *Port Ellen* (NR 358 458).

Paisley and district (Map 64) was the cotton centre of Scotland and still retains a thread industry. One of the finest surviving early mills is *Cartside Mill*, Milliken Park, Johnstone (NS 415 625). Built *c* 1790 with six storeys, it has semi-octagonal bays and Palladian windows. Notable mills in Paisley itself include: *Anchor Mills*, Seedhill (NS 490 635), where the main surviving buildings date from 1899–1900; *Ferguslie Mills*, Maxwellton Road (NS 467 634), a very large complex founded in 1826; and *Underwood Mill*, Underwood Road (NS 478 642), rebuilt in the 1860s and now a wool store. An earlier phase of the textile industry is illustrated in surviving weavers' cottages, of which the best example is at *Kilbarchen* (NS 401 632). Built in 1723, it has been restored by the National Trust for Scotland as a memorial to the local weaving industry with a workshop containing a 200-year-old loom and living accommodation.

Shotts, Iron Works (65/NS 879 598) was founded in 1802. The surviving structures include an L-plan rubble furnace bank; remains of an 1830s engine house and an earlier one; a tall steel foundry, *c* 1900 with earlier cupola arches; pattern stores; a brass foundry; and one gatehouse.

Tiree, Harbour and lighthouse establishment, Hynish (46/NL 98 39) were constructed in 1837–43 by Alan Stevenson. There is a masonry dock and pier; a pair of workers' houses; ancillary buildings; a signal tower; and a block of keepers' cottages.

TAYSIDE

Textiles, particularly jute and cotton, and distilling have been the main industries.

Arbroath (Map 54) is a harbour and flax-spinning town. The *Harbour* (NO 643 405) consists of the outer New Harbour of 1841–6, a rectangular tidal basin and a rectangular wet dock, rebuilt from the Old Harbour in 1871–7. Nearby at Ladyloan is a *tower* (NO 641 404) built in 1813 to signal to the Bell Rock Lighthouse; it is now a museum. Examples of flax-spinning mills can be seen at the *Baltic Spinning Mills*, Dens Road (NO 640 415), 1866; *Inch Mill*, Lindsay Street (NO 641 413); and in *Millgate* (NO 641 410 and 642 409); while *sailcloth factories* are to be found in Catherine Street (NO 640 411) and Chalmers Street and East Mary Street (NO 641 406).

Auchterarder, Glenruthven Weaving Mill, Abbey Road (58/NN 955 129) is a weaving factory built in 1877. The looms have gone but the late-19th-century steam engine survives. *Tel.* Auchterarder (076 46) 2427.

Blair Atholl Watermill (43/NN 872 653). An early 17th-century three-storey mill with a kiln and granary added about 1800, it went out of use in 1929 but has recently been restored and now grinds daily.

Dundee (Map 54) is known for the production of jute and many mills can be seen in the town: *Bowbridge Jute Works*, Dens Road (NO 408 317), 1857–8; *Constable Jute Works*, Dens Road (NO 407 314), *c* 1850 and later; *Clepington Jute Works* (NO 413 317), late 19th century; *Dens Works* (NO 408 309), 1850 and later; *Eagle Jute Mills*, Victoria Street and Brown Constable Street (NO 409 312), 1864; *East Port Jute Works* (NO 407 308), late 19th century; the *Logie Works*, Polepark Road and Douglas Street (NO 392 303), 1828–65; *Meadow Mill*, West Henderson's Wynd (NO 394 304), 1874; the *Tay Works*, Lochee Road (NO 398 304), 1865 and later; and a warehouse of 1828 in Dens Street and Constable Street (NO 408 308). See also the *Camperdown Works* in Lochee (NO 383 317) which has a remarkable Italianate chimney. There are a number of examples of workers' housing: see, for example, that built by the Baxster Brothers in 1866–7 in Lyon Street (NO 408 309). The *Tay Railway Bridge* (NO 395 263–392 293), when built in 1882–7 the longest bridge in Britain, incorporates trusses of the first bridge, destroyed in 1879. The piers of the old bridge can be seen downstream.

Glamis, Angus Folk Collection (54/NO 386 468). This museum has a collection of domestic and agricultural utensils, gear and implements.

Montrose (Map 54): the rectangular *Harbour* (NO 716 571) was built in 1843 by James Leslie; note the hand-operated crane at the north end and the manually-operated capstan on the lock gates. The *lighthouse* at the mouth of the inlet (NO 722 570) was built by Robert Stevenson early in the 19th century and is now a beacon. Around the harbour are the mid-19th-century *Harbour Buildings* (NO 716 573); the remains of the *Harbour Station* (NO 717 574) of 1848; and the mid-19th-century *Brechin Agricultural Product Company warehouse* (NO 715 572). The *Lochside Distillery* (NO 715 590) of 1889 includes a French Renaissance tower; and nearby the octagonal three-storey Tudor style *Lochside Cistern* (NO 716 589), 1841, has been converted into a house. At *Fisherhills* (Map 45) the main road crosses the North Esk by a fine seven-span bridge of 1770–5 (NO 723 622) and alongside it can be seen the now disused 11-span *North Water railway viaduct* (NO 724 622) of 1865.

Perth (Map 53). An exploration can begin appropriately at the information centre (NO 120 232) which is housed in the circular waterworks building of 1832. The late-18th-century *Upper City Mills* (NO 114 237) have been converted into a hotel retaining the two internal low-breast wheels while the *Lower City Mills* alongside survive largely intact with a large pyramidal-roofed

Dundee – Lower Dens Mill

kiln and an unusual four-storey granary. The large **Perth General Station** (NO 112 232) of 1848 has awnings and an overall roof supported on cast-iron columns although the central offices have been modernized.

Stanley Cotton Mills (53/NO 114 328) were founded in 1785 by Sir Richard Arkwright and others. They consist of three main blocks forming a 'U'. The oldest is the Bell Mill to the west with a later circular stair tower between it and the Mid Mill, a 22-bay mid-19th-century rubble building which runs along the river and links with the 1840 East Mill. There are a number of ancillary buildings on the site and to the north-west is **Stanley Village**, which was built in the late 18th and early 19th centuries for the workers at the mills; some of the original two-storey houses remain, the best examples being on the north side of Percy Street and in Store Street.

THE WESTERN ISLES

In the Western Isles, where clothmaking and quarrying were of importance but the main life of the islands was determined by the sea, sites worth visiting include:

Harris, Iron bridge, Meavaig (13, 14/NB 101 063). A light two-span bridge over the mouth of Meavaig River. Two similar but shorter spans with four small approach spans can be seen at **Amhuinnsuidhe** (13/NB 053 078).

Harris, Rodel harbour (18/NG 047 827) is a basin formed by two rubble piers built in the mid-19th century; the curved pier has a wooden post-crane at its head. Other piers can be seen at **Amhuinnsuidhe** (13/NB 047 078), a mid-19th-century rubble structure; **West Loch Tarbert**, an old rubble pier and quay (14/NB 147 002) and a new concrete pier (14/NB 144 006); and **East Loch Tarbert** (14/NB 158 998), a 20th-century concrete-piled structure with some interesting wooden buildings at its head.

Harris, Weaving mill, Geocrab (14/NG 112 905). A single-storey rubble and corrugated iron building powered by a water turbine supplied from the loch behind through a cast-iron pipe aqueduct which at one point crosses a stream on five rubble piers.

Harris, Whaling Station, Bunavoneadar (13, 14/NB 131 038). A tapering brick chimney is all that survives of this once large plant.

Lewis, South Shawbost Norse Mill (8/NB 244 463). A thatched-roofed oval rubble-stone building which was restored in 1968. A number of ruined Norse mills can be seen in the area, most notably a group of three with a long built-up lade bringing the water supply at **Sandavat** (13/NB 007 303).

Stornoway, Harbour (8/NB 423 330), built c 1870 and improved since, has two piers, a breakwater and extensive quays. There is a handsome three-storey warehouse (8/NB 422 328) built about 1780, probably as a fish and gear store, and close by a small Doric-style custom house of c 1830, now used as offices. See also the late-19th-century **Port of Ness Harbour** (8/NB 538 638) and the piers on the west coast at **Breasclete** (8/NB 209 352) – early-20th-century concrete; **Callanish** (8/NB 213 325) – 19th-century rubble; and **Carloway** (8/NB 207 427) – late-19th- to early-20th-century concrete.

Stornoway, Woollen Mill (8/NB 427 327). A range of late-19th- and early-20th-century red-brick buildings.

Lighthouses are important on such rugged coastlines. See in particular **Arnish Point** (8/NB 433 308), south of Stornoway, a short circular tapering tower of 1852 by Alan Stevenson; **Butt of Lewis** (8/NB 519 665), at the tip of the island, a complex of light-tower, fog-horn-tower and ancillary buildings of c 1863 by D. & T. Stevenson; and **Tiumpan Head** (8/NB 573 377), on the Eye Peninsula, a short tapering circular tower and ancillary buildings of 1900 by D. Alan Stevenson.

What to Read

General works

Brian Bailey, *The industrial heritage of Britain* (Ebury Press, 1981)

Brian Bracegirdle, *The archaeology of the industrial revolution* (Heinemann, 1973)

Robert Angus Buchanan, *Industrial archaeology in Britain* (Pelican, 1972; 2nd ed. Allen Lane, 1980)

Anthony Burton, *The past at work* (André Deutsch, 1980)

——, *The National Trust guide to our industrial past* (Philip, 1983)

John Butt and Ian Donnachie, *Industrial archaeology in the British Isles* (Elek, 1979)

Neil Cossons, *The BP book of industrial archaeology* (David & Charles, 1975)

Keith Falconer, *A guide to England's industrial heritage* (Batsford, 1980)

Kenneth Hudson, *Industrial archaeology: a new introduction* (rev. ed. Baker, 1976)

J. Kenneth Major, *Fieldwork in industrial archaeology* (Batsford, 1975)

Arthur Raistrick, *Industrial archaeology: an historical survey* (Eyre Methuen, 1972; Paladin, 1973)

Rex Wailes, *A source book of the industrial past* (Ward Lock, 1980)

Area studies

David Alderton, *Industrial archaeology in and around Norfolk* (Association for Industrial Archaeology, 1981)

David Alderton and John Booker, *The Batsford guide to the industrial archaeology of East Anglia: Cambridgeshire, Essex, Norfolk and Suffolk* (Batsford, 1980)

Owen Ashmore, *The industrial archaeology of north-west England* (Manchester University Press, 1981)

Frank Atkinson, *The industrial archaeology of north-east England* (2 vols, David & Charles, 1974)

William Awdry, *Industrial archaeology in Gloucestershire* (Gloucestershire Society for IA, 1973)

Michael Bone, *Barnstaple's industrial archaeology: a guide* (Exeter IA Group, 1973)

Frank Booker, *The industrial archaeology of the Tamar valley* (rev. ed. David & Charles, 1971)

Fred Brook, *Industrial archaeology of the British Isles, I: The West Midlands* (Batsford, 1977)

Charles A. Buchanan and Robert Angus Buchanan, *The Batsford guide to the industrial archaeology of central southern England* (Batsford, 1980)

Amina Chatwin, *Cheltenham's ornamental ironwork* (the author, 1975)

Michael Chitty, *Industrial archaeology of Exeter: a guide:* (Exeter IA Group, 1974)

—— et al., *A guide to the industrial heritage of Merseyside* (2nd ed. NW Society for IA and History, 1978)

Michael C. Corfield, *A guide to the industrial archaeology of Wiltshire* (Wiltshire County Council, 1978)

East Midlands Tourist Board, *Industrial heritage* (1977)

Christine Edginton, *Tiverton's industrial archaeology: a guide* (Exeter IA Group, 1976)

Enfield Archaeological Society, *Industrial archaeology in Enfield* (1971)

Larch S. Garrad, T. A. Bawden, J. K. Qualtrough and J. W. Scatchard, *The industrial archaeology of the Isle of Man* (David & Charles, 1972)

Helen Harris, *The industrial archaeology of Dartmoor* (David & Charles, 1968)

——, *The industrial archaeology of the Peak District* (David & Charles, 1971)

Cyril Hart, *Industrial history of Dean* (David & Charles, 1971)

Arthur J. Haselfoot, *The Batsford guide to the industrial archaeology of south-east England: Kent, Surrey, East Sussex, West Sussex* (Batsford, 1978)

The Heart of England Tourist Board, *Steam historic vehicles and industrial archaeology in the heart of England* (1979)

John Hoare and John Upton, *Sussex industrial archaeology: a field guide* (Phillimore, 1972)

Kenneth Hudson, *The industrial archaeology of southern England* 2nd ed. (David & Charles, 1968)

John Hume, *The industrial archaeology of Glasgow* (Blackie, 1974)

——, *The industrial archaeology of Scotland: vol. 1, The Lowlands and Borders* and vol. 2, *The Highlands and Islands* (2 vols, Batsford, 1976, 1977)

William B. Johnson, *The industrial archaeology of Hertfordshire* (David & Charles, 1970)

Peter Laws, *Industrial archaeology in Bedfordshire* (Bedfordshire County Council, 1967)

Leicestershire County Council, *Leicestershire's industrial heritage* (1983)

London Transport, *London's industrial archaeology* (1977)

John Marshall and Michael Davies-Shiel, *Industrial archaeology of the Lake District* (2nd ed. David & Charles, 1977)

Walter Minchinton, *Industrial archaeology in Devon* (4th ed. Dartington Amenity Research Trust, 1984)

Pamela Moore, ed., *A guide to the industrial archaeology of Hampshire and the Isle of Wight* (Southampton University IA Group, 1984)

Frank Nixon, *The industrial archaeology of Derbyshire* (David & Charles, 1969)

Gordon A. Payne, *Surrey industrial archaeology: a field guide* (Phillimore, 1977)

David Morgan Rees, *The industrial archaeology of Wales* (David & Charles, 1975)

Christopher S. Rule, *The industrial archaeology of south east London* (SELIA, 1983)

Robert Sherlock, *The industrial archaeology of Staffordshire* (David & Charles, 1976)

David Smith, *Industrial archaeology of the east Midlands* (David & Charles, 1965)

Geoffrey Starmer, *Industrial archaeology in Northamptonshire* (Northamptonshire Museums and Art Gallery, 1970)

Derek Studder, *A guide to the industrial archaeology of the Reigate and Banstead district* (Surrey Industrial History Group, 1979)

William J. Thompson, *Industrial archaeology of north Staffordshire* (Moorland, 1975)

Arthur C. Todd and Peter Laws, *The industrial archaeology of Cornwall* (David & Charles, 1972)

John Van Laun, *The problem of past industry in the national park* (Brecon Beacons National Park Committee, 1976)

Welsh Tourist Board, *Wales, a glimpse of the past* (1978)

Anthony Wilson, *London's industrial heritage* (David & Charles, 1967)

Neil R. Wright, *A guide to the industrial archaeology of Lincolnshire including South Humberside* (Association for Industrial Archaeology, 1983)

Studies of particular aspects

Kenneth J. Allison, *East Riding water-mills* (East Yorkshire Local History Society, 1970)

Michael Atkinson with Roger Burt and Peter Waite, *Dartmoor mines: the mines of the granite mass* (Exeter IA Group, 1983)

Bertram Baxter, *Stone blocks and iron rails* (David & Charles, 1966)

Anthony Bird, *Roads and vehicles* (Longman, 1969)

Godfrey Body and R. L. Eastleigh, *Cliff railways* (David & Charles, 1974)

Fred Brook and Martin Allbutt, *The Shropshire lead mines* (Moorland, 1973)

Robert Angus Buchanan and George Watkins, *The industrial archaeology of the stationary steam engine* (Longman, 1976)

William A. Campbell, *The chemical industry* (Longman, 1971)

Robert T. Clough, *The lead smelting mills of the Yorkshire Dales and northern Pennines* (rev. ed. the author, 1979)

T. E. Crowley, *The beam engine* (Senecio, 1981)

Joan Day, *Bristol brass* (David & Charles, 1973)

Walter English, *The textile industry* (Longman, 1969)

Trevor D. Ford and J. H. Rieuwerts, *Leadmining in the Peak District* (Peak Park Planning Board, 1975)

William K. V. Gale, *Iron and steel* (Longman, 1969)

Alan R. Griffin, *Coal mining* (Longman, 1971)

Douglas Hague and Rosemary Christie, *Lighthouses: their architecture, history and archaeology* (Gomer Press, 1975)

Nigel Harvey, *Industrial archaeology of farming in England and Wales* (Batsford, 1980)

Geoffrey Hayes, *A guide to stationary steam engines* (Moorland, 1981)

Kenneth Hudson, *Building materials* (Longman, 1972)

Geraint Jenkins, *The craft industries* (Longman, 1972)

John Kanefsky, *Devon tollhouses* (Exeter IA Group, 1984)

Michael J. T. Lewis, *Early wooden railways* (Routledge, 1970)

J. Kenneth Major, *Animal-powered engines* (Batsford, 1978)

Ian McNeil, *Hydraulic power* (Longman, 1972)

Walter Minchinton, *Windmills of Devon* (Exeter IA Group, 1976)

—— *Exeter's water supply: history and archaeology* (Exeter IA Group, 1984)

Walter Minchinton and John Perkins, *Tidemills of Devon and Cornwall* (Exeter IA Group, 1971)

Bryan Morgan, *Civil engineering: railways* (Longman, 1971)

Peter Naylor, *Discovering lost mines* (Shire, 1981)

Ken Powell, *Pennine mill trail* (SAVE, 1981)

Philip J. G. Ramsden, *The archaeology of canals* (World's Work, 1979)

——, *The archaeology of railways* (World's Work, 1981)

John Reynolds, *Windmills and watermills* (Hugh Evelyn, 1970)

Kenneth H. Rogers, *Wiltshire and Somerset woollen mills* (Pasold Research Fund, 1976)

Lionel T. C. Rolt, *Navigable waterways* (Longman, 1969)

Peter L. Smith, *Discovering canals in Britain* (Shire, 1981)

John B. Snell, *Mechanical engineering: railways* (Longman, 1971)

Jennifer Tann, *Gloucestershire woollen mills* (David & Charles, 1967)

John Vince, *Discovering watermills* (Shire, 1980)

——, *Discovering windmills* (Shire, 1980)

George Watkins, *The textile mill engine* (2 vols, David & Charles, 1970, 1971)

——, *The steam engine in industry* (2 vols, Moorland, 1978, 1979)

Martin Watts, *Corn milling* (Shire, 1983)

Jenny West, ed., *Windmills and watermills open to view* (SPAB, 1981)

John Winter, *Industrial architecture: a survey of factory building* (Studio Vista, 1970)

Acknowledgements

No one can compile a book of this sort without incurring a multitude of obligations and it is impossible to list separately everyone who has helped. Nonetheless, I would like to say how grateful I am to the owners, operators, museum curators and administrators (whatever term is appropriate) of individual sites who have checked the information relating to them and have provided addresses and telephone numbers. I would also like to thank staff of the English, Scottish and Welsh tourist boards, staff in many county planning departments and borough councils, officers of museums and art galleries, staff of the Welsh Office, the Scottish Office, the Royal Commission on Ancient Monuments and statutory bodies like the Severn-Trent Water Authority for their help.

A number of photographs are from my collection but many came from elsewhere. I would therefore like to thank the following for permission to use their photographs: Anstruther Museum, the Avoncroft Museum of Buildings, the Bass Museum of Brewing History, Big Pit Museum Trust (Blaenavon), Birmingham City Museums and Art Gallery, Black Country Museum Trust, the Boat Museum (Ellesmere Port), A. Booth (courtesy of South Yorkshire County Council), Bradford City Museum, the British Engineerium, British Waterways Board, Buckler's Hard Maritime Museum, Camden Museum (Bath), Carew Castle Estate, Carisbrooke Castle (Isle of Wight), Chatterley Whitfield Mining Museum, Cheddleton Flint Museum, City of Leicester Arts and Recreation Department, City of Swansea Environment Department, Clearwell Caves, Cleveland County Council, Clwyd County Council, Anthony J. Cooke, Crofton Beam Engines Trust, Michael Davies-Shiel and Dr J. D. Marshall, Department of the Environment, Dogdyke Pumping Station Preservation Trust, W. A. Fairhurst & Partners, Finch Foundry, the Friends of the Woodbridge Tidemill, the Gladstone Pottery Museum, Glasgow Museum of Transport, Gwynedd County Council, Ironbridge Gorge Museum Trust, the Lake District Special Planning Board, Leighton Buzzard Narrow Gauge Railway Society, Liverpool Road Station Society (Manchester), Lound Hall Mining Museum, Manx Museum and National Trust, Merthyr Tydfil Borough Council, Monkwearmouth Station Museum, Morwellham Recreation Company, Brian Murless, Museum of East Anglian Life, Museum of Lakeland Life and Industry, National Coal Board, National Museum of Wales, National Railway Museum (crown copyright), National Trust, New Lanark Conservation, Newport Council, Papplewick Pumping Station Trust, Pilkington Glass Museum, Derek Pratt, Quarry Bank Mill Trust, Royal Commission on the Ancient and Historical Monuments of Scotland, Royal Committee for Aerial Photography, Royal Navy, Royal Scottish Museum, Ruddington Framework Knitters' Shops Preservation Trust, Ryhope Engines Trust, St Austell China Clay Museum, Scottish Development Department (Ancient Monuments), Severn-Trent Water Authority, Sheffield Museum, Sheffield Trades Historical Society, Southend Council, Southern Industrial History Centre, Stretham Engine Preservation Trust, Swindon Railway Museum, Talyllyn Railway, Tramway Museum (Crich), Martin Watts, Weald and Downland Open Air Museum, the Welsh Office, the Welsh Tourist Board, West Glamorgan County Council, Wookey Hole Caves, Wycombe Chair and Local History Museum.

Then, in obtaining both photographs and information, I have been helped by a number of my IA friends including David Alderton, Owen Ashmore, Rev W. Awdry, Hugh Bodey, James Bond, John Crompton, Michael Davies-Shiel, Ian Donnachie, Keith Falconer, L. S. Garrad, A. D. and A. M. George, Stephen Hughes (for information from the Royal Commission on Ancient and Historical Monuments in Wales), S. J. Lavender, Kenneth Major, John Marshall, Amber Patrick, David Perrett (and other members of GLIAS), Philip Riden, Geoffrey Starmer, John Stengelhofen, Jenny West, John Williams-Davies and Neil Wright.

The completion of this book was delayed by my absence overseas and it may not have been possible to check precisely and acknowledge properly every obligation. If any person or organization should feel that they have been overlooked or inadequately thanked, I would like them to know that this will be through ignorance or inadvertence and not through design. I ask them to accept my sincere apologies. Further, I will gladly undertake to make appropriate alterations (with the co-operation of my publisher) in future editions.

Finally, this manuscript would not have been successfully transformed into a printed volume but for the devoted work of my secretaries, Elaine Harrison and Celia Manning, and of Celia King and the careful editorial work of Ian Paten.

Index